Restorying Indigenous Leadership

RESTORYING INDIGENOUS LEADERSHIP

Wise Practices in Community Development

**Edited by Cora Voyageur,
Laura Brearley, and Brian Calliou**

Banff Centre Press

Warning: Readers should be aware that this book includes names of deceased people, which may cause sadness or distress to Indigenous peoples.

Banff Centre Press

Box 1020, Station 21
107 Tunnel Mountain Drive
Banff, Alberta, Canada T1L 1H5
www.banffcentrepress.ca

20 19 18 17 16 15 14   9 8 7 6 5 4 3 2 1

Cover designed by Grace Cheong.
Cover photo: Lonny Kalfus/Getty Images.
Interior designed and typeset by Brian Morgan.

Banff Centre Press is pleased to acknowledge the generous donors who have given financial support to the Indigenous Leadership and Management program and the Wise Practices Symposium at The Banff Centre, especially the Rural Alberta Development Fund.

Rural Alberta
Development Fund

Library and Archives Canada
Cataloguing in Publication

Restorying indigenous leadership :
wise practices in community development /
edited by Cora Voyageur, Laura Brearley,
and Brian Calliou.

Includes bibliographical references.
Issued in print and electronic formats.

ISBN 978-1-894773-68-3 (pbk.)
ISBN 978-1-894773-71-3 (epub)
ISBN 978-1-894773-72-0 (mobi)

1. Indian leadership.
2. Community leadership.
3. Leadership—Cross-cultural studies.
4. Indigenous peoples—Politics and government.
5. Indigenous peoples—Economic conditions.
6. Art, Aboriginal Australian.
7. Native peoples—Canada.
8. Indians of North America—United States.
9. Aboriginal Australians.

I. Voyageur, Cora Jane, 1956–, editor
II. Calliou, Brian, editor
III. Brearley, Laura, editor

GN380.R63 2014   305.8   C2014-903457-1
C2014-903458-X

Printed and bound in Canada

Dedication

We would like to dedicate this book about restorying Indigenous leadership to two Indigenous elders who have been very influential to the work we do in our Indigenous Leadership and Management program area at The Banff Centre. First, we dedicate it to Elder Tom Crane Bear, a member of the Siksika Nation, part of the Blackfoot Confederacy, in Treaty 7 territory in southern Alberta, Canada. Elder Tom has been an elder and cultural advisor to The Banff Centre's Indigenous programming for over fifteen years and is a respected elder who does important work in sharing and preserving Blackfoot culture and traditional teachings. Second, we dedicate it to Uncle Albert Mullett, a member of the Gunai/Kurnai peoples in Victoria, Australia. Uncle Albert is a respected elder who has been actively involved in Aboriginal education and the preservation of Koorie cultural heritage.

Acknowledgements

We would like to acknowledge Treaty 7 territory upon which The Banff Centre is located and where we do our important work in Indigenous leadership development. We would like to acknowledge and thank all the Treaty 7 elders, leaders, and citizens who work in supporting the work we do. We would like to acknowledge and thank two sponsors whose financial contributions allowed us to begin important applied research into documenting and telling the stories of wise practices case studies: Nexen Energy, which funded our Nexen Chair in Indigenous Leadership, and Rural Alberta Development Fund (RADF), which funded our Wise Practices Symposium and case studies, upon which this book was based. We would like to thank the staff at The Banff Centre who assisted, in many ways, in implementing our vision of applied research into wise practices success stories, especially Nick Nissley, Lisa Jackson, Anna Wowchuk, and Katie Smith. We would also like to acknowledge and thank our former Nexen Chair in Indigenous Leadership, Cynthia Wesley-Esquimaux, for her active role in the Alberta wise practices case studies, especially for her work with the Indigenous youth cohort. We would like to thank the film and media team at The Banff Centre for their terrific work in documenting our RADF wise practices research project. We would like to thank W. Brett Wilson for his inspiring talk at our symposium and for agreeing to write the foreword, and each of the contributors to this collection. Finally, we would like to thank the Banff Centre Press in taking on this important book project, especially Robyn Read and May Antaki whose attention to fine details and superb editing ensured this book would be of top quality.

Table of Contents

Foreword

I'm often asked about the secret to success. You've likely heard that it lies within each of us—that we are truly responsible for determining how to achieve our own goals. It's certainly true that we choose our paths to success. But whatever paths we choose, when others start to follow us, we are no longer just individuals searching for success: we become leaders. To me, learning to be great leaders means broadening both our visions and our aspirations. There's always the chance that we may, collectively, decide to change our path or direction. If success begins and ends with leadership, then leadership begins and ends with questioning and rethinking the very paths we choose to follow, and on which paths we lead others.

The Indigenous leaders featured within this book are great leaders because they are great listeners. They have listened closely to traditional, Western stories of leadership and governance, have been able to hear the silences in the gaps within these stories, and have heard and invited new voices to contribute. As a form of storytelling, "restorying" involves recollecting the stories of the past, paying attention to the stories of our present, and appealing for new voices in these compelling narratives. These are the voices that will raise alternative and innovative suggestions for how social change can be enacted in Indigenous communities, today and into the future.

So, while I'm often asked about the key to success, the truth is, there really isn't just one key, one single answer, or one path. The collection *Restorying Indigenous Leadership* demonstrates this, abounding with stories, testimonials, and case studies that offer a variety of models, approaches, and conceptions of success. You will find in this book inspiring research and groundbreaking methodologies of Indigenous leaders whose identities as leaders are very closely tied to the assets and needs of their Indigenous communities and cultures. These are stories of Indigenous leaders who define success by the search, not the answer; by remaining open to new inspirations, opportunities, and possibilities; and by knowing that sustaining the economic development of Indigenous communities means never assuming the story is over.

Restorying is not only an active and ongoing process, it is an invitation to listen, and to speak into the silences. Welcome.

W. Brett Wilson

Indigenous Leadership and Approaches to Community Development

Cora Voyageur, Laura Brearley, and Brian Calliou

Since leadership plays an important role in any community, Indigenous leadership scholarship advocates opportunities for leaders within Indigenous communities to gain the knowledge and skills required to fulfill the needs and aspirations of their peoples and to foster economic development. Yet over the years, states have imposed their laws and institutions upon Indigenous peoples, resulting in the loss of traditional leadership and governance. There has been a pattern of non-Indigenous leadership practices being forced upon Indigenous communities, exacerbated by the media portraying Indigenous communities and their leaders in a negative light, which sociologists have termed a "deficit paradigm" (Ponting and Voyageur 2001). *Restorying Indigenous Leadership: Wise Practices in Community Development* shares different stories that collectively could be referred to as a "strength-based" paradigm: specific examples of wise practices and successful leadership in Indigenous communities.

Stories have been bringing us together for thousands of years; storytelling is not only a way we make sense of our worlds (Ellis 2004), but it is "a creative act of leadership through which we manifest our solidarity and strengthen our people to take their next steps in encouraging good and healthy lives" (Kenny 2012, 1). *Restorying Indigenous*

Leadership uses a storytelling model that interweaves lived experiences with extensive research to stimulate progressive and informed action through not just sharing stories but a process of *restorying*.

Restorying is a dynamic form of storytelling that revisits and recuperates in order to restore—a central theme in the work of Indigenous writers Thomas King (2008) and Lewis Mehl-Madrona (2007). While Indigenous scholars Audra Simpson and Dale Turner argue that Indigenous leaders need to understand and use the narratives of modernity and globalization, they also emphasize the necessity of incorporating Indigenous knowledge, practices, and ideas *into* the global discourse in order to assert their respective community rights and interests (2008). Thus, restorying not only helps readers become aware of "the power and beauty of our stories to educate and heal people" (Archibald 2008, 371), but enacts a kind of storytelling that encompasses the past, the present, and the future, and is a participatory and reciprocal process between writer and reader.

Indigenous researcher Judy Atkinson (2001, 8) advocates the form of listening that brings a sense of responsibility to the stories that are told, called Deep Listening, and stresses the importance of respect and relationality in the relationship between the storyteller and the listener. At its most profound level, Deep Listening is the search for understanding and meaning by paying attention to the spaces within and between stories. Being awake and attuned in this way develops a critical awareness of our relationship to the stories being told and those being silenced. John Berger (2008) contends that we need to listen to what is said, what is not said, what is waiting to be said, and what is crying out to be expressed. This kind of awareness requires an understanding that there is not just one kind of listening—that listening is a complicated, nuanced process that requires practice.

In his work on learning by contemplating the future, Otto Scharmer (2007, 7–8) describes four types of listening:

1. **Downloading:** Confirming what you already know.
2. **Objective or Attentive Listening:** Paying attention to what differs from your own concepts.

3. **Empathic Listening:** Seeing the world through someone else's eyes.
4. **Generative Listening:** Listening from the emerging field of the future.

Scharmer's fourth concept, Generative Listening, aligns closely with the concept of Deep Listening. It incorporates a confirmation of what is known, an attention to what is different, and a listening beyond what is heard with the ears. It invites work teams or communities to be fully present with each other and to identify what is happening and emerging in the moment. For leaders, it means getting out of the way in order to open a space in which genuine contact can be made. That space is a place of possibility where current and emerging needs can be expressed and explored.

Listening deeply opens the way to developing collective mindfulness. Being collectively mindful is about being aware of the complexities within a situation and the different perspectives from which it can be viewed. When leaders are present, they are attuned to other people and to their context. Scharmer refers to this as "presencing"—a term that blends *presence* and *sensing*. The paradox is that the more a leader is present, the more she or he is able to get out of the way and become more available for other people. Scharmer contends that a kind of deepened presence gives access to greater levels of authentic awareness, new dimensions of power, and a clearer direction. It bridges inner experience and collective experience in creative, non-linear ways.

One of the key elements of Karl Weick's (2006) work on collective mindfulness is the capacity to seek a complete and nuanced picture of any difficult situation. Reflecting on issues from different perspectives requires a degree of comfort with complexity and a reluctance to simplify. It helps leaders pull out threads and insights from knotty issues, working in co-operation with people's commonalities and differences. Collective mindfulness is an important element of how Indigenous peoples come together to present their diverse perspectives in a dialogue until a consensus emerges. It is the key to the work that needs to be done to co-create communities where we can work together in sustainable ways.

The Study of Leadership

The literature on leadership is vast, and yet leadership theory, for the most part, reflects only a Western conceptualization of leadership; rarely does it reflect any cross-cultural leadership perspectives (Pfiefer 2005, 10). There is not a consensus on a definition of leadership, but Joseph Rost (1993, 102), after an extensive review and critique of leadership definitions, defined it as "an influence relationship through which leaders and followers intend real change that is mutually acceptable and has individual commitment." Gary Yukl (1998, 3), in his review of definitions of leadership, argued that the notion of influence underpins most leadership definitions, and concluded that most definitions "reflect the assumption that it involves a social influence process whereby the intentional influence is exerted by one person over other people to structure the activities and relationships" of the group. This definition of leadership is at odds with Indigenous leadership practices, which place the emphasis on community and collective perspective rather than autonomy and a single point of view.

In his analysis of the vast literature on leadership, sociologist Keith Grint (2000) isolated four main approaches to leadership: trait approach, situational approach, contingency approach, and constitutive approach. A trait approach (also known as the study of "great men") was an early attempt at leadership theorization that suggested leaders possessed inherent qualities and characteristics that made them great leaders, and that through studies we could identify such traits. These great leaders supposedly could lead under any conditions. The situational approach, in contrast, emphasized the importance of the context or circumstances that leaders faced. The right situation had to arise before a leader had an opportunity to excel. The contingency approach combines the two previous approaches by looking at the essence of a leader but also the situation or context that leader faced. If a leader's strengths aligned with the situation, then the leader would be able to lead effectively. This contingency approach recognizes that different leaders may require different circumstances in order to lead. Lastly, the constitutive approach was described by Grint as a "pro-active affair" for leaders (4). Leaders actively shape a group's interpretation of the situation and try to persuade others that their interpretation is the truth, and that their vision or plan is the right response. Leaders may actually influence an organizational culture and help shape an organization's interpretation of their context and, by extension, how to deal effectively with given situations.

One other main theoretical area of study is that of transformational leadership, which moves beyond leadership behaviours and situations to the exploration of leadership as a more dynamic and complex phenomenon. Transformational leadership theories differ from situational or contingency theories by focusing on the importance of collective identity and the reciprocal relationship involved (Conger 1999). Leaders make meaning for the group by creating an inspirational vision and strategic direction, persuading the group of the importance of such change, and mobilizing energy to carry out these goals. This approach to leadership through inspiration is often referenced in contrast to transactional leadership, which sees leaders using the carrot or the stick to get followers or staff to perform (Griffin and Rafferty 2004). Transformational leadership also recognizes the important role followers play in leadership effectiveness: a leader's vision, values, and knowledge have to resonate with his or her followers in order to be effective—which seems to contend that a leader listen deeply to his or her followers' needs.

Whether leadership differs between cultures is a question that has received attention in leadership studies. Indeed, Geert Hofstede (1980, 1983, 1991) led a movement exploring cultural differences in leadership and management, arguing that culture is the mind's software and it collectively programs leaders, thereby distinguishing them, and their values, from leaders of other cultures. Cross-cultural leadership studies have shown that culture is an important factor to consider when exploring leadership, and that the major leadership schools of thought, which come from Western countries, do not provide a complete cross-cultural picture (Dorfman et al. 2004). *Restorying Indigenous Leadership* opens up a different kind of conversation, considering a full range of leadership behaviours.

Research and writing on Indigenous leadership may not be extensive, but it is a growing area. There are a variety of themes that one sees in this emerging literature on Indigenous leadership. Most of the research and publishing on Indigenous leadership has been in the form of biographical studies of chiefs and other political leaders, often written for the general public (Sluman 1967; Dempsey 1972, 1986, 1995; MacEwan 1973; Goodwill and Sluman 1984; Smith 1987; MacGregor 1989; Comeau 1993; Botting 2005; Harper 2013; Madsen 1999; Smith 1986; Baird 1972; Utley 1993; Sugden 1997; Kohere 1949; Rutherford 1947; Binney, Chaplin, and Wallace 1979; Horner 1974; Coe 1989; Attwood and Markus 2004). This line of research takes the trait approach to leadership, although these biographers also use the situational approach to some extent, placing the leaders in their legal and historical context or situation. What we see is that Indigenous peoples in the various colonies were similarly dealing with the effects of colonization, especially the rapid influx of white settlers, displacement from their traditional lands and resources, and their attempts at protest and resistance in an effort to stand up for their Indigenous rights (Elliott and Fleras 1992; Havemann 1999; Langton et al. 2004; Knafla and Westra 2010). Soon after settlement, these Indigenous leaders had similar experiences with the colonial governments imposing assimilation policies upon them and restricting their governance and sovereignty (Armitage 1995; Franks 2000; Hocking 2005; Ivison, Patton, and Sanders 2000). Thus, the Indigenous leaders in each of these countries had similar issues and challenges facing them and their communities, with similar results, such as loss of cultural practices, dispossession from traditional lands, and a marginalization from the mainstream economy. The resulting social impacts are still being felt today in Indigenous communities.

Scholarly studies of Indigenous leadership have also been undertaken by social scientists, including many ethnohistorians who attempted some generalized characterizations (Macleod 1923; MacNeish 1956; Rogers 1965; Smith 1973; Morantz 1982, Chute 1998; Fenton 1946; Bee 1969, 1979; Berkhofer 1978; Holm 1982; Schusky 1986; Tollefson 1986; Abler 2004; Hauptman 2008). There were also collections published by Indigenous leaders (Monture 1960; Quan 2003; Josephy 1962; Fielder 1975; Foreman 1976; Dockstader 1977; Nagelfell 1995; Edmunds 2001). Some research focused on leaders and the Indigenous organizations they represented (Mitchell 1977;

Patterson 1978; Dobbin 1981; Tennant 1982; O'Donnell 1985; Krosen-brink-Gelissen 1989; McFarlane 1993; Sawchuk 1998; Calliou 2011; Drucker 1958; Svensson 1980; Hauptman 1983; Morrison 1991). In Canada, sociologist Menno Boldt from the University of Lethbridge led a new wave of published scholarly works on Indigenous leadership studies in the early 1980s, exploring leaders' attitudes, values, political activism, and Indigenous nationalism, including extra-legal action (Boldt 1973, 1980, 1981a, 1981b, 1981c, 1982, 1993; Boldt and Long 1987; Hedican 1986, 1991). In the United States during this period, research was being published on contemporary Indigenous leadership issues led by R. David Edmunds and others (Edmunds 1980; Holm and Jordan 1979; Cornell 1980; Williams 1984a, 1984b; Holm 1985; Fenton 1986; Fixico 1986; Lurie 1986; Ervin 1987; Martin 1987; Hoxie 1984, 1992; Moses and Wilson 1985). In Australia, New Zealand, and the Pacific Islands during this period, most studies were by anthropologists exploring traditional leadership, especially the concepts around chiefdoms and authority (Douglas 1979; Blackwood 1981; Allen 1984; Marcus 1989; Lawson 1990; Sutton 1990; Rose 1992; Diamond 2003; Lindstrom and White 1997).

There has been a considerable amount of research and publishing on Indigenous educational leadership (Sealy 1985; Urion 1993; Robbins and Tippeconnic 1985; Charleston and Lynch 1990; Jules 1999; Muskego 1995; Ambler 1992; Eagleeye and Stein 1993; Jennings 2005; Johnson 1997; Benham et al. 2003; Fitzgerald 2003, 2006; Montes 2007; Benham and Murakami-Ramalho 2010; Pidgeon 2012). Another area that has received much attention is Indigenous women in leadership in a variety of sectors, including politics, business, and education (Voyageur 2002, 2003, 2005, 2008, 2011a, 2011b; Maracle 2003; Fraser and Kennedy 2012; Johnson 2000; Hauptman 1979, 1985; Vernon 1985; Antell 1990; Griffen 1987; Mathes 1990; McCoy 1992; Halsey and Jaimes 1992; Miller 1992, 1994; Mankiller and Wallis 1993; Gomez and Prindeville 1999; Stauss and Taylor 2006). There has been some exploration of Indigenous leadership in the urban environment and its associated issues (McKinney 1980; Straus and Valentino 2003; Lickers 2006). Problems associated with factionalism, questions of authority, and what has been termed the "crisis in Indigenous tribal leadership" have been covered by several scholars (Sawchuk 1995; Shepardson 1971; Moulton 1979; Holm 1985).

Scholars and practitioners have carried out research on Indigenous leadership training (Calliou 2005, 2008; Ottmann 2005a, 2005b; Kotowich-Laval 2005; Begay 1991, 1997; Finley 1997; Wakshul 1997; Hassin and Young 1999; Allicock et al. 2010; Foley 2008). Manley Begay (1997) has argued that training of Indigenous leaders requires a focus on knowledge and skills to carry out nation building after the effects of colonialism, stating that "native leaders have become responsible for the tasks of rebuilding, reuniting, reshaping, and revitalizing these nations." Jacqueline Ottmann (2005a, 2005b) reported that Indigenous leaders she interviewed felt that any leadership development program would have to be cognizant of specifically Indigenous culture, needs, and issues, as well as aware of current and innovative leadership practices.

The comparison of traditional Indigenous leadership and Western leadership is an area that has garnered some attention (Bruhn 2009; Delorme 2012; Nielson and Redpath 1997; Badwound and Tierney 1988; Pfiefer 2005). This stream of research still makes quite broad generalized statements about Western and Indigenous leaders and the leadership they carry out. R. David Edmunds (1980, ix) argued that, rather than making generalizations about the nature of American Indian leadership, it was perhaps better to study the diversity of leadership through biographical research that illustrates how "Indian leadership has manifested itself in a wide variety of patterns." Indeed, the varieties of Indigenous leadership and the difficulties of researching and explaining them have been discussed by some scholars (Berkhofer 1978; Williams 1984a). Understanding a particular Indigenous community, its historical and legal context, and its world view may be challenging, but it is a necessary prerequisite for truly appreciating a leader, and his or her values and accomplishments. Carolyn Kenny (2012, 4) argues that, for Indigenous leaders, the road to leadership is "paved with land, ancestors, Elders, and story—concepts that are rarely mentioned in the mainstream leadership literature" and that such a perspective "embodies concepts unique to Native leadership." Cheryl A. Metoyer (2010) argues that Indigenous leadership is rooted in culture, and that any study of, or development of, leadership must consider specific traditions and ways of knowing, just as Ottmann (2005b) argues that culture and language play a major role in defining the roles and expectations of Indigenous leadership.

Others have argued that we need to rethink leadership, that we need to explore leadership concepts appropriate to building strong Aboriginal communities, and that we have to pay attention to the original philosophies and practices of our people (Fraser and Kennedy 2012). Survival of specific Indigenous identities will require a continuation of traditional knowledge and practices. Laurence M. Hauptman (2008, xxi) argued in his study of Iroquois leadership that they were able to survive the onslaught of Euro-American contact by being adaptable to change by relying on their traditions, cultural strengths, and ceremonies. Some Indigenous scholars argue that leaders need to learn from an ancestral knowledge perspective (Nicholas-MacKenzie 1999; Washington 2004).

Another line of argument calls for a need to break away from the colonial mindset and a state of dependency. For example, Strater Crowfoot (1997, 323), a Blackfoot leader, argues that Indigenous leaders "need a paradigm shift in [their] thinking, away from the cynical, defensive, dependent, entitlement mindset that has been articulated in [them] under the colonial Indian Act regime, and toward a more trusting, assertively proactive, persevering, visionary, affirming, meritocratic, and inclusive orientation...." Selwyn Katene (2010, 6), exploring what makes good Maori leadership, especially in response to the colonial encounter, argues that Indigenous peoples "looked to a leader that would lead them forward through the difficult times that lay ahead, someone who could present an identifiable vision or future state that they could aspire to, someone who could clearly map out a way forward and who had a plan which was mutually beneficial." Thus, Indigenous leaders are expected to lead change in the community that not only meets current needs, but anticipates the challenges and opportunities that lie ahead. Taiaiake Alfred (1995, 1999), a Mohawk political theorist, argues that Indigenous leaders today must ensure that they work to revitalize their community's traditional values, which will serve as a foundation for re-establishing the community's leadership and governance systems in order to preserve its identity and nationhood.

Even though Indigenous scholars and practitioners are calling for more research on traditional forms of Indigenous leadership and governance, many continue to argue that contemporary Indigenous leaders need to learn both modern Western knowledge and traditional knowledge related to knowing, being, and doing as a leader (Calliou 2005, 2008; Ottmann 2005a; Simpson and Turner 2008). Indeed, leadership today requires "new expertise and old wisdom" (Perkinson and Reihana, n.d., 1). Training and developing Indigenous leadership is an important aspect of community economic development. *Restorying Indigenous Leadership* presents positive steps, research, and models to inspire Indigenous leaders to develop new, and reconsider established, practices.

Wise Practices in Community Development

Brian Calliou and Cynthia Wesley-Esquimaux's chapter, "A Wise Practices Approach to Indigenous Community Development in Canada," provides a context and rationale for The Banff Centre's wise practices approach to community economic development. The authors present and describe the wise practices model developed by The Banff Centre, which integrates insights from a literature review, critique of the term "best practices," the notion that there is wisdom in stories of success, and the importance of traditional teachings. Their chapter explores some important ideas about strength-based approaches to Indigenous community economic development, issues of perception, and the legacy of colonization.

Christopher Wetzel's chapter, "The Field of Tribal Leadership Training, Cultures of Expertise, and Native Nations in the United States," applies a sociological perspective to the issue of training and capacity building for Indigenous organizations. The work paints an ecological picture of the field of Indigenous leadership training in the United States. Wetzel provides an overview of how the field is organized, who the key organizational players are, and the kinds of training offered. He introduces a typological model of tribal training to explore internal and external issues and the question of how to be critical consumers of training services. He interweaves stories and research to explore the implications of three key questions: How can First Nations thoughtfully and strategically use the services of these organizations? What leadership and community development training is best handled by First Nations? And how does the field impact expressions of self-determination and sovereignty?

Laura Brearley's chapter, "Deep Listening and Leadership: An Indigenous Model of Leadership and Community Development in Australia," contains a series of stories and messages generated from the Deep Listening Project. It articulates the links between ancient wisdom and leading community development practices. The Deep Listening Project began in 2004 with a group of Indigenous leaders, artists, and researchers in Australia undertaking their MA and PhD degrees. They included Indigenous ways of knowing in their research and used research as a framework for telling stories and passing on messages for future generations. The Deep Listening Project brings together an inclusive and creative cross-cultural community. The project includes a cross-cultural exchange that has been occurring between Indigenous leaders and creative artists in Australia and Canada through The Banff Centre since 2008. In the chapter, project participants tell stories about the importance of Deep Listening in the subject areas of leadership, research, diversity, community, relationship, regeneration, and sustainability.

Cora Voyageur's chapter, "Restorying the Leadership Role: Indigenous Women in Politics and Business in Canada," presents some of her research into women's experiences of leadership and entrepreneurship in Indigenous communities in Canada, and brings to life stories of leadership and community development, as well as the links between them. In her research, Voyageur describes the detrimental impact of colonization and the accompanying patriarchal attitudes on the subjugation of women's social, economic, and political statuses in the community. She describes how women's subordination and exclusion from power was embedded within the Indian Act of 1876. In addition to Voyageur's compelling accounts about the loss of women's visibility and agency through colonization, her research reveals another story that is both restorative and emergent: the post-colonial complexities that characterize the context in which women leaders and business entrepreneurs are working. The women who were interviewed for this chapter tell stories about the impact education has had on their professional lives and the challenges they faced when returning to their Indigenous communities with broadened perspectives and a heightened awareness of what Indigenous leadership means to them. The women leaders are perceived by others to be courageous, responsible, and innovative, with a sense of commitment to the health and well-being of the community. The interviewees identify leaders in the Indigenous community as being critical thinkers who draw on their networks and relationships to solve problems. The female Indigenous leaders are described not necessarily as charismatic but as skilled communicators and better listeners. The vitality, persistence, and resilience of the women whose stories are shared in Voyageur's research exemplify Indigenous women's "restored" and "restoryed" capacity to lead.

Michelle Evans's chapter, "Exploring Australian Indigenous Artistic Leadership," draws on stories and insights from her recent doctoral research, which explores the nexus between Indigenous arts and leadership. Evans provides an overview of the Australian historical and political context of the associated traumas of colonization and dispossession. She discusses the emotional, historical, socio-economic, and cultural contexts of arts leadership in the Australian Indigenous community through personal narratives and leadership literature. By analyzing narratives of creative practitioners speaking about their practice, Evans identifies the influences and pressures on Indigenous arts leaders. The stories reveal the complexities of the cultural navigation required of them. In particular, she focuses on family relationships, cultural connections, and creative traditions. Evans explores the ego needs of arts leaders, the impact of entrenched power relations, and the complexities of managerialism. What she finds is that leadership involves an ongoing negotiation amongst Indigenous culture, business imperatives, and managerial processes.

In her chapter, "Four Contemporary Tensions in Indigenous Nation Building: Challenges for Leadership in the United States," Miriam Jorgensen looks at the big picture, articulating the complexities of contemporary nation building and the associated leadership principles and practices that are needed to respond effectively to the current and future needs of Indigenous nations. She explores inter-related areas of self-governance, self-determination, and boundaries in politics and business, and the imperatives of shifting from indi-vidualized present-day perspectives to the collective, future-oriented approach of seventh-generation thinking. Drawing on decades of research and stories, Jorgensen weaves together a compelling and nu-anced analysis of nation building, sustainable Indigenous community development, and informed leadership practices.

Dennis Foley's chapter, "Aboriginal Approaches to Business Leader-ship and Entrepreneurship in Australia," outlines the long history of entrepreneurialism in Indigenous culture in Australia. He identifies four levels of Australian Aboriginal businesses: the Nursery Industries; the Complex Retail and Service Industry; the Professional Industry; and the Multinational and National Industry. He presents a broad de-scription of current Indigenous businesses in Gippsland, a regional area of Victoria, Australia. Foley's chapter also explores Indigenous ways of knowing and includes stories of the impact of racism on Indigenous entrepreneurs and researchers of Indigenous entrepreneurialism.

Bob Kayseas's chapter, "Leadership Success in Overcoming the Environmental Constraints to Indigenous Entrepreneurial Activity in Canada," is also broad in its scope and explores the economic development of Canadian Indigenous communities based on his doc-toral research. His research is grounded in three case studies of wise practices in Indigenous entrepreneurship: the Osoyoos Indian Band, British Columbia; the Lac La Ronge Indian Band, Saskatchewan; and the Membertou First Nation, Nova Scotia. His research is directed to a core question: What has enabled the success of entrepreneurial ven-tures in Canadian Indigenous reserves despite all the legal, historical, and social constraints? Kayseas explores the impact of welfare and the resulting dependence on government, and examines the geographical, social, and legal complexities of entrepreneurship, including a lack of access to information channels, minimal networking opportun-ities, small markets, higher costs, few role models, and an inability to leverage land for borrowing. He also describes the detrimental effects of federal legislation and policy, the legacy of the Indian Act, and the exogenous and endogenous factors in development. He identifies the cultural opportunities and accompanying complexities of linking economic and philosophical principles, maintaining a collectivist orientation within a competitive context, linking business development to language and cultural retention, and seeing land as a renewable heritage resource. He explores the phenomenon of entrepreneurship and entrepreneurial characteristics, and examines the principles of capacity building and the positive impact of educated band members. There is certainly a connection between Kayseas's research and the examinations of entrepreneurial training opportunities in Christopher Wetzel's and Dennis Foley's chapters.

The stories in *Restorying Indigenous Leadership* share with readers the inspiring processes and wise practices by which we may concurrently develop retrospective awareness, recognize current capacities, and become aware of future possibilities for Indigenous leadership—deeply awake to our present moment as well as our responsibility to the future. *Restorying* is not just about the stories told, but about the significant questions that surface in the spaces that exist between stories: What matters? What matters most?

References

Abler, Thomas S. 2004. "Seneca Moieties and Hereditary Chieftainships: The Early-Nineteenth-Century Political Organization of an Iroquois Nation." *Ethnohistory* 51 (3): 459–88.

Alfred, Taiaiake (Gerald R.). 1995. *Heeding the Voices of Our Ancestors: Kahnawake Mohawk Politics and the Rise of Native Nationalism.* Toronto: Oxford University Press.

———. 1999. *Peace, Power, Righteousness: An Indigenous Manifesto.* Toronto: Oxford University Press.

Allen, Michael. 1984. "Elders, Chiefs, and Big Men: Authority, Legitimation and Political Evolution in Melanesia." *American Ethnologist* 11 (1): 20–41.

Allicock, Sydney, Lynne Hately, Michael Lickers, and Christine Wihak. 2010. "Eagle and the Condor: Indigenous Alliances in Leadership Development." *Diaspora, Indigenous, and Minority Education* 1 (2): 135–48.

Ambler, Marjane. 1992. "Women Leaders in Indian Education: More Women are Running Tribal Colleges – What Does This Mean for the Future of Native American Societies?" *Tribal College Journal* 3 (4): 10–14.

Antell, Judith Anne. 1990. "American Indian Women Activists."' Unpublished PhD diss., University of California.

Archibald, Jo-ann (Q'um Q'um Xiiem). 2008. "An Indigenous Storywork Methodology." In *Handbook of the Arts in Qualitative Research: Perspectives, Methodologies, Examples and Issues,* edited by Ardra L. Cole and J. Gary Knowles, 371–76. Thousand Oaks, California: Sage Publications.

Armitage, Andrew. 1995. *Comparing the Policy of Aboriginal Assimilation: Australia, Canada, and New Zealand.* Vancouver: University of British Columbia Press.

Atkinson, Judy. 2001. "Privileging Indigenous Research Methodologies." Paper presented at the *National Indigenous Researchers Forum,* University of Melbourne.

Attwood, Bain, and Andrew Markus. 2004. *Thinking Black: William Cooper and the Australian Aborigines League.* Canberra: Aboriginal Studies Press.

Badwound, Elgin, and William Tierney. 1988. "Leadership and American Indian Values: The Tribal College Dilemma." *Journal of American Indian Education* 28 (1): 9–15.

Baird, W. David. 1972. *Peter Pitchlynn: Chief of the Choctaws.* Norman: University of Oklahoma Press.

Bee, Robert L. 1969. "Tribal Leadership in the War on Poverty: A Case Study." *Social Science Quarterly* 50 (3): 676–86.

——. 1979. "To Get Something For the People: The Predicament of Native American Leaders." *Human Organization,* 38 (3), 239–47 .

Begay, Jr., Manley. 1991. "Designing Native American Management and Leadership Training: Past Efforts, Present Endeavours, and Future Options." Harvard Project Report Series No. 91–3. Cambridge: John F. Kennedy School of Government, Harvard University.

——. 1997. "Leading by Choice, Not Chance: Leadership Education for Native Chief Executives of American Indian Nations." Unpublished PhD diss., Graduate School of Education, Harvard University.

Benham, Maenette K. P., Valorie Johnson, W. K. Kellogg, and Matthew Jason VanAlstine. 2003. "Native Leadership: Advocacy for Transformation,

Culture, Community, and Sovereignty." In *The Renaissance of American Indian Higher Education: Capturing the Dream*, edited by Maenette K. P. Benham and Wayne J. Stein, 149–66. Mahwah, New Jersey: Lawrence Erlbaum Associates.

Benham, Maenette, and Eliabeth Murakami-Ramalho. 2010. "Engaging in Educational Leadership: The Generosity of Spirit." *International Journal of Leadership in Education* 13 (1): 77–91.

Berger, John. January 14, 2008. "In Conversation with Ramona Kaval." *The Book Show*. Radio National, Australia.

Berkhofer, Robert F., Jr. 1978. "Native Americans." In *Ethnic Leadership in America*, edited by John Higham, 119–49. Baltimore: John Hopkins University Press.

Binney, Judith, Gillian Chaplin, and Craig Wallace. 1979. *Mihaia: The Prophet Rua Kenana and His Community*. Wellington: Oxford University Press.

Blackwood, Peter. 1981. "Rank, Exchange and Leadership in Four Vanautu Societies." In *Vanautu: Politics, Economics, and Ritual in Island Melanesia* edited by Michael Allen, 35–84. Sydney: Academic Press.

Boldt, Menno. 1973. "Indian Leaders in Canada: Attitudes Toward Equality, Identity, and Political Status." Unpublished PhD diss., Yale University.

——. 1980. "Canadian Native Indian Leadership: Context and Composition." *Canadian Ethnic Studies* 12: 15–33.

——. 1981a. "Enlightenment Values, Romanticism, and Attitudes Toward Political Status: A Study of Native Indian Leaders in Canada." *Canadian Review of Sociology and Anthropology* 18 (4): 545–65.

——. 1981b. "Philosophy, Politics and Extralegal Action: Native Indian Leaders in Canada." *Ethnic and Racial Studies* 4 (2): 205–21.

——. 1981c. "Social Correlates of Nationalism: A Study of Native Indian Leaders in a Canadian Internal Colony." *Comparative Political Studies* 14 (2): 205–31.

——. 1982. "Intellectual Orientations and Nationalism Among Leaders in an Internal Colony: A Theoretical and Comparative Perspective." *British Journal of Sociology* 33 (4): 484–510.

——. 1993. *Surviving As Indians: The Challenge of Self-Government*. Toronto: University of Toronto Press.

Boldt, Menno, and J. Anthony Long. 1987. "Leadership Selection in Canadian Indian Communities: Reforming the Present and Incorporating the Past." *Great Plains Quarterly* 7 (2): 103–15.

Botting, Gary. 2005. *Chief Smallboy: In Pursuit of Freedom*. Calgary: Fifth House Books.

Bruhn, Jodi. 2009. "In Search of Common Ground: Reconciling Western-Based Governance Principles and First Nations Traditions." Report for the Institute on Governance, Ottawa.

Calliou, Brian. 2005. "The Culture of Leadership: North American Indigenous Leadership in a Changing Economy." In *Indigenous Peoples and the Modern State*, edited by Duane Champagne, Karen Jo Torjesen, and Susan Steiner, 47–68. Walnut Creek: AltaMira Press.

———. 2008. "The Significance of Building Leadership and Community Capacity to Implement Self-Government." In *Aboriginal Self-Government in Canada: Current Trends and Issues*, edited by Yale Belanger, 332–48. 3rd ed. Saskatoon: Purich Publishing.

———. 2011. "From Paternalism to Partnership: The Challenges of Aboriginal Leadership." In *Visions of the Heart: Canadian Aboriginal Issues*, edited by Olive Patricia Dickason and David Long, 258–91. 3rd ed. Oxford: Oxford University Press.

Charleston, G. Mike, and Patrick D. Lynch. 1990. "The Emergence of American Indian Leadership in Education." *Journal of American Indian Education* 29 (2): 1–10.

Chute, Janet E. 1998. "Ojibwa Leadership During the Fur Trade Era at Sault Ste. Marie." In *New Faces of the Fur Trade: Papers of the Seventh North American Fur Trade Conference*, edited by Jo-Anne Fiske, Susan Sleeper-Smith, and William Wicken, 153–72. East Lansing: Michigan State University Press.

Coe, Mary. 1989. *Windrayne: A Wiradjuri Koorie*. Canberra: Aboriginal Studies Press.

Comeau, Pauline. 1993. *Elijah: No Ordinary Hero*. Vancouver: Douglas & McIntyre.

Conger, Jay A. 1999. "Charismatic and Transformational Leadership in Organizations: An Insider's Perspective on These Developing Streams of Research." *Leadership Quarterly* 10 (2): 145–79.

Cornell, Stephen E. 1980. "American Indian Political Resurgence: The Historical Sociology of Group Incorporation and Response." Unpublished PhD diss., University of Chicago.

Crowfoot, Strater. 1997. "Leadership in Frist Nation Communities: A Chief's Perspectives on the Colonial Millstone." In *First Nations in Canada: Perspectives in Opportunity, Empowerment, and Self-Determination*, edited by J. Rick Ponting, 299–325. Toronto: McGraw-Hill Ryerson.

Delorme, Marie Yvonne. 2012. "Leadership: The Role of Interaction of Aboriginal and Non-Aboriginal Leaders in the Context of Economic Development." Unpublished PhD diss., University of Calgary.

Dempsey, Hugh A. 1972. *Crowfoot: Chief of the Blackfeet*. Norman: University of Oklahoma Press.

——. 1986. *The Gentle Persuader: A Biography of James Gladstone, Indian Senator*. Saskatoon: Western Producer Prairie Books.

——. 1995. *Red Crow: Warrior Chief*. 2nd ed. Saskatoon: Fifth House.

Diamond, Paul. 2003. *A Fire in Your Belly: Maori Leaders Speak*. Wellington: Huai Publishers.

Dobbin, Murray. 1981. *The One-and-a-Half Men: The Story of Jim Brady and Malcom Norris, Metis Patriots of the 20th Century*. Vancouver: New Star Books.

Dockstader, Frederick J. 1977. *Great North American Indians: Profiles in Life and Leadership*. New York: Van Nostrand Reinhold.

Dorfman, Peter W., Vipin Gupta, Paul J. Hanges, Robert J. House, and Mansour Javidan, eds. 2004. *Culture, Leadership, and Organizations: The GLOBE Study of 62 Societies*. Thousand Oaks: Sage Publications.

Douglas, Bronwen. 1979. "Rank, Power, Authority: A Reassessment of Traditional Leadership in South Pacific Societies." *Journal of Pacific History* 14 (1): 2–27.

Drucker, Philip. 1958. *The Native Brotherhoods: Modern Intertribal Organizations on the North West Coast*. Washington: U.S. Printing Office.

Eagleeye, Dan, and Wayne Stein. 1993. "Learned Leadership: Preparing the Next Generation of Tribal College Administrators." *Tribal College Journal* 5 (2): 33–36.

Edmunds, R. David, ed. 1980. *American Indian Leaders: Studies in Diversity*. Lincoln: University of Nebraska Press.

——. 2001. *The New Warriors: Native American Leaders Since 1900*. Lincoln: University of Nebraska Press.

Elliott, Jean Leonard, and Augie Fleras. 1992. *The 'Nations Within': Aboriginal-State Relations in Canada, the United States and New Zealand*.

Toronto: Oxford University Press.

Ellis, Carolyn. 2004. *The Ethnographic I: A Methodological Novel about Autoethnography*. Walnut Creek: AltaMira Press.

Ervin, Alexander M. 1987. "Styles and Strategies of Leadership During the Alaskan Native Land Claims Movement: 1959–71." *Anthropologica* 29 (1): 21–38.

Fenton, William N. 1946. "An Iroquois Condolence Council for Installing Cayuga Chiefs in 1945." *Washington Academy of Social Sciences Journal* 36 (4): 110–27.

———. 1986. "Leadership in the Northeastern Woodlands of North America." *American Indian Quarterly* 10 (1): 21–45.

Fielder, Mildred. 1975. *Sioux Indian Leaders*. Seattle: Superior.

Finley, Vernon. 1997. "Designing a Cultural Leadership Program." *Tribal College Journal* 9 (2): 19–22.

Fitzgerald, Tanya. 2003. "Changing the Deafening Silence of Indigenous Women's Voices in Educational Leadership." *Journal of Educational Administration* 41 (1): 9–23.

———. 2006. "Walking Between Two Worlds: Indigenous Women and Educational Leadership." *Educational Management Administration & Leadership* 34 (2): 201–13.

Fixico, Donald L. 1986. "Tribal Leaders and the Demand for Natural Energy Resources on Tribal Lands." In *The Plains Indians in the Twentieth Century*, edited by Peter Iverson, 219–35. Norman: University of Oklahoma Press.

Foley, Dennis. 2008. "Australian Aboriginal Leadership in Modernity: Born or Trained?" *Journal of Australian Indigenous Issues* 11 (4): 36–47.

Foreman, Carolyn Thomas. 1976. *Indian Women Chiefs*. Washington: Zenger.

Franks, C. E. S. 2000. "Indian Policy: Canada and the United States Compared." In *Aboriginal Rights and Self-Government: The Canadian and Mexican Experience in North American Perspective*, edited by Curtis Cook and Juan D. Lindau, 221–64. Montreal & Kingston: McGill-Queen's University Press.

Fraser, Tina Ngaroimata, and Carolyn Kennedy, eds. 2012. *Living Indigenous Leadership: Native Narratives on Building Strong Communities*. Vancouver: University of British Columbia Press.

Gomez, Teresa Braley, and Diane-Michele Prindeville. 1999. "American

Indian Women Leaders, Public Policy, and the Importance of Gender and Ethnic Identity." *Women and Politics* 20 (2): 17–32.

Goodwill, Jean, and Norma Sluman. 1984. *John Tootoosis*. Winnipeg: Pemmican Publications.

Griffen, Connie. 1987. "Relearning to Trust Ourselves: Interview with Chief Wilma Mankiller." *Women of Power* 7: 38–40.

Griffin, Mark A., and Alannah E. Rafferty. 2004. "Dimensions of transformational leadership: Conceptual and empirical extensions." *The Leadership Quarterly* 15 (2004): 329–54.

Grint, Keith. 2000. *The Arts of Leadership*. Oxford: Oxford University Press.

Halsey, Theresa, and M. Annette Jaimes. 1992. "American Indian Women: At the Center of Indigenous Resistance in North America." In *The State of Native America: Genocide, Colonization, and Resistance*, edited by M. Annette Jaimes, 311–44. Boston: South End Press.

Harper, Joan. 2013. *He Moved a Mountain: The Life of Frank Calder and the Nisga'a Land Claims Accord*. Vancouver: Ronsdale Press.

Hassin, Jeannette, and Robert S. Young. 1999. "Self-Sufficiency, Personal Empowerment, and Community Revitalization: The Impact of a Leadership Program on American Indians in the Soutwest." *American Indian Culture and Research Journal* 23 (3): 265–86.

Hauptman, Laurence M. 1979. "Alice Jemison: Seneca Political Activist, 1901–1964." *The Indian Historian* 12 (2): 15–62.

——. 1983. "The American Indian Federation and the Indian New Deal: A Reinterpretation." *Pacific Historical Review* 52 (4): 378–402.

——. 1985. "Designing Women: Minnie Kellogg, Iroquois Leader." In *Indian Lives: Essays on Nineteenth and Twentieth-Century Native American Leaders*, edited by Lester George Moses and Raymond Wilson, 158–79. Albuquerque: University of New Mexico Press.

——. 2008. *Seven Generations of Iroquois Leadership: The Six Nations Since 1800*. Syracuse: Syracuse University Press.

Havemann, Paul. 1999. *Indigenous Peoples Rights in Australia, Canada and New Zealand*. Oxford: Oxford University Press.

Hedican, Edward J. 1986. *The Ogoki River Guides: Emergent Leadership Among the Northern Ojibwa*. Waterloo: Wilfred Laurier University Press.

——. 1991. "On the Ethno-Politics of Canadian Native Leadership and Identity." *Ethnic Groups* 9: 1–15.

Hocking, Barbara, ed. 2005. *Unfinished Constitutional Business: Rethinking Aboriginal Self-Determination*. Canberra: Aboriginal Studies Press.

Hofstede, Geert. 1980. *Culture's Consequences: International Differences in Work Related Values*. Beverly Hills: Sage Publications.

——. 1983. "The Cultural Relativity of Organizational Practices and Theories." *Journal of International Business* 14 (2): 75–89.

——. 1991. *Cultures and Organizations: Software of the Mind*. London: McGraw Hill.

Holm, Tom. 1982. "Indian Concepts of Authority and the Crisis of Tribal Governments." *Social Science Journal* 19 (2): 59–72.

——. 1985. "The Crisis in Tribal Government." In *American Indian Policy in the Twentieth Century*, edited by Vine Deloria, Jr., 135–54. Norman: University of Oklahoma Press.

Holm, Tom M., and Glenn Jordan, eds. 1979. *Indian Leaders: Oklahoma's First Statesmen*. Oklahoma City: Oklahoma Historical Society.

Horner, Jack. 1974. *Vote Ferguson for Aboriginal Freedom*. Sydney: Australia and New Zealand Book Co.

Hoxie, Frederick E. 1984. "Building a Future on the Past: Crow Indian Leadership in an Era of Division and Reunion." In *Indian Leadership*, edited by Walter L. Williams, 76–84. Manhatten: Sunflower University Press.

——. 1992. "Crow Indian Leadership Amidst Reservation Oppression." In *State and Reservation: New Perspectives on Federal Indian Policy*, edited by George Pierre Castile and Robert L. Bee, 38–60. Tucson: University of Arizona Press.

Ivison, Duncan, Paul Patton, and Will Sanders. 2000. *Political Theory and the Rights of Indigenous Peoples*. Cambridge: Cambridge University Press.

Jennings, Michael. 2005. *Alaska Native Political Leadership and Higher Education: One University, Two Universes*. Walnut Creek: AltaMira Press.

Johnson, Shelly. 2000. "Reclaiming Their Places: Seven Women Chiefs of Northern B.C." Unpublished master's thesis, Faculty of Social Work, University of Northern British Columbia.

Johnson, V. J. 1997. "Weavers of Change: Portraits of Native American Women Educational Leaders." Unpublished PhD diss., Michigan State University.

Josephy, Alvin M., Jr. 1962. *The Patriot Chiefs: Studies of Nine Great Leaders of American Indians*. London: Eyre and Spottiswoode.

Jules, F. 1999. "Native Indian Leadership." *Canadian Journal of Native Education* 23 (1): 40–56.

Katene, Selwyn. 2010. "Modelling Māori Leadership: What Makes for Good Leadership?" *MAI Review* 2010 (2): 1–16.

Kenny, Carolyn. 2012. "Liberating Leadership Theory." In *Living Indigenous Leadership: Native Narratives on Building Strong Communities,* edited by Carolyn Kenny and Tina Ngaroimata Fraser, 1–16. Vancouver: University of British Columbia Press.

King, Thomas. 2008. "The art of indigenous knowledge: A million porcupines crying in the dark." In *Handbook of the Arts in Qualitative Research: Perspectives, Methodologies, Examples, and Issues,* edited by Ardra L. Cole and J. Gary Knowles, 13–27. Thousand Oaks: Sage Publications.

Knafla, Louis A., and Haijo Westra. 2010. *Aboriginal Title and Indigenous Peoples: Canada, Australia and New Zealand.* Vancouver: University of British Columbia Press.

Kohere, Reweti T. 1949. *The Story of a Maori Chief: Mokena Kohere and His Forebears.* Wellington: Reed Publishing.

Kotowich-Laval, Marian. 2005. "Indigenous Leadership, Challenges and Leadership Training." Unpublished master's thesis, Royal Roads University, British Columbia.

Krosenbrink-Gelissen, Lilianne E. 1989. "The Metis National Council: Continuity and Change among the Canadian Metis." *European Review of Native American Studies* 3 (1): 33–42.

Langton, Marcia, Lisa Palmer, Kathryn Shain, and Maureen Tehan, eds. 2004. *Honour among Nations? Treaties and Agreements with Indigenous Peoples.* Melbourne: Melbourne University Press.

Lawson, Stephanie. 1990. "The Myth of Cultural Homogeneity and Its Implications for Chiefly Power and Politics in Fiji." *Comparative Studies in Society and History* 32 (4): 795–821.

Lickers, Michael. 2006. "Urban Aboriginal Leadership." Unpublished master's thesis, Royal Roads University, British Columbia.

Lindstrom, Lamont, and Geoffrey M. White, eds. 1997. *Chiefs Today: Traditional Pacific Leadership and the Postcolonial State.* Stanford: Stanford University Press.

Lurie, Nancy Oesterich. 1986. "Money, Semantics, and Indian Leadership," *American Indian Quarterly* 10 (1): 47–63.

MacEwan, Grant. 1973. *Sitting Bull: The Years in Canada*. Edmonton: Hurtig Publishers.

MacGregor, Roy. 1989. *Chief: The Fearless Vision of Billy Diamond*. Toronto: Penguin Books Canada Ltd.

Macleod, William Christie. 1923. "On the Significance of Matrilineal Chiefship." *American Anthropologist* 25 (4): 495–524.

MacNeish, June Helm. 1956. "Leadership Among the Northeastern Athabascans." *Anthropologica* 2: 131–63.

Madsen, Brigham D. 1999. *Chief Pocatello*. Moscow: University of Idaho Press.

Mankiller, Wilma, and Micheal Wallis. 1993. *Mankiller: A Chief and Her People*. New York: St. Martin's Press.

Maracle, Sylvia. 2003. "The Eagle Has Landed: Native Women, Leadership and Community Development." In *Strong Women Stories: Native Vision and Community Survival*, edited by Kim Anderson and Bonita Lawrence, 70–80. Toronto: Sumach Press.

Marcus, George E. 1989. "Chieftainship." In *Developments in Polynesian Ethnology*, edited by Robert Borofsky, Jr., and Alan Howard, 175–209. Honolulu: University of Hawaii Press.

Martin, John F. 1987. "Havasupai Political Structure and Leadership." In *Coast, Plains, and Deserts: Essays in Honor of Reynold J. Ruppe*, anthropological research papers, edited by Silvia Gaines. Phoenix: Arizona State University.

Mathes, Valerie Sherer. 1990. "Nineteenth-Century Women and Reform: The Women's National Indian Association." *American Indian Quarterly* 14 (1): 1–18.

McCoy, Melanie. 1992. "Gender or Ethnicity: What Makes a Difference? A Study of Women Tribal Leaders." *Women and Politics* 12 (3): 57–68.

McFarlane, Peter. 1993. *From Brotherhood to Nationhood: George Manuel and the Making of the Modern Indian Movement*. Toronto: Between the Lines.

McKinney, Edward A. 1980. "A School of Social Work Trains Urban Indigenous Leadership in Cleveland." *Community Development Journal* 15 (3): 200–207.

Mehl-Madrona, Lewis. 2007. *Narrative Medicine: The Use of History and Story in the Healing Process*. Vermont: Bear & Company.

Metoyer, Cheryl A. 2010. "Leadership in American Indian Communities: Winter Lessons." *American Indian Culture and Research Journal* 34 (4): 1–12.

Miller, Bruce G. 1992. "Women and Politics: Comparative Evidence from the Northwest Coast." *Ethnology* 31 (4): 367–83.

——. 1994. "Women and Tribal Politics: Is There a Gender Gap in Indian Elections?" *American Indian Quarterly* 18 (1): 25–41.

Mitchell, Marybelle. 1977. *From Talking Chiefs to a Native Corporate Elite: The Birth of Class and Nationalism among Canadian Inuit.* Montreal & Kingston: McGill-Queen's Press.

Montes, Claudine. 2007. "Leadership in Native American Higher Education: A Call for a Collective Vision and Contemporary Warriors." *BC Educational Leadership Research EJournal* 8. www.slc.educ.ubc.ca/ejournal/issue8/Leadership_journal_article_Claudine_Montes.pdf.

Monture, Ethel Brant. 1960. *Famous Indians: Canadian Portraits.* Toronto: Clarke, Irwin.

Morantz, Toby. 1982. "Northern Algonquian Concepts of Status and Leadership Reviewed: A Case Study of the Eighteenth-Century Trading Captain System." *Canadian Review of Sociology and Anthropology* 19 (4): 482–501.

Morrison, Dorothy Nafus. 1991. *Chief Sarah: Sarah Winnemucca's Fight for Indian Rights.* Portland: Oregon Historical Society Press.

Moses, L. G., and Raymond Wilson, eds. 1985. *Indian Lives: Essays on Nineteenth and Twentieth Century Native American Leaders.* Albuquerque, University of New Mexico Press.

Moulton, Gary E. 1979. "Chief John Ross and the Internal Crises of the Cherokee Nation." In *Indian Leaders: Oklahoma's First Statesmen,* edited by H. Glenn Jordan and Thomas M. Holm, 114–25. Oklahoma City: Oklahoma Historical Society.

Muskego, Pauline. 1995. "Leadership in First Nations Schools: Perceptions of Aboriginal Education Administrators." Unpublished master's thesis, University of Saskatchewan.

Nagelfell, Karl. 1995. *North American Indian Chiefs.* North Dighton, Massachusetts: JG Press.

Nicholas-MacKenzie, Lea. 1999. "Lessons From Our Ancestors: A Legacy of Leadership." Unpublished PhD diss., Royal Roads University, British Columbia.

Nielsen, Marianne O., and Lindsay Redpath. 1997. "A Comparison of Native Culture, Non-Native Culture and New Management Ideology." *Canadian Journal of Administrative Sciences* 14 (3): 327–39.

O'Donnell, Jacqueline. 1985. "The Native Brotherhood of British Columbia 1931-1950: A New Phase in Native Political Organization." Unpublished master's thesis, University of British Columbia.

Ottmann, Jacqueline. 2005a. "First Nations Leadership Development within a Saskatchewan Context." Unpublished PhD diss., Department of Educational Administration, University of Saskatchewan.

——. 2005b. "First Nations Leadership Development." Report for The Banff Centre, Indigenous Leadership and Management, www.banffcentre.ca/departments/leadership/aboriginal/library/pdf.

Patterson, E. Palmer., II. 1978. "Andrew Paull and the Early History of British Columbia Organizations." In *One Century Later: Western Canadian Reserve Indians Since Treaty 7*, edited by Ian A. L. Getty and Donald B. Smith, 43–54.Vancouver: University of British Columbia Press.

Perkinson, Martin, and Franceen Reihana. n.d. "Tikanga Māori Leadership: Understanding the Dynamics of Maori Leadership in a Changing World." Research project abstract, http://www.firstfound.org/reihana.htm.

Pfiefer, Dale Marie. 2005. "Leadership in Aotearoa New Zealand: Māori and Pākehā Perceptions of Outstanding Leadership." Unpublished master's thesis, Massey Univeristy, Wellington, New Zealand.

Pidgeon, Michelle. 2012. "Transformation and Indigenous Interconnections: Indigeneity, Leadership, and Higher Education." In *Living Indigenous Leadership: Native Narratives on Building Strong Communities*, edited by Tina Ngaroimata Fraser and Carolyn Kenny, 136–49. Vancouver: University of British Columbia Press.

Ponting, J. Rick, and Cora J. Voyageur. 2001. "Challenging the Deficit Paradigm: Grounds for Optimism Among First Nations in Canada." *Canadian Journal of Native Studies* 21 (2): 275–307.

Quan, Holly. 2003. *Native Chiefs and Famous Métis: Leadership and Bravery in the Canadian West*. Canmore: Altitude Publishing Canada Ltd.

Robbins, Rebecca, and John W. Tippeconnic, III. 1985. *American Indian Education Leadership*. Tempe: Center for Indian Education, Arizona State University.

Rogers, Edward S. 1965. "Leadership Among the Indians of Eastern

Subarctic Canada." *Anthropologica* 7 (2): 263–84.

Rose, Bruce. 1992. *Aboriginal Land Management Issues in Central Australia.* Alice Springs, Northern Territory: Central Land Council.

Rost, Joseph C. 1993. *Leadership for the Twenty-First Century*, Westport, Connecticut: Praeger.

Rutherford, James. 1947. *Hone Heke's Rebellion, 1844–1846: An Episode in the Establishment of British Rule in New Zealand.* Auckland: Auckland University College.

Sawchuk, Joe. 1995. "Fragmentation and Realignment: The Continuing Cycle of Métis and Non-Status Indian Political Organizations in Canada." *Native Studies Review* 10 (2): 77–95.

——. 1998. *The Dynamics of Native Politics: The Alberta Metis Experience.* Saskatoon: Purich Publishing.

Scharmer, C. Otto. 2007. *Theory U: Leading from the Future as it Emerges.* San Francisco: Berrett-Koehler.

Schusky, Ernest L. 1986. "The Evolution of Indian Leadership on the Great Plains, 1750–1950." *American Indian Quarterly* 10 (1): 65–82.

Sealy, Jonathan. 1985. "Leadership Styles of Principles in Native Schools in Saskatchewan." Unpublished master's thesis, University of Saskatchewan.

Shepardson, Mary. 1971. "Navajo Factionalism and the Outside World." In *Apachean Culture, History and Ethnology*, edited by Keith H. Basso and Morris E. Opler, 83–89. Tucson: University of Arizona Press.

Simpson, Audra, and Dale Turner. 2008. "Indigenous Leadership in a Flat World." Research paper, National Centre for First Nations Governance, Vancouver, British Columbia. http://fngovernance.org/ncfng_research/turner_and_simpson.pdf.

Sluman, Norma. 1967. *Poundmaker.* Toronto: Ryerson Press.

Smith, Donald B. 1987. *Sacred Feathers: The Reverend Peter Jones (Kahkewaquonaby) and the Mississauga Indians.* Toronto: University of Toronto Press.

Smith, James G. E. 1973. *Leadership Among the Southwestern Ojibway.* Publication in Ethnology No. 7. Ottawa: National Museum of Canada.

Smith, P. David. 1986. *Ouray: Chief of the Utes.* Ridgeway: Wayfinder Press.

Stauss, Kimberley, and Mary Jane Taylor. 2006. "Native American Women Who Lead Human Services Organizations." *Journal of Ethnic & Cultural Diversity in Social Work* 15 (1-2): 123–46.

Straus, Anne Terry, and Debra Valentino. 2003. "Gender and Community

Organization Leadership in the Chicago Indian Community." *American Indian Quarterly* 27 (3/4): 523–32.

Sugden, John. 1997. *Tecumseh: A Life*. New York: Henry Holt & Co.

Sutton, Douglas G. 1990. "Organisation and Ontology: The Origins of the Northern Maori Chiefdom, New Zealand." *Man* 25 (4): 667–92.

Svensson, Frances. 1980. "Ethnicity Versus Communalism: The American Indian Movement and the Politics of Survival." In *The Mobilization of Collective Identity: Comparative Perspectives*, edited by Ann Baker Cottrell and Jeffrey A. Ross 65–88. Lanham: University Press of America.

Tennant, Paul. 1982. "Native Indian Political Organization in British Columbia 1900-1969: A Response to Internal Colonialism." *BC Studies: The British Columbian Quarterly* 55 (Autumn): 3–49.

Tollefson, Kenneth D. 1986. "The Snoqualmie: A Puget Sound Chiefdom." *Ethnology* 26 (2): 121–36.

Urion, Carl. 1993. "Honour-Song Leadership." *Canadian Journal of Native Education* 20 (1): 1–4.

Utley, Robert M. 1993. *The Lance and the Shield: The Life and Times of Sitting Bull*. New York: Henry Holt & Co.

Vernon, H. A. 1985. "Maris Bryant Pierce: The Making of a Seneca Leader." In *Indian Lives: Essays on Nineteenth and Twentieth-Century Native American Leaders*, edited by Lester George. Moses and Raymond Wilson, 17–42. Albuquerque: University of New Mexico.

Voyageur, Cora J. 2002. "Keeping All The Balls in The Air: The Experience of Canada's Women Chiefs." In *Women and Leadership: Feminist Voices*, edited by A. MacNevin, F. O'Reilly, E. Silverman, and A. Taylor, 206–24. Ottawa: Canadian Research Institute for the Advancement of Women.

———. 2003. "The Community Owns You: Experiences of Canada's Women Chiefs." In *Out of the Ivory Tower: Taking Feminist Research to the Community*, edited by Andrea Martinez and Meryn Stuart, 228–50. Toronto: Sumach Press.

———. 2005. "They Called Her Chief: A Profile of Chief Dorothy McDonald." In *Unsettled Pasts: Reconceiving the West Through Women's History*, edited by Sarah Carter, Lesley Erickson, Patricia Roome, and Char Smith, 355–61. Calgary: University of Calgary Press.

———. 2008. *Firekeepers of the Twenty-First Century: First Nation Women Chiefs*. Montreal & Kingston: McGill-Queen's University Press.

———. 2011a. "Out in the Open: Elected Female Leadership in Canada's First Nation Community." *Canadian Review of Sociology* 48 (1): 67–85.

———. 2011b. "Female First Nations Chiefs and the Colonial Legacy." *American Indian Culture and Research Journal* 35 (3): 59–78.

Wakshul, Barbra. 1997. "Training Leaders for the 21st Century: The American Indian Ambassadors Program." *Winds of Change* 12 (2): 24–28.

Washington, Siemthlut Michelle. 2004. "Bringing Traditional Teachings to Leadership." *American Indian Quarterly* 28 (3/4): 583–603.

Weick, Karl E. 2006. "Organizing for Mindfulness: Eastern Wisdom and Western Knowledge." *Journal of Management Inquiry* 15 (3): 275–87.

Williams, Walter. 1984a. *Indian Leadership*. Manhattan: Sunflower University Press.

———. 1984b "Twentieth-Century Indian Leaders: Brokers and Providers." Journal of the West 23 (3): 3–6.

Yukl, Gary A. 1998. *Leadership in Organizations*. Upper Saddle River, New Jersey: Prentice-Hall International.

Chapter 1

A Wise Practices Approach to Indigenous Community Development in Canada

Brian Calliou and Cynthia Wesley-Esquimaux

Introduction

Indigenous peoples in Canada face many challenges because of the impact of globalization, rapid technological change, and a neo-liberal market economy with its shrinking governmental support. Many Indigenous peoples continue to live in substandard conditions and poverty. However, they also face many opportunities, since much of the industrial development of natural resources occurs on their traditional territories. Recent Supreme Court of Canada case law states that they need to be consulted and accommodated in any development projects that might impact their Aboriginal rights. Thus, there is an urgent need for effective leadership for Indigenous communities to adapt to this external change and to build the internal capacity to take advantage of economic opportunities. Developing effective Indigenous leaders requires a blended approach of revitalizing traditional cultural principles and values while teaching them the core competencies required for success in the modern business world. The wisdom of Indigenous knowledge systems must also be developed, along with Western knowledge and skills to run the governments, organizations, and businesses of today's Indigenous communities.

In this chapter, we describe a wise practices approach to successful community economic development. This wise practices approach is informed by a review of literature on best practices in Indigenous business, economic development, and community development. From this literature review, we identified seven elements that are essential for modern Indigenous leaders to cultivate in order to lead their communities through the rapid changes that are occurring. In addition, the modern Indigenous leader must meet the community's needs and aspirations, while preserving his or her community's culture and traditions.

Approaches to Indigenous Economic Development

There have been many approaches to Indigenous economic development, most often imposed upon First Nations communities by governments or non-governmental organizations. Such approaches have often been assimilationist in nature. They argued that adhering to cultural values, traditions, and knowledge actually placed Indigenous peoples at a disadvantage. Within the assimilationist stream is modernization theory, which views industrialization and technological advances as part of an inevitable progress (Calliou and Voyageur 2007). Thus, modernists argue that economic underdevelopment among most Indigenous peoples is due to outmoded economic organization and ideas. Modernists further state that if Indigenous peoples do not undergo industrialization and are unable to change with the times, then their disadvantaged position vis-à-vis the Canadian economy is really of their own doing. This "blaming the victim" stance does not recognize the societal, institutional, and structural barriers that restrict Indigenous participation in the market economy. The modernization theory is reflected in the neo-liberal view of a capitalist, market-driven economic system that supports Western liberal democratic values such as individualism, consumerism, individual property ownership, and wealth accumulation. Such notions often set up a clash of cultural values with Indigenous peoples, who generally have a strong belief in collectivism, a spiritual connection to the land and its resources, and a history of sharing the land rather than exclusive ownership of it.

Other theories have challenged modernization theory by highlighting the overt and systemic structures that marginalize Indigenous peoples from the economy. The metropolis-hinterland theory argues that at the root of legal and political barriers are the metropolitan centres run by elites who exploit the raw materials of the hinterland regions, where Indigenous peoples generally live, and then sell the finished products back to the outlying areas (Davis 1971). Colonialist theory argues that Indigenous communities are essentially internal colonies that are exploited for economic gain by the dominant society, which uses them as a source for cheap resources and unskilled labour (Frideres 1988; Abele 1997, 129). Dependency theory argues that underdevelopment can only be understood by analyzing the economic and power relationships between developed and underdeveloped economies (Dos Santos 1971; Frank 1966). Indigenous peoples have become dependent upon the productive relationships established by the capitalist metropolises of developed countries. Thus, world systems related to a global capitalist economy benefit some regions and lead to the underdevelopment of others (Wallerstein 2004). Robert Anderson (1999) set out a "contingency" theory wherein he argues that while there are world systems at play, Indigenous peoples' participation in the global economy is contingent upon a number of factors, many of which can be controlled by Indigenous peoples themselves. This contingency approach takes agency and social relations seriously, and emphasizes a community-driven approach to economic development where the community is an active agent in development and controls its pace and nature. Indigenous peoples in Canada have been advocating for greater self-government, respect for their rights to their traditional lands and resources, and an active role in economic development on their traditional lands. Government policy has been established through history to play a role in Indigenous economic development.

Federal Government Policy on Indigenous Economic Development

Historically, Indigenous peoples in Canada adapted well to the presence of the new settler populations, especially during the fur trade, where they played prominent roles (Ray 1974). Indigenous peoples also began to adapt somewhat successfully to the new agricultural economy, and it was government policy that began to impede Indigenous communities' agricultural success by restricting their ability to sell their products (Carter 1990). Indigenous peoples in Canada also adopted seasonal labour as a way to earn an income and continue their traditional livelihood of hunting, fishing, and trapping (High 1996; Elias 1990). It is only relatively recently that Indigenous peoples have been marginalized from the economy—from the early 1920s onward (Tough 1992).

Federal government policy had an assimilationist agenda early on, and residential school policy had a significant impact on Indigenous identity and cultural capital (Tobias 1976; Milloy 1999). State-sponsored welfare programs also led many Indigenous citizens to become dependent (Helin 2006). Furthermore, policy and laws such as the Indian Act imposed further barriers to Indigenous involvement in the national economy and limited the possibilities of success (Calliou and Voyageur 2007, 140). As one commentator stated, in all liberal democracies such as Canada, Indigenous peoples are transformed into "politically weak, economically marginal and culturally stigmatized members of national societies" (Dyck 1985, 1).

More recently, the Canadian federal government has attempted to deal with Indigenous involvement in the economy through a variety of policies. The federal government instituted a policy in 1989 entitled the Canadian Aboriginal Economic Development Strategy (CAEDS), which was a partnership between three federal government departments. The Department of Indian and Northern Development funded programs in community economic and resource development; the Department of Employment and Immigration funded training and skills development; and the Department of Industry, Science and Technology funded programs in business development.

More recently, in 2009, the Conservative federal government instituted a new policy entitled the Federal Framework for Aboriginal Economic Development (FFAED), which strongly reflects the Conservative government's neo-liberal approach to the "good society." Their policy efforts are focused on opening up Canada's natural resources for the world to exploit. Of course, the natural resources are on traditional Indigenous lands. This market-driven approach to Indigenous participation in the national economy sees the policy focus on partnerships with private industry, a strong emphasis on northern development, especially of its natural resources, a results-based approach to any funding investments, and enabling legislation (Oppenheimer and Weir 2010).

Much government policy and many non-governmental organizational approaches to Indigenous economic development focused on capacity development and training, particularly in business, management, and leadership development. Some Indigenous institutions were established to carry out such training, including the Council for the Advancement of Native Development Officers, the Indigenous Leadership Institute, the Aboriginal Financial Officers Association, and the National Centre for First Nations Governance. Many post-secondary institutions also established training programs to meet this need (O'Connell, Oppenheimer, and Weir 2010). Each of these institutions uses a variety of methods to deliver the training. One method to learning in the areas of leadership, management, and business is the best practices approach.

Best Practices in Business and Management

Leadership development programs use a variety of methods and approaches to teach leadership and management (McGonagill and Pruyn 2010). Besides formal lectures in post-secondary institutions, many organizational or community leaders also rely on the best practices case study approach to develop leaders and look for ways to improve (Leskiw and Singh 2007).

So what are best practices? One definition states that best practices are the "methodologies, strategies, procedures, practices and/or processes that consistently produce successful results" (Foy, Krehbiel, and Plate 2009, i). A best practice is "a proven method, technique, or process for achieving a specific outcome under a specific circumstance and in an effective way" (Calliou and Wesley-Esquimaux 2010, 5).

Best practices are essentially documented case histories of innovation and performance success in a specific practice area. They provide guidelines for others to learn from because of the detailed analysis of the practice under study.

There have been a number of studies that reviewed and documented best practices of Indigenous communities in their economic or community development. We gathered many of the main studies of best practices and analyzed them and drew our own conclusions.

Literature Review of Best Practices in Indigenous Community Economic Development

We now provide an overview of some of the literature and studies of best practices in Indigenous community and economic development. These studies have generally identified certain key elements of success that provide a basis for understanding how or why some Indigenous communities achieve results.

Harvard Project on American Indian Economic Development

One of the best-known studies of successful Indigenous economic development is the Harvard Project on American Indian Economic Development (HPAIED). The HPAIED began in the mid-1980s and explored why some Native American tribes were defying the odds and achieving economic success and strong community growth. There were some tribes who stood out from the others in achieving success, while the majority were struggling with poverty and dependence. Initially, the study focused narrowly on tribal economics, especially employment and businesses, but what the researchers found was much broader and was as much social and political. One could not really understand tribal economic development without considering the entire community structure, systems, and institutions. In other words, the study of tribal economic development required a holistic approach where a broader set of success factors could be identified and explored.

The HPAIED concluded that in order to achieve successful tribal economic development, there had to be a strong self-governing community that had a stable environment in which investors were willing to risk investment dollars. Only once these factors were in place could they achieve success in their economic development ventures. The HPAIED study came up with four main success factors: 1) de facto sovereignty, that is, the exercise of local autonomy; 2) effective institutions that match the culture, that is, they set up rules of engagement in the community that resonate with the community's cultural values; 3) strategic direction, that is, long-term strategic planning rather than short-term decisions; 4) strong, action-oriented leadership, that is, effective leaders who move their strategic vision and ideas into action to achieve results. These were strong leaders who led drastic changes in their communities, who were willing to break with the status quo so there would be improved conditions in their communities. The HPAIED termed this the nation-building approach to Indigenous community economic development (Cornell and Kalt 1988, 1990, 2000; Cornell and Gil-Swedberg 1995; Kalt 1993; Jorgensen 2007).

National Centre for First Nations Governance
The National Centre for First Nations Governance, an independent, non-profit, Indigenous-run institution, has developed an approach to assist in leadership development and governance that includes a set of key components: the people (citizens); the land (territory and community lands); laws and jurisdiction; institutions; and resources. Through the governance of these key components, they also identified the following leadership and governance principles necessary to lead and govern First Nations successfully: strategic vision; meaningful information sharing; participation in decision making; territorial integrity; economic realization; respect for the spirit of the land; expansion of jurisdiction; rule of law; transparency and fairness; results-based organizations; cultural alignment of institutions; effective intergovernmental relations; human resource capacity; financial management capacity; performance evaluation; accountability and reporting; diversity of revenue sources. They also published a best practices report that uses case studies to illustrate these leadership and governance principles (NCFNG 2009).

Institute on Governance
The Institute on Governance, an independent, non-profit public interest agency located in Ottawa with a mission to advance better governance in the public interest, carried out a number of reports on Aboriginal governance. In some of their reports, they have set out a model with five principles of good governance: legitimacy and voice; direction; performance; accountability; and fairness (Amos, Graham, and Plumptre 2003; Bruhn and Graham 2009; Bruhn 2009).

UN Development Program

The United Nations' Development Program (UNDP) has identified nine principles of good governance for assistance to developing countries: participation; consensus orientation; strategic vision; responsiveness; effectiveness and efficiency; accountability; transparency; equity; and rule of law (Amos, Graham, and Plumptre 2003).

DIAND Governance Action Plan

The federal government of Canada's Department of Indian Affairs and Northern Development (DIAND) created a governance action plan to guide its work with First Nations building their capacity for self-government. In their governance action plan, they identified seven "key drivers or levers of capacity development for good governance": a vision or sense of self as self-governing; stable and effective leadership; effective governing institutions; culture match; strategic orientation; citizen engagement; and effective and stable intergovernmental relations (INAC 2000).

Friendship Centre Movement Best Practices in Governance and Management

The Friendship Centre movement in Canada has done great work in bringing culturally appropriate services and programs to urban Aboriginals and off-reserve Indians. The National Association of Friendship Centres partnered with the Institute on Governance to document various Friendship Centres' best practices. The key factors of successful practices include: board governance; executive leadership; staffing; volunteers; strategic planning; evaluation; adaptive capacity; external relations; sustainability; fundraising; and human resource management. They documented one best practice case study on each of these practice areas to illustrate that specific Friendship Centre's approach to achievement (Graham and Kinmond 2008; Graham and Mitchell 2009).

Conference Board of Canada

The Conference Board of Canada produced a report that examined ten Aboriginal communities and identified six key factors to success in creating wealth and employment as part of Aboriginal economic development efforts: strong leadership and vision; strategic community economic development plan; access to capital, markets, and management expertise; good governance and management; transparency and accountability; and the positive interplay of business and politics (Loizides and Wuttunee 2005). In another report on best practices in Aboriginal businesses, they set out the following factors of success: purpose; clear corporate vision; winning attitude; using creativity to overcome obstacles; good location; experience and expertise; hiring people from outside the community; recruitment and retention; and developing partnerships (Nelson and Sisco 2008). In yet another report on successful Aboriginal businesses, they looked at ten case studies to form the basis of their conclusion on three main factors of success: leadership; sound business practices; and strong relationships and partnerships (Sisco and Stewart 2009).

Royal Commission on Aboriginal Peoples
The RCAP report identified five critical factors of success in community economic development in the following manner: restoration of power and control over lands and resources; development of a positive and encouraging social/political/cultural climate for Aboriginal economic development; development of enabling instruments for use in surmounting the problems facing Aboriginal economic development; development of a skilled and positive, forward-looking labour force; and acceptance and willingness to engage in economic activity by the mainstream in collaboration with Aboriginal people (Wein 1999; Newhouse 1999).

Human Resources Development Canada
The federal government's Human Resources Development Canada department produced a report on Aboriginal social and economic development that set out lessons learned that they feel are important as factors for successful Aboriginal development: governance; planning and policy development; control over resources and funding arrangements; program delivery and management; accountability; capacity building; and other requirements such as coordin-

ation across programs, combining human resource and economic development, and linking education and training to employment (HRDC 1999).

Comprehensive Community Planning Workshop
The Okanagan Indian Band in British Columbia hosted a workshop on comprehensive community planning, and Indian and Northern Affairs Canada (INAC) wrote a report on it setting out the lessons learned, which include: community-based and community-driven planning; building a planning team and process; financial resources mobilization; capacity building, planning tools, and resources; intergovernmental relations; and linkages, networking, and sharing of best practices (INAC 2005).

Public Works Management in First Nations Communities
Public Works and Government Services Canada and Indian Affairs Canada developed a report on good public works management in First Nations communities that explored the experiences of six communities to identify the following keys to success: vision; leadership; policies; management and administration; self-sufficiency; human resources; asset protection and management; accountability; and fiscal accountability (INAC and PWGSC 2002).

Indigenous Research and Education, Charles Darwin University
Indigenous scholar Darryl Cronin, of the Indigenous Research and Education faculty at Charles Darwin University in Australia, developed a paper exploring what Aboriginal people think about governance and community development. He identified the following key elements of a governance and development approach: Aboriginal authority; jurisdictional authority; cultural appropriateness; research, education, and training; leadership; strengthening families; direct and adequate funding; private-sector and non-profit-sector partnerships; and capacity of government agencies (Cronin 2003).

The studies reviewed above informed our own "seven elements of success" model described below. However, before we describe our model, we will critique the concept of "best practices" and rationalize why we chose instead to adopt the concept of "wise practices."

Critique of the "Best Practices" Concept

There is an assumption that calling practices "best practices" means they can inspire others and encourage leaders to improve their own practices. The assumption is that these documented stories can make a difference to those who study them, and that the knowledge can be transferred into action using the best practice case study as a guide. Best practices case studies are also used as a benchmark against which to compare one's own community or organization. Although there is some truth to each of these assumptions, there is a growing skepticism about the universality of best practices.

There is much utility in learning from best practices case studies. However, as one education scholar put it, best practices can unrealistically elevate expectations, best practices' "too confident hope ordinarily smashes against the rocks of reality," and the attempt to implement best practices "ordinarily diverts attention away from the practical to the theoretic" (Davis 1997, 1). Some commentators caution that we cannot assume that what is successful in one situation, context, or culture will necessarily work in a completely different one (Krajewski and Silver, n.d.). Others have raised the issue of universality, asking the following: How could this supposed objective, universal standard of best practice "take into account context and values, subjectivity and plurality? How could it accommodate multiple perspectives, with different groups in different places having different views of what quality was or different interpretations of criteria?" (Dahlberg, Moss, and Pence 1999, 4). Thus, the term "best practices" is often decontextualized and cannot always be generalized into another context or culture.

Furthermore, another question arises: What criteria determine what is "best"? It is often a Western corporate standard. It reflects a certain ideological lens—that of the neo-liberal market. Certainly, the criteria of what successful or best practice is can differ between Western liberal democracies and Indigenous peoples. Cornell (1987) argues that the middle-class dream of success in the United States is not necessarily the same definition of success that most Native Americans have. Thus, best practices tend to reflect hierarchical evaluative criteria that also tend to exclude local and Indigenous knowledge and ways of doing. For case studies to resonate and be relevant, they need to allow for other perspectives, knowledge, and experiences. There has been a similar assumption that Western-based knowledge and experience with respect to leadership, management, and business practices have an objective quality that can be universally applied to other cultures. Hofstede (1980, 1983) has argued that the failure of many international development initiatives during the 1960s and 1970s was partly due to the lack of cultural sensitivity in the transfer of management ideas. In fact, culture matters. Many Indigenous scholars are arguing that modern management and business practices and knowledge are important for Indigenous peoples, but that they must be reconciled with and built upon traditional cultural values and knowledge (Wuttunee 2004; Smith 2000; Neilsen and Redpath 1997; Newhouse 2000; Calliou 2005).

Finally, some commentators have argued that best practices in adult education are running the risk of eroding the traditional grounding in an ethic of the common good and of social justice (Bartlette 2008). Indigenous communities that involve themselves in successful business enterprises do so for the collective good, for social purposes, and to maintain their cultural identity (Anderson 2001; Champagne 2004).

More Indigenous people have argued that there is something missing in how Indigenous community and leadership development is approached (Snowball and Wesley-Esquimaux 2010; Thoms 2007). They argue that an approach other than best practices must be developed, one that makes a space for Indigenous knowledge, experiences, and stories "learned on the frontlines through socio-cultural insight, ingenuity, intuition, long experience, and trial and error" (Thoms 2007, 8).

The Wise Practices Approach to Economic and Leadership Development

Taking the foregoing critique into account, and in order to resonate with Indigenous leaders, we adopt the notion of "wise practices" as an alternative term to "best practices." Wise practices are best defined as "locally-appropriate actions, tools, principles or decisions that contribute significantly to the development of sustainable and equitable conditions" (Calliou and Wesley-Esquimaux 2010, 19). Rather than aspiring to be universal, as best practices try to be, wise practices are "idiosyncratic, contextual, textured, and not standardized" (Davis 1997). Thus, wise practices recognize the wisdom in each Indigenous community and in the community's own stories of achieving success. The concept of wise practices recognizes that culture matters.

Wise practices are thus based on what so many Indigenous scholars have argued: the importance of an Indigenous identity and strong cultural ties (King 2008; Calliou 2005; Grint and Warner 2006; Cowan 2008; Ottmann, 2005b). Indigenous perceptions of leaders' characteristics also inform the wise practices approach, as is illustrated by the words of Taiaiake Alfred (1999, 10) citing Leroy Little Bear, a Blackfoot philosopher and scholar:

> A culture attempts to mold its members into ideal personalities. The ideal personality in Native American cultures is a person who shows kindness to all, who puts the group ahead of individual wants and desires, who is a generalist, who is steeped in spiritual and ritual knowledge—a person who goes about daily life and approaches "all his or her relations" in a sea of friendship, easygoing-ness, humour, and good feelings.... She or he is a person expected to display bravery, hardiness, and strength against enemies and outsiders. She or he is a person who is adaptable and takes the world as it comes without complaint.

These characteristics of ideal persons reflect the principles of wisdom: fluid intelligence; ethical judgement; actions undertaken for noble and worthwhile purposes; working for the welfare of others; and having a metaphysical or spiritual quality (Kok 2009). Theorists and practitioners in organizational studies and leadership development are increasingly becoming interested in wisdom. They see a need for wisdom to be practised by leaders, managers, and business persons who must make complex decisions in this period of rapid change, uncertainty, and paradox, all the while considering the welfare of others and the planet (Cooperrider and Srivastva 1998;

Korac-Kakabadse, Korac-Kakabadse, and Kouzmin 2001; Weick 2004; Kageler et al. 2005; Sternberg 2005; Knudtson and Suzuki 1992). In order for leaders to practise wisely, they need to have well-developed intuitive powers to move beyond existing ideas or rules. In fact, wisdom "requires one to respect tradition and experience," and issues a leader faces "can be considered reflexively from a cultural-historical perspective" (Kok 2009, 54). Collective knowledge impacts learning, and many theorists now see knowledge as a socially shared resource. Knowledge "can only be exploited to its maximum degree when complemented by wisdom" (Kok 2009, 55). Indigenous traditional knowledge offers traditional teachings in order to prepare people to live as good human beings who can coexist respectfully and who have a respectful relationship with their environment.

Ottmann (2005b) argues that Indigenous leadership development began with childhood encouragement and direction from the elders, and with inspiration and support from other leaders. Thus, the shared values and beliefs of the community shaped a future leader. Indeed, Little Bear (2011, 77) has stated that individuals are going to have their own "personal interpretation of the collective cultural code; however, the individual's worldview has its roots in the culture—that is, in the society's shared philosophy, values, and customs."

A wise practices approach to developing Indigenous leadership examines the "wisdom of practice" and documents case studies that are "thickly textured, robust, subject matter specific, and richly contextualized" (Davis 1997, 3). The expansion of these detailed, descriptive, and interpretive case studies will illuminate the wisdom of successful practices, especially the construction of the meaning of culturally appropriate leadership practices in the service of the common wealth.

There is a growing body of Indigenous scholarship exploring the use of wise practices and wisdom in a variety of disciplines, such as business (Erakovic et al. 2011), mental health and addiction (Snowball and Wesley-Esquimaux 2010), and social work (Nabigon and Wenger-Nabigon 2012).

A wise practices model also reflects a strengths-based approach to community economic development. It recognizes that there are many gifts and strengths in a community that strategies for growth can build upon. This assets-based planning method provides for an inventory of assets, including cultural assets (Cunningham and Mathie 2002). This is also referred to as an appreciative inquiry approach, where strengths are identified as a starting point rather than problems or shortcomings (Cooperrider and Whitney 2005; Bushe 1998). Certainly, one of the strengths of an Indigenous community is its local knowledge and experience, that is, the oral histories and traditional teachings held by elders and other wisdom keepers.

The methodology for researching and documenting wise practices is multidisciplinary, using arts-based research methods to visually capture the wise practice case study story (Brearley, Calliou, and Tanton 2009; Brearley and Darso 2008). The wise practices approach uses a qualitative research method to carry out a naturalistic inquiry that allows for a community to find its voice and narrate its own story of achievement, highlighting its strengths and local knowledge and experience. It also uses a participatory action research method that embraces principles of community participation and reflection, empowerment, and emancipation of the people seeking to improve their social situation (Walter 2006).

The wise practices approach involves a journey that goes backwards in order to move forwards. Interviews of community or organizational leaders elicit the story from when the idea for the venture began, documenting all its characters and its journey, including the assorted trials and tribulations that led to ultimate success. The resulting case studies use the storytelling method to inform and inspire other leaders to undertake their own community initiatives in a wise way. This is merely a wise practice in itself, since traditionally Indigenous leaders learned from past stories before making a decision about future action.

Wise Practices Seven Elements of Success Model

Drawing on the conclusions from the best practices literature review that we explained earlier, we have identified seven key factors of success for Indigenous community economic development. Our selection of the success factors was also informed by competency map research we undertook through focus groups at The Banff Centre.

The findings supported the importance of culture and identity for Indigenous leaders (Calliou 2005). We call this our wise practices model, which sets out the following seven elements of success:

1. Identity and culture
2. Leadership
3. Strategic vision and planning
4. Good governance and management
5. Accountability and stewardship
6. Performance evaluation
7. Collaborations, partnerships, and external relationships

We will discuss each of these seven key success factors in turn.

Identity and Culture

The first key factor is *identity and culture,* which is to say that leaders of Indigenous communities have stated clearly that for any Indigenous leader to be competent in advocating and representing their community's interests, they must have a strong understanding of, and grounding in, their culture, traditional knowledge, and historical connection to their traditional territories (King 2008; Grint and Warner 2006; Cowan 2008). This became very clear in our competency map research (Calliou 2005). Other Indigenous scholars have also found this to be the case (Ottmann, 2005b). This key success factor supports current claims about the importance of identity at work and authentic leadership (Gini 1998; Jaros 2012; Cooper, Scandura, and Schriesheim 2005; Gooty and Michie 2005).

Leadership

The second factor is *leadership.* Effective leadership is key to successful community economic development. The term "leadership" is a verb, that is, it refers to action taken by someone to turn ideas into actions and thus into results. It does not need to be related to someone in authority; leadership can be practised by essentially anyone at any level. Warren Bennis and Burt Nanus (1985) defined leadership as that which "gives an organization its vision and its ability to translate the vision into reality." Leaders must be action oriented in order to transform ideas into action, lead change, and achieve results. They must practise courageous leadership in order to change the status quo and improve the conditions of the community. Also, Sonia Ospina and others argue that values-based leadership towards social justice, what they term "social change leadership," is about leadership that is collective or shared, and that both beliefs and behaviours are important (Foldy and Ospina 2005).

Strategic Vision and Planning

Third is the key factor *strategic vision and planning*. Leaders must set out long-term visions for the community that inspire and motivate community members to support strategic plans that bring positive change. Such strategic plans provide a basis for decision making and help to focus scarce resources on their collective strategic goals. They allow the community or organization to be proactive rather than reactive (Cornell 1998; Anderson and Smith 1998; Guyette 1996).

Good Governance and Management

The fourth factor is *good governance and management*. Leaders must set up good governance and management structures and systems to effectively carry out the goals and program needs for their communities (Cornell and Kalt 1990; Cornell 2007; Cornell and Jorgensen 2007; Calliou 2008). Building effective institutions and processes allows leaders and managers to come and go while the government or organization continues to operate. Stable governance and management sends a strong message to potential external partners that they can rest assured that the Indigenous community or organization operates professionally.

Accountability and Stewardship

The fifth factor relates to *accountability and stewardship*. Good leaders and managers act as stewards of the community resources and are accountable for their decisions and actions (Block 1993; Davis, Donaldson, and Schoorman 1997; Hernandez 2008; Leithwood 2001; Fox 1992). Being open and transparent about their decision making and spending builds community trust in them. Leaders or managers can show how they are accountable by openly reporting how decisions were made, scarce resources allocated, and results achieved.

Performance Evaluation

Next is the sixth factor, *performance evaluation*. This refers to being accountable and practising stewardship of community resources by measuring for results of decisions made and dollars invested in the various strategies undertaken. Evaluating the performance of the initiatives undertaken by leaders ensures that they are achieving the most value for each dollar invested in their projects (Martz 2013; Meier 2003). Evaluation of human resources is another important measurement that ensures that staff performance is tied to strategic objectives and that results are being achieved. Thus, one is essentially carrying out performance management (Bacal 1999). However, there is a growing literature critiquing evaluation approaches and calling for an Indigenous evaluation framework that makes room for culturally competent evaluations (Chouinard and Cousins 2007; LaFrance and Nichols 2010; Aton et al. 2007).

Collaborations, Partnerships, and External Relationships

Finally, the seventh factor is *collaborations, partnerships, and external relationships*. External partnerships are often necessary for an Indigenous community's success. Indigenous communities often need external financial support, as well as external support in other areas. Thus, good working relationships with external funders, bankers, investors, suppliers, and trading partners are key to success. Being self-governing means being interdependent, that is, having networks and external trading partners. Many Indigenous communities enter into partnerships, co-operatives, or joint ventures (Wuttunee 2002; Fraser 2002; Hammond Ketilson and MacPherson 2002).

Conclusion

Through a literature review of best practices in Indigenous community and economic development, we were able to provide an empirical basis for our wise practices model for successful community economic development, with its seven elements that increase the likelihood of success. The concept of wise practices, in contrast to the concept of best practices, provides a space for Indigenous knowledge and local experience in order to lay a foundation for a strengths-based approach to community economic development. It recognizes that culture matters, and that wise practices case studies can inspire and provide wisdom that can teach us ways to build our communities and our local economies. It also recognizes that each community has its own wisdom, experiences, and strengths to build upon.

The wise practices model sets out various elements for Indigenous leaders to become familiar with and learn aspects of, so that they have the competencies to lead change, inspire hope, and take advantage of economic opportunities for their communities. The economic success that can be achieved through such a model is not merely for wealth accumulation, but rather is for the public good. It is for what one commentator described as "tribal capitalism," and another called "capitalism with a red face" (Champagne 2004; Newhouse 2000). This represents capitalism as a means to an end—a triple bottom-line approach to economic development that seeks to protect and enhance an Indigenous community's identity and culture.

As Indigenous communities face rapid changes coming from external sources, they are in need of competent leadership to adapt to this change. Developing leaders' knowledge, skills, and virtues can be accomplished in part by learning from and being inspired to action by wise practices case studies. Leadership for change is necessary, but a wise practices approach also supports the continuance of traditional knowledge as a foundation for the change, so that identity and culture are preserved.

References

Abele, Frances. 1997. "Understanding What Happened Here: The Political Economy of Indigenous Peoples." In *Understanding Canada: Building on the New Canadian Political Economy*, edited by Wallace Clement, 118–40. Montreal: McGill-Queen's University Press.

Alfred, Taiaiake. 1999. *Peace, Power, Righteousness: An Indigenous Manifesto*. Toronto: Oxford University Press.

Amos, Bruce, John Graham, and Tim Plumptre. 2003. "Principles for Good
    Governance in the 21st Century: Policy Brief No. 15." Unpublished
    report, Institute on Governance, Ottawa. http://iog.ca/wp-content/
    uploads/2012/12/2003_August_policybrief15.pdf.
Anderson, Robert B. 1999. *Economic Development Among the Aboriginal
    Peoples in Canada: The Hope for the Future*. North York: Captus Press.
———. 2001. "Aboriginal People, Economic Development and Entrepre-
    neurship." *Journal of Aboriginal Economic Development* 2 (1): 33–42.
Anderson, Joseph S., and Dean Howard Smith. 1998. "Managing Tribal
    Assets: Developing Long-Term Strategic Plans." *American Indian Cul-
    ture and Research Journal* 22 (3): 139–49.
Aton, Kanani, Fiona Cram, Alice J. Kawakami, Morris K. Lai, and Laurie
    Porima. 2007. "Improving the Practice of Evaluation Through Indigen-
    ous Values and Methods: Decolonizing Evaluation Practice – Returning
    the Gaze From Hawai'i and Aotearoa." *Hulili: Multidisciplinary Research
    on Hawaiian Well-Being* 4 (1): 319–48.
Bacal, Robert. 1999. *Performance Management*. New York: McGraw-Hill.
Bartlette, Deborah. 2008. "Are 'Best Practices' Hurting Adult Ed: McIntyre
    and the Globalisation of Practice." Unpublished paper presented at
    Thinking Beyond Borders: Global Ideas, Global Values 27th National
    Conference, online proceedings of the Canadian Association for the
    Study of Adult Education, University of British Columbia, Vancouver.
Bennis, Warren, and Burt Nanus. 1985. *Leaders: Strategies for Taking Charge*.
    New York: Harper & Row.
Block, Peter. 1993. *Stewardship: Choosing Service Over Self-Interest*. San
    Francisco: Berrett-Koehler.
Brearley, Laura, and Lotte Darso. 2008. "Vivifying Data and Experience
    Through Artful Approaches." In *Handbook of the Arts in Qualitative Re-
    search: Perspectives, Methodologies, Examples and Issues*, edited by Ardra
    L. Cole and Gary J. Knowles, 639–52. Thousand Oaks: Sage Publications.
Brearley, Laura, Brian Calliou, and Janice Tanton. 2009. "An Aesthetic
    Approach to Leadership and Organizational Development: The Deep
    Listening Model for Research and Cultural Renewal." Unpublished
    paper presented at the Asia-Pacific Researchers in Organization Studies
    13 Conference, Monterrey, Mexico, December 7–9.
Bruhn, Jodi. 2009. "In Search of Common Ground: Reconciling West-

ern-based Governance Principles and First Nations Traditions." Unpublished report, Institute on Governance, Ottawa. www.iog.ca/sites/iog/files/2009_Traditions.pdf.

Bruhn, Jodi, and John Graham. 2009. "Improving Health Governance in First Nations Communities: Model Governance Policies and Tools." Unpublished report, Institute on Governance, Ottawa. http://iog.ca/wp-content/uploads/2012/12/2009_January_healthgov_modelpolicies.pdf.

Bushe, Gervase R. 1998. "Appreciative Inquiry with Teams." *Organization Development Journal* 16 (3): 41–50.

Calliou, Brian. 2005. "The Culture of Leadership: North American Indigenous Leadership in a Changing Economy." In *Indigenous Peoples and the Modern State*, edited by Duane Champagne, Karen Jo Torjesen, and Susan Steiner, 47–68. Walnut Creek: AltaMira Press.

———. 2008. "The Significance of Building Leadership and Community Capacity to Implement Self-Government." In *Aboriginal Self-Government in Canada: Current Trends and Issues*, edited by Yale Belanger, 332–47. 3rd ed. Saskatoon: Purich Publishing.

Calliou, Brian, and Cora J. Voyageur. 2007. "Aboriginal Economic Development and the Struggle for Self-Government." In *Power and Resistance: Critical Thinking About Canadian Social Issues*, edited by Wayne Antony and Les Samuelson. 4th ed. Halifax: Fernwood Publishing.

Calliou, Brian, and Cynthia Wesley-Esquimaux. 2010. "Best Practices in Aboriginal Community Development: A Wise Practices Approach." Unpublished report, the Banff Centre, Indigenous Leadership and Management. http://www.banffcentre.ca/indigenous-leadership/library/pdf/best_practices_in_aboriginal_community_development.pdf.

Carter, Sarah. 1990. *Lost Harvests: Prairie Indian Reserve Farmers and Government Policy*. Montreal: McGill-Queen's University Press.

Champagne, Duane. 2004. "Tribal Capitalism and Native Capitalists: Multiple Pathways of Native Economy." In *Native Pathways: American Indian Culture and Economic Development in the Twentieth Century*, edited by Brian Hosmer and Colleen O'Neill, 308–29. Boulder: University Press of Colorado.

Chouinard, Jill A., and J. Bradley Cousins. 2007. "Culturally Competent Evaluation for Aboriginal Communities: A Review of the Empirical

Literature." *Journal of Multidisciplinary Evaluation* 4 (8): 40–57.

Cooper, Cecily D., Terry A. Scandura, and Chester A. Schriesheim. 2005. "Looking Forward But Learning From Our Past: Potential Challenges to Developing Authentic Leadership Theory and Authentic Leaders." *The Leadership Quarterly* 16 (3): 475–93.

Cooperrider, David L., and Suresh Srivastva, eds. 1998. *Organizational Wisdom and Executive Courage*. San Francisco: New Lexington Press.

Cooperrider, David L., and Diana Whitney. 2005. *Appreciative Inquiry: A Positive Revolution in Change*. San Francisco: Berrett-Koehler.

Cornell, Stephen. 1987. "American Indians, American Dreams, and the Meaning of Success." *American Indian Culture and Research Journal* 11 (2): 59–70.

———. 1998. "Strategic Analysis: A Practical Tool for Building Indian Nations." Harvard Project Report No. 98–10. Cambridge: John F. Kennedy School of Government, Harvard University.

———. 2007. "Remaking the Tools of Governance: Colonial Legacies, Indigenous Solutions." In *Rebuilding Native Nations: Strategies for Governance and Development*, edited by Miriam Jorgensen, 57–77. Tucson: University of Arizona Press.

Cornell, Stephen, and Marta Cecilia Gil-Swedberg. 1995. "Sociohistorical Factors in Institutional Efficacy: Economic Development in Three American Indian Cases." *Economic Development and Cultural Change* 43 (2): 239–68.

Cornell, Stephen, and Miriam Jorgensen. 2007. "Getting Things Done for the Nation: The Challenge of Tribal Administration." In *Rebuilding Native Nations: Strategies for Governance and Development*, edited by Miriam Jorgensen, 146–72. Tucson: University of Arizona Press.

Cornell, Stephen, and Joseph P. Kalt. 1988. "Sovereignty and Nation-Building: The Development Challenge in Indian County Today." *American Indian Culture and Research Journal* 22 (3): 187–214.

———. 1990. "Pathways from Poverty: Economic Development and Institution-Building on American Indian Reservations." *American Indian Culture and Research Journal* 14 (1): 89–125.

———. 2000. "Where's the Glue? Institutional Bases of American Indian Economic Development." *Journal of Socio-Economics* 29 (3): 443–70.

Cowan, David A. 2008. "Profound Simplicity of Leadership Wisdom: Exemplary Insight From Miami Nation Chief Floyd Leonard." *International Journal of Leadership Studies* 4 (1): 51–81.

Cronin, Darryl. 2003. "Rethinking Community Development, Resources and Partnerships for Indigenous Governance." Unpublished paper, Faculty of Indigenous Research and Education, Charles Darwin University, Northern Territory, Australia.

Cunningham, Gord, and Alison Mathie. 2002. "From Client to Citizens: Asset-Based Community Development as a Strategy for Community Driven Development." The Coady International Institute, St. Francis Xavier University, Nova Scotia. http://dspace.cigilibrary.org/jspui/bitstream/123456789/10369/1/From%20Clients%20to%20Citizens%20Asset%20Based%20Community%20Development%20as%20a%20Strategy%20For%20Community%20Driven%20Development.pdf?1.

Dahlberg, Gunilla, Peter Moss, and Alan Pence. 1999. *Beyond Quality in Early Childhood Education and Care: Postmodern Perspectives.* London: Routledge.

Davis, Arthur K. 1971. "Canadian Society and History as Hinterland Versus Metropolis." In *Canadian Society: Pluralism, Change and Conflict,* edited by Richard J. Ossenberg, 6–32. Scarborough: Prentice-Hall.

Davis, O. L., Jr. 1997. "Beyond 'Best Practices' Toward Wise Practices." *Journal of Curriculum and Supervision* 13 (1): 1–5.

Davis, James H., Lex Donaldson, and F. David Schoorman. 1997. "Toward a Stewardship Theory of Management." *Academy of Management Review* 22 (1): 20–47.

Dos Santos, Theotonio. 1971. "The Structure of Dependence." In *Readings in the U.S. Imperialism,* edited by K. T. Fann and Donald C. Hodges, 225–36. Boston: Extending Horizons.

Dyck, Noel, ed. 1985. *Indigenous People and the Nation-State: Fourth World Politics in Canada, Australia and Norway.* St. John's: Memorial University of Newfoundland.

Elias, Peter Douglas. 1990. "Wage Labour, Aboriginal Relations, and the Cree of the Churchill River Basin, Saskatchewan." *Native Studies Review* 6 (2): 43–64.

Erakovic, Lijijana, Manula Henare, Edwina Pio, and Chellie Spiller. 2011. "Wise Up: Creating Organizational Wisdom Through an Ethic of *Kaitiakitanga.*" *Journal of Business Ethics* 104 (2): 223–35.

Foldy, Erica, and Sonia Ospina. 2005. "Toward a Framework of Social Change Leadership." Research paper no. 2010-05, NYU Wagner. http://

ssrn.com/abstract=1532332.

Fox, Jonathan. 1992. "Democratic Rural Development: Leadership Accountability in Regional Peasant Organizations." *Development and Change* 23 (2): 1–36.

Foy, Malcom, Rick Krehbiel, and Elmar Plate. 2009. "Best Practices for First Nations Involvement in Environmental Assessment Review of Development Projects in British Columbia." Unpublished report, New Relationship Trust, Vancouver. http://www.newrelationshiptrust.ca/downloads/environmental-assessments-report.pdf.

Frank, Andre Gunder. 1966. "The Development of Underdevelopment." *Monthly Review* XVII (2): 17–31.

Fraser, Sarah Jane. 2002. "An Exploration of Joint Ventures as a Sustainable Development Tool for First Nations." *Journal of Aboriginal Economic Development* 3 (1): 40–44.

Frideres, James. 1988. "The Political Economy of Natives in Canada." In *Native Peoples in Canada: Contemporary Conflicts*, edited by James Frideres, 366. 3rd ed. Scarborough: Prentice-Hall.

Gini, Al. 1998. "Work, Identity and Self: How We Are Formed by the Work We Do." *Journal of Business Ethics* 17 (7): 707–14.

Gooty, J., and S. Michie. 2005. "Values, Emotions, and Authenticity: Will the Real Leader Please Stand Up?" *Leadership Quarterly* 16 (3): 441–57.

Graham, John, and Mackenzie Kinmond. 2008. "Friendship Centre Movement Best Practices in Governance and Management." Unpublished report, National Association of Friendship Centres and Institute on Governance, Ottawa. http://iog.ca/wp-content/uploads/2012/12/2008_August_nafc_bestpractices.pdf.

Graham, John, and Laura Mitchell. 2009. "A Legacy of Excellence: Best Practices Board Study Aboriginal Healing Foundation." Unpublished report, Institute on Governance, Ottawa. http://iog.ca/wp-content/uploads/2012/12/2009_October_AHFBoard.pdf.

Grint, Keith, and Linda Sue Warner. 2006. "American Indian Ways of Leading and Knowing." *Leadership* 2 (2): 225–44. doi:10.1177/1742715006062936.

Guyette, Susan. 1996. *Planning for Balanced Development: A Guide for Native American and Rural Communities*. Santa Fe: Clear Light Publishers.

Hammond Ketilson, L., and I. MacPherson. 2002. "Aboriginal Co-operatives in Canada: A Sustainable Development Strategy Whose Time Has Come." *Journal of Aboriginal Economic Development* 3 (1): 45–57.

Helin, Calvin. 2006. *Dances with Dependency: Indigenous Success Through Self-Reliance*. Vancouver: Orca Spirit Publishing.

Hernandez, Morela. 2008. "Promoting Stewardship Behavior in Organizations: A Leadership Model." *Journal of Business Ethics* 80 (2008): 121–28. doi:10.1007/s10551-007-9440-2.

High, Steven. 1996. "Native Wage Labour and Independent Production During the Era of Irrelevance." *Labour/Le Travail* 37 (Spring): 243–64.

Hofstede, Geert. 1980. *Culture's Consequences: International Differences in Work Related Values*. Beverley Hills: Sage.

——. 1983. "The Cultural Relativity of Organizational Practices and Theories." *Journal of International Business* 14 (2): 75–89.

HRDC (Human Resources Development Canada). 1999. "Aboriginal Social and Economic Development: Lessons Learned Summary Report." Unpublished report, Evaluation and Data Development, Strategic Policy, HRDC, Ottawa.

INAC (Indian and Northern Affairs Canada). 2000. "Towards Sustainable, Successful First Nation Communities: Good Governance, the Governance Continuum and Governance Programming." Unpublished report, Self Government Branch, INAC, Ottawa.

——. 2005. "Comprehensive Community Planning: Lessons Learned and Networking Workshop." Unpublished report, Strategic Planning and Communications, INAC, Ottawa.

INAC (Indian and Northern Affairs Canada) and PWGSC (Public Works and Government Services Canada). 2002. "Good Public Works Management in First Nations Communities: Sharing the Story— Experiences of Six Communities." Unpublished report, INAC and PWGSC, Ottawa.

Jaros, Stephen. 2012. "Identity and the Workplace: An Assessment of Contextualist and Discursive Approaches." *Tamara: Journal for Critical Organization Inquiry* 10 (4): 45–59.

Jorgensen, Miriam, ed. 2007. *Rebuilding Native Nations: Strategies for Governance and Development*. Tucson: University of Arizona Press.

Kageler, W., V. L. Goodwin, T. M. Pitts, and J. L. Whittington. 2005. "Legacy Leadership: The Leadership Wisdom of the Apostle Paul."

Leadership Quarterly 16 (5): 749–70.

Kalt, Joseph P. 1993. "Sovereignty and Economic Development on American Indian Reservations: Lessons from the United States." In *Sharing the Harvest: The Road to Self-Reliance – Report of the National Round Table on Aboriginal Economic Development and Resources,* edited by the Royal Commission on Aboriginal Peoples, 35. Ottawa: Minister of Supply and Services and Canada Communication Group.

King, Tracey. 2008. "Fostering Aboriginal Leadership: Increasing Enrollment and Completion Rates in Canadian Post-Secondary Institutions." *College Quarterly* 11 (1). http://www.collegequarterly.ca/2008-vol11-num01-winter/king.html.

Knudtson, Peter, and David Suzuki. 1992. *Wisdom of the Elders.* Toronto: Stoddart Publishing.

Kok, Ayse. 2009. "Realizing Wisdom Theory in Complex Learning Networks." *Electronic Journal of e-Learning* 7 (1): 53–60. http://www.ejel.org/volume7/issue1.

Korac-Kakabadse, A., N. Korac-Kakabadse, and A. Kouzmin. 2001. "Leadership Renewal: Towards the Philosophy of Wisdom." *International Review of Administrative Sciences* 67 (2): 207–27.

Krajewski, Henryk, and Yvonne Silver. n.d. "Announcing the Death of 'Best Practices': Resurrecting 'Best Principles' to Retain and Engage High Potentials." Unpublished article, Human Resources Association of Calgary. Accessed February 6, 2014. www.right.com/documents/newsroom/20080620141835_420216525.pdf

LaFrance, Joan, and Richard Nichols. 2010. "Reframing Evaluation: Defining an Indigenous Evaluation Framework." *Canadian Journal of Program Evaluation* 23 (2): 13–31.

Leithwood, Kenneth. 2001. "School Leadership in the Context of Accountability Policies." *International Journal of Leadership in Education: Theory and Practice* 4 (3): 217–35. doi:10.1080/13603120110057082.

Leskiw, Sheri-Lynne, and Parbudyal Singh. 2007. "Leadership Development: Learning From Best Practices." *Leadership and Organization Development Journal* 28 (5): 444–64.

Little Bear, Leroy. 2011. "Jagged Worldview Colliding." In *Reclaiming Indigenous Voice and Vision,* edited by Marie Battiste, 77–85. Vancouver: University of British Columbia Press.

Loizides, Stelios, and Wanda Wuttunee. 2005. "Creating Wealth and Employment in Aboriginal Communities." Unpublished report, Conference Board of Canada, Ottawa.

Martz, Wes. 2013. "Evaluating Organizational Performance: Rational, Natural, and Open System Models." *American Journal of Evaluation* 34 (3): 385–401. doi:10.1177/1098214013479151.

McGonagill, Grady, and Peter W. Pruyn. 2010. "Leadership Development in the U.S.: Principles and Patterns of Best Practice." Unpublished report, Bertelsmann Stiftung, Gütersloh, Germany. http://www.bertelsmann-stiftung.de/cps/rde/xbcr/SID-57313EB7-4601475F/bst_engl/Leadership-Development-in-the-US.pdf.

Meier, Werner. 2003. "Results-Based Management: Towards a Common Understanding Among Development Cooperation Agencies." Discussion paper ver. 5.0, Canadian International Development Agency, Performance Review Branch, Ottawa.

Milloy, John. 1999. *A National Crime: The Canadian Government and the Residential School System.* Winnipeg: University of Manitoba Press.

Nabigon, Herbert C., and Annie Wenger-Nabigon. 2012. "'Wise Practices': Integrating Traditional Teachings With Mainstream Treatment Approaches." *Native Social Work Journal* 8 (2012): 43–55.

NCFNG (National Centre for First Nations Governance). 2009. "Governance Best Practices Report." http://fngovernance.org/publication_docs/NCFNG_Best_Practice_Report.pdf.

Nelson, Rodney, and Ashley Sisco. 2008. "From Vision to Venture: An Account of Five Successful Aboriginal Businesses." Unpublished report, Conference Board of Canada, Ottawa.

Newhouse, David. 1999. "The Development of the Aboriginal Economy Over the Next 20 Years." *Journal of Aboriginal Economic Development* 1 (1): 68–77.

——. 2000. "Modern Aboriginal Economies: Capitalism with a Red Face." *Journal of Aboriginal Economic Development* 1 (2): 55–61.

Nielsen, Marianne O., and Lindsay Redpath. 1997. "A Comparison of Native Culture, Non-Native Culture and New Management." *Canadian Journal of Administrative Sciences* 14 (3): 327–39.

O'Connell, Tom, Robert J. Oppenheimer, and Warren Weir. 2010. "Training Opportunities in Aboriginal Business, Community and Economic

Development: Being Offered Through Aboriginal Organizations."
Journal of Aboriginal Economic Development 7 (1): 19–28.

Oppenheimer, Robert, and Warren Weir. 2010. "The New Federal Framework for Aboriginal Economic Development: The Base Upon Which Future Canadian Government Policies and Programs Are Being Built." *Journal of Aboriginal Economic Development* 7 (1): 86–94.

Ottmann, Jacqueline. 2005a. "First Nations Leadership Development." Report for the Banff Centre, Indigenous Leadership and Management. www.banffcentre.ca/departments/leadership/aboriginal/library/First_Nations_Leadership_Ottmann.pdf.

——. 2005b. "First Nations Leadership Development within a Saskatchewan Context." EdD diss., Department of Educational Administration, University of Saskatchewan.

Ray, Arthur J. 1974. *Indians in the Fur Trade: Their Role as Trappers, Hunters, and Middlemen in the Lands Southwest of the Hudson Bay, 1660-1870.* Toronto: University of Toronto Press.

Sisco, Ashley, and Nicole Stewart. 2009. "True to Their Visions: An Account of 10 Successful Aboriginal Businesses." Unpublished report, Conference Board of Canada, Ottawa.

Smith, Dean Howard. 2000. *Modern Tribal Development: Paths to Self-Sufficiency and Cultural Integrity in Indian Country.* Walnut Creek: AltaMira Press.

Snowball, Andrew, and Cynthia Wesley-Esquimaux. 2010. "Viewing Violence, Mental Illness and Addictions Through a Wise Practice Lens." *International Journal of Mental Health and Addictions* 8 (2): 390–407.

Sternberg, Robert J. 2005. "A Model of Educational Leadership: Wisdom, Intelligence, and Creativity, Synthesized." *International Journal of Leadership in Education* 8 (4): 347–64.

Thoms, Michael J. 2007. "Leading an Extraordinary Life: Wise Practices for an HIV Prevention Campaign With Two-Spirited Men." Unpublished paper, 2-Spirited People of the First Nations, Toronto.

Tobias, John. 1976. "Protection, Civilization, Assimilation: An Outline of Canada's Indian Policy." *Western Canadian Journal of Anthropology* 6 (2): 39–53.

Tough, Frank. 1992. "Regional Analysis of Indian Aggregate Income, Northern Manitoba." *Native Studies Review* 12 (1): 95–146.

Wallerstein, Immanuel. 2004. *World-Systems Analysis.* Durham: Duke

University Press.

Walter, Maggie. 2006. "Participatory Action Research." In *Social Research Methods*, edited by Maggie Walter, chapter 21. Online excerpt, accessed June 9, 2014. http://lib.oup.com.au/he/study_skills/walter2e/walter_ch21.pdf.

Weick, K. E. 2004. "Mundane Poetics: Searching for Wisdom in Organization Studies." *Organization Studies* 25 (3): 653–68.

Wein, Fred. 1999. "The Royal Commission Report: Nine Steps to Rebuild Aboriginal Economies." *Journal of Aboriginal Economic Development* 1 (1): 102–19.

Wuttunee, Wanda. 2002. "Partnering Among Aboriginal Communities: Tribal Council Investment Group (TCIG)." *Journal of Aboriginal Economic Development* 3 (1): 9–17.

———. 2004. *Living Rhythms: Lessons in Aboriginal Economic Resilience.* Montreal: McGill-Queen's University Press.

Chapter 2

The Field of Tribal Leadership Training, Cultures of Expertise, and Native Nations in the United States

Christopher Wetzel

Abstract

This paper theorizes the emergent field of expert organizations that provide training, technical assistance, and capacity-building work for Native American tribal leaders. The development of the field of expert training organizations has occurred in the context of federal policies of Self-Determination and a pervasive faith in neo-liberalism. Analyzing the organization of institutions in the field, this paper argues for the presence of four types of groups based on their orientation to the market (public versus private) and the breadth of knowledge and services offered (specialist versus generalist). Recognizing that expertise needs to be perceived as legitimate by consumers of knowledge, four case studies of training organizations are presented to illustrate how each category represents a unique culture of expertise. Finally, questions are raised about the implication of tribal training for sovereignty.

Introduction[1]

In 2002, citizens of the Eastern Band of Cherokee Indians, an Indigenous nation based in the Qualla Boundary region of western North Carolina, voted to audit the listing of their enrolled citizens. When the review process started several years later, an Associated Press State and Local Wire (2005) article noted the Eastern Band's decision to retain the services of the Falmouth Institute:

> The Eastern Band of Cherokee Indians has hired outside auditors to review birth and death certificates and other documents to separate legitimate members from gold-diggers.... An auditing team from the Falmouth Institute, a Fairfax, Va., consulting company to American Indian tribes, arrived in Cherokee late last month to begin work.

As a for-profit generalist "consulting company to American Indian tribes" that aspires to be "the premier provider of culturally relevant education and information services for North American Indian tribes and organizations," the Falmouth Institute (2012a) serves Native American tribal nations in a multitude of ways. In this instance, the Eastern Band hired Falmouth to review the Nation's membership roll—a logistically challenging, politically fraught process in any context.

Emerging from the current experiences of an Indigenous community in the United States, this narrative highlights the expanding field of training, technical assistance, and capacity-building organizations that work with Native nations. This field's development has coincided with an era of federal Indian policy that privileges Self-Determination, where tribal nations can assume responsibility for providing services and running programs previously administered by the federal government, as well as a broader neo-liberal moment that celebrates free markets and small government (Castile 1999, 2006; Harvey 2007; Stark and Wilkins 2011). Key questions for this project include: How is the field organized? Who are the organizational players? What kinds of training services are offered to tribal clients? What are the consequences of outsourcing training and expertise on the ways Indigenous peoples envision possible futures?

Expertise is a dual relationship between people and the knowledge being produced, as well as between experts who produce knowledge and the communities that consume it (Goldman 2006). To successfully work with tribal clients, organizations necessarily rely on the ability to articulate their unique, relevant knowledge about a range of laws and practices. As such, training organizations actively cultivate ideals of expertise. Academic studies have examined the development and deployment of expertise in fields such as economics (Fourcade-Gourinchas 2006; Reay 2007); medicine, science, and technology (Collins and Evans 2002; Epstein 1996; Hilgartner 2000); and public policy (Brint 1994; Eyal 2006). Although social scientists have researched the interrelationships between expertise, organizations, and policy-making, attention must be paid to the particular and peculiar relationships between experts and Indigenous peoples. Consider here Vine Deloria, Jr.'s (1969) classic critique of how anthropologists exploit Indians by producing vast amounts of abstract knowledge that is of little use to tribal nations, yet impacts and declares authority over them. Since these relationships are often asymmetrical and replete with challenges, it is imperative to examine the field of organizations that provide training, technical assistance, and capacity-building work in Indian Country.

This article begins by describing a pair of key historical forces that shaped the field's milieu, specifically the Indian Self-Determination and Education Assistance Act and a wide embrace of neo-liberal tenets. Next I outline a typology for the field, arguing that training organizations can be divided into four broad categories based on the services offered by a group and their orientation to the market. In the subsequent section I closely analyze the four categories, arguing that each represents a distinct culture of training. Finally, the paper concludes by considering the implications of the field's emergence and highlighting areas for future research.

Shaping the Context: Self-Determination and Neo-Liberalism

The emergence of tribal training groups has been significantly shaped by the rise of Self-Determination as a framework for federal Indian policy. Federal policies have long vacillated between affirming the inherent sovereignty of tribes and imposing a state of subsidiary wardship (Corntassel and Witmer 2011; Deloria and Lytle 1998). Responding to demands articulated by the Red Power Movement (Cornell 1988; Johnson 2008; Nagel 1997) and a growing urban Indigenous population (Fixico 2000), President Richard Nixon repudiated the doctrine of termination that sought to end the government-to-government relationship between the state and tribes. Congress also passed the Indian Self-Determination and Education Assistance Act in 1975 (Public Law 93-638). Title I of the Act established a process for tribal nations to contract with the Bureau of Indian Affairs to take over federal programs such as education and housing. Unlike in the past, when federal agencies and bureaucrats operated programs, Self-Determination made it possible to transfer authority for specifically agreed-upon tasks to tribes:

> The philosophy underlying this concept of self-determination revolved around the vesting of both management and control of governmental service programs in the tribal governments on the theory that tribes knew best their own problems and could therefore allocate their resources and energies in the proper direction. (Deloria and Lytle 1983, 103)

When tribes elected to regain control of a program and negotiated a contract, the Self-Determination Act required that grant dollars be used specifically and exclusively to support the designated program or to cover indirect costs related to administering the program.

When Congress amended the Self-Determination Act in 1988 (Public Law 100-581), the "Tribal Self-Governance Demonstration Project" was added. Title III reiterated the federal government's commitment to the trust relationship and provided for tribal nations to negotiate self-governance compacts. Starting with a small number of tribes and expanding with subsequent re-authorizations, the Self-Governance Demonstration Project allowed for tribes that completed planning projects and demonstrated financial stability to negotiate an annual funding agreement with the federal government. Unlike contracts that required grant dollars to be used for specific programs, annual funding compacts afforded Native governments the choice of whether or not to take over services, as well as flexibility and discretion about how to allocate funds. Initiated as a five-year pilot project, compacting has become an established element of the federal government's approach to Self-Determination.

Self-Determination in general, and the implementation of contracting and compacting specifically, represents a critical development in federal policy. Some describe the Act as producing substantial benefits. Self-Governance Communication and Education (2009, 2), a tribally based information clearing house, posits that "Self-Governance returns decision-making authority and management responsibilities to Tribes and their governing bodies.... Tribes are accountable to their own people for resource management, service delivery, and development." The return of "decision-making authority" to tribal nations, as well as the financial resources necessary to implement these visions, benefits tribal citizens while strengthening tribal governments. Others highlight Self-Determination's international benefits, asserting that "the compacting process in a real sense is the modern-day equivalent of the historic treaty making period" (Stark and Wilkins 2011, 100). By contrast, others are ambivalent about the consequences of Self-Determination. The Act enables the Bureau of Indian Affairs to retain significant power through an orientation towards bureaucratic planning rather than tribal needs (Nelson and Sheley 1985). At best, the Act facilitates the limited exercise of "relative powerlessness" while participation in compacting "carries with it a divisiveness that draws some participants toward assimilation while it creates alienation among factions that choose not to participate" (Esber 1992, 213, 221).

Suspending any judgement about the Self-Determination Act's consequences for assertions of tribal nationhood or relations between sovereigns, I argue that specific provisions of the Act have been extremely consequential for the emergence of tribal training organizations. First, while having more control over programs, compacting or contracting tribes are statutorily obligated to meet government financial auditing and reporting standards. Complying with these terms requires substantial technical knowledge, thorough bookkeeping, and staffing to complete audits in a timely manner. Second, the federal government's shift towards being a grant-issuing and auditing body also transforms relationships between sovereigns. Relative to the federal government, tribes become applicants for necessarily limited pools of funding rather than coequal sovereigns. Between tribal nations, the grant-making process is often competitive and zero-sum, with the awarding of dollars to one community signalling the failure of another to garner much-needed resources. Third, with the growing desire to reclaim programs, tribes rightly want to fill administrative positions with community members. Yet when Native nations lack the requisite human capital, experience, or technical knowledge to direct programs, they often turn to training organizations for assistance.

At the present time, tribal leadership development programs are critical. Responding to opportunities for Self-Determination, tribal nations have embraced the opportunity to plan and direct services for their citizens. Yet individual leaders, tribal governments, and larger communities have to be prepared to assume these diverse responsibilities and address the cultural, economic, social, political, and legal complexities of implementing effective programs (Begay 1991; Calliou 2005). Brian Calliou (2008) insists that tribal leadership training programs must build capacity within the community while also enhancing the skills of individual leaders. Moreover, emerging leadership programs have to do this work in a way that reflects the tremendous dynamism of Native nations while simultaneously remaining consonant with specific cultures, knowledges, traditions, and sacred responsibilities (Ottmann 2005).

Neo-liberalism also shapes the field of tribal training. Generally speaking, neo-liberalism connotes a series of interconnected trans-formations: the globalization of economic markets, privatization of previously state-run industries, and a significant downsizing of gov-ernment and regulation to allow the "free market" to rule (Beckfield, Brady, and Zhao 2007; Babb and Fourcade-Gourinchas 2002; Harvey 2007). Too often, Native peoples are perceived as economically and politically backward, with people citing disparities in educational attainment, income, and poverty rates as evidence. While real and consequential (Ogunwole 2006; Stark and Wilkins 2011), these inequalities are rooted in structural conditions rather than cultural beliefs. The United States Commission on Civil Rights (2003, ix) highlights structural barriers: "Small in numbers and relatively poor, Native Americans often have had a difficult time ensuring fair and equal treatment on their own. Unfortunately, relying on the goodwill of the nation to honor its obligation to Native Americans clearly has not resulted in desired outcomes." The Commission's report continues: "In short, the Commission finds evidence of a crisis in the persistence and growth of unmet needs. The conditions in Indian Country could be greatly relieved if the federal government honored its commitment to funding, paid greater attention to building basic infrastructure in Indian Country, and promoted self-determination among tribes" (United States Commission on Civil Rights 2003, xii). Many of the problems on reservations are institutional and structural. Despite this, some proponents of neo-liberalism still blame the victims. James Watt, secretary of the interior under President Ronald Reagan and the cabinet official directly responsible for the Bureau of Indian Affairs, captured these dubious perceptions, stating in a speech: "If you want an example of the future of socialism, don't go to Russia—come to America and go to the Indian reservations.... Every social problem is exaggerated because of socialistic government policies on the Indian reservation" (Morris 1992, 72).

Nevertheless, Native nations are deeply integrated into and impacted by the growth of a neo-liberal milieu. Whether in the form of gaming (Cattelino 2008; Mason 2000), tourism (Bunten 2010; Nesper 2003), or other enterprises, tribes engage in economic development and diversification in order to provide needed revenues that support critical social services and create jobs for Natives and non-Natives alike. Regardless of the form of economic development, many explicitly invoke the Harvard Project's (HPAIED 2007) vision of success: sovereignty, institutions, strategic direction, strong leadership, and culture are the building blocks of any profitable and sustainable economic development. Although Harvard Project (129) scholars assert that their model does not require tribes to be more "Western" or embrace a neo-liberal political-economic model, others question this conclusion (Mowbray 2006; Sullivan 2006). Maggie Walter (2010, 123) notes that although neo-liberalism was originally seen as potentially empowering and granting rights, it has ultimately overrun Indigenous Australians: "Disregarding the lack of fit between Indigenous lives and rights and a free market paradigm it was Indigenous Australia that had to alter to fit the template; rational economic man was not open to Indigenization.... Whatever the issue, the market economy or market solutions were the answer." Maggie Bolton (2007) found similar challenges in her research on how non-governmental organizations in Bolivia use grants to produce disciplined Indigenous subjects. Although most of these critiques come from beyond the continental United States, one ought to be cognizant of how the ideas and practices of neo-liberalism affect tribal nations. Much like with Self-Determination, the point is that the idea of dynamic markets being able to solve problems, coupled with the challenges of creating economically, environmentally, and socially sustainable industries, shapes the situation from which training organizations have emerged.

Towards a Typology of Training

A central goal of this paper is to paint an "ecological" picture of the field of training, technical assistance, and capacity-building organizations (Abbott 1988). That is, the project looks beyond specific groups to theorize the contours of the whole professional field. A coherent structure becomes evident in thinking about what groups do and how they work with tribal nations. My research started by documenting which groups constitute the field. I asked elected tribal leaders, scholars, and practitioners about organizations with which they were familiar; I reviewed web pages, industry publications, and conference announcements; and I analyzed tribal and Native news sources for details about decisions to hire consultants. Although the list of fifty-four groups generated to date may not be exhaustive, it is sufficient to begin conceptually mapping the larger field. A list of training groups is included in the chapter's Appendix.

At first glance, one sees that the groups are geographically clustered. A critical mass of training groups is present in Arizona and New Mexico, with ten organizations located between Albuquerque, Phoenix, and Tucson. Clusters of expert groups are also evident in the Washington, D.C., area and throughout the upper Midwest. These locations make sense because they are near either Indigenous population clusters (whether reservations or cities in the Southwest and upper Midwest) or federal agencies and decision makers (Washington, D.C.). For the groups where founding dates could be determined, one was founded in the 1950s, two in the 1960s, one in the 1970s, nine in the 1980s, eleven in the 1990s, and nine in the 2000s. These figures reflect the field's novelty as well as the correlation with Self-Determination and neo-liberalism.

I propose that the field can best be understood by organizing groups into four categories based on two dimensions associated with how they work with Indigenous communities. Figure 1 presents this typology. The horizontal axis reflects a group's orientation to the market. The difference here is between public organizations that are either non-profit or affiliated with university research centres and private organizations that are market driven and explicitly seek to generate profits. The vertical axis, by comparison, indicates the breadth of services offered by training organizations. Here the distinction is between generalist groups that promote themselves as capable of working in a number of substantive areas (including, but certainly not limited to, accounting, auditing, constitutional reform, economic development, education, elections, environment, gaming, health, housing, Indian Child Welfare Act, justice systems, policing, and professional development) and specialist groups that typically work in only one or two specific areas.

Figure 1: Map of Organizational Typologies

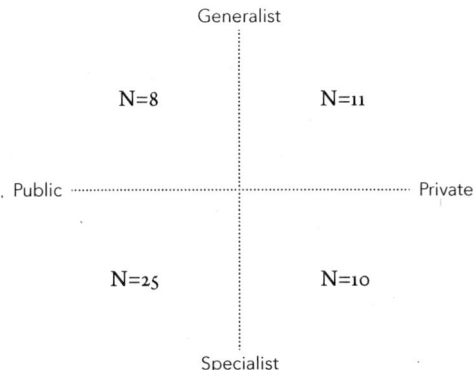

This typology yields a number of important insights. First, the field is far from monolithic, as we can see a fair amount of differentiation. The preponderance of expert groups are public-specialist organizations (46 percent, n=25), with smaller numbers of private-generalists (20 percent, n=11), private-specialists (19 percent, n=10), and public-generalists (15 percent, n=8). As will be detailed in the next section, these categories connote particular cultures of expertise that orient how organizations work with tribal nations. To put it another way, where groups are located in the field indicates not the substance of their work with tribal clients but rather the style of training.

Second, the field is highly interconnected. Sometimes these inter-actions can be largely in the realm of ideas or visions, such as when a number of practitioners mentioned their perception of the public-generalist Harvard Project as the field's "philosophers" or as "driving the big ideas" about the meaning of sovereignty (Wetzel 2009, int. 3), which other groups then work to implement. At other times, depending on the content of a program, specific grant requirements, or the needs of a tribal client, training organizations will collaborate to provide useful services, such as how the Native American Training Institute and the Tribal Law and Policy Institute jointly operate the National Child Welfare Resource Center for Tribes.

Third, we see the robust presence of Native actors and organizations. Approximately 55 percent of all the private groups are Indian or tribally owned, as are more than 60 percent of the public-specialist groups. This at least suggests the possibility of a strong Indigenous influence on the field's practices and visions.

Analyzing the Field's Terrain: Four Organizational Types

Having described the field in a general sense, our attention now turns to the four specific types: public-generalist, private-generalist, private-specialist, and public-specialist.[2] For each category I present an organizational case study to highlight the general approach to training.

Public-Generalist Category

Of the eight public-generalist training groups, seven are affiliated with universities. Perhaps the best known of these groups is the Harvard Project on American Indian Economic Development. Founded in 1987 by economist Joseph Kalt and sociologist Stephen Cornell, "through applied research and service, the Harvard Project aims to understand and foster the conditions under which sustained, self-determined social and economic development is achieved among American Indian nations" (HPAIED 2012b). Based out of the John F. Kennedy School of Government at Harvard University, the Harvard Project regularly collaborates with the Native Nations Institute at the University of Arizona to offer expert services such as research, Honoring Nations, and some courses to tribal leaders.

Research is a particular strength for the Harvard Project. Based on extensive work by scholars, practitioners, and students, the Harvard Project has produced a substantial body of research that has frequently been published in peer-reviewed academic forums (Cornell and Kalt 1992, 1998, 2000). More recently, a pair of books highlighting key findings from more than two decades of research were published: *Rebuilding Native Nations: Strategies for Governance and Development* (Jorgensen 2007) and *The State of Native Nations: Conditions Under U.S. Policies of Self-Determination* (HPAIED 2007). Written in accessible language and featuring extensive profiles of tribal successes, both volumes are designed for consumption by leaders of Indigenous nations, scholars, and the general public. Working papers and article reprints from Harvard Project–affiliated scholars are also published online through the Joint Occasional Papers on Native Affairs series. As mentioned above, the research is organized around the importance of factors that shape successful governance and economic development: robust institutions; the match between policies, practices, and institutions and a community's culture; capable leadership; and real sovereignty where tribes own their own decisions (Jorgensen 2012).

A second major capacity-building initiative is the Harvard Project's Honoring Nations program. Honoring Nations celebrates best practices by tribal nations in a range of endeavours:

> Honoring Nations serves as a vehicle for shifting the focus from what does not work to what does, fostering pride and confidence in the ability of American Indian governments to make positive contributions to the wellbeing of their respective communities and citizens. The program is also founded on the idea that Native nations can benefit from having greater access to innovative ideas

and effective governing approaches. Honored programs serve as important sources of knowledge and inspiration, and our experience shows that they are drawn upon by communities throughout Indian Country and far beyond. (HPAIED 2012a)

Communities can self-nominate for the recognition, with applications being evaluated by a board of scholars and community leaders based on factors that resonate with the Harvard Project's central principles: effectiveness, sovereignty, cultural relevance, transferability, and sustainability. Finalists receive site visits from and make presentations to the Honoring Nations board members. Ultimately, awardees receive a grant of $10,000 or $20,000 as well as being asked to participate in future Harvard Project conferences (HPAIED 2012c).

Private-Generalist Category

The eleven private-generalist groups confront significant challenges when seeking to establish their professional legitimacy and expertise. These groups represent that they are knowledgeable in diverse topics, from teaching secretaries how to properly answer telephones to completely rewriting tribal governing documents. This range and breadth invariably raises questions about how private-generalist groups envision their role and how they convince tribal nations to rely on the group's unique expertise for training or to provide technical assistance.

For this category, we turn our attention to the Falmouth Institute, founded in 1985 by Richard Phelps. Phelps, who had previously worked for a management and leadership training organization, based the group in northern Virginia because the location's proximity to agencies and bureaucrats in Washington, D.C., added value for tribal clients. The Falmouth Institute's (2012a) mission is to be "the premier provider of culturally relevant education and information services for North American Indian tribes and organizations." Relying on its knowledge of laws, histories, and policies related to Indian Country, as well as how federal programs work helps the Falmouth Institute create an advantage. Phelps (Richard Phelps, pers. comm.) explained the project of providing tribal nations with accessible, informed expertise: "Tribes don't have a lot of trust for the government. Our organization offers never-ending service to tribes. They get answers with no strings attached. If we don't know the answer in the office, we draw on a network of extended faculty who conduct trainings." Because expertise is a field and a competitive marketplace, employees saw the importance of building a solid corporate reputation including service to communities. The group's extended faculty are not only leaders in their fields who teach outstanding courses, they are also available to address any questions or concerns once attendees return home from training seminars.

To offer training on such a wide range of topics, the Falmouth Institute relies on a network of faculty. As of November 2012, the Falmouth web page lists forty-one instructors who work or worked for tribal governments, tribal enterprises, universities, industries, or as independent consultants. Educational backgrounds of faculty include accounting, anthropology, business, counselling, economics, and law (Falmouth 2012d). They perceive themselves, and by extension the organization, as technocrats who provide knowledge to tribes. One person explained: "We aren't really advocates and we aren't giving advice. We show tribes what their options are." Her colleague picked up on this point and continued: "We just give them knowledge, and knowledge is power." In this instance, the pair contends that the Falmouth Institute shows tribes how to do things but does not tell them what to do. The information they provide is neither normative nor is it meant to point tribes towards any particular decision or outcome. This vision of expertise reflects a deep knowledge of the minutiae of federal policies and regulations, of generally accepted accounting practices, and of best practices in ethics. As an organization, the Falmouth Institute has a unique depth and breadth of knowledge with which to assist their tribal clients.

Falmouth offers general training programs and thematic conferences on dozens of topics. The organization had more than forty training sessions scheduled in areas ranging from basic budgeting to background investigations of vendors between December 2012 and February 2013—a period when training sessions slow down due to several major holidays (Falmouth 2012b). Frequently held in Las Vegas, Nevada, training sessions typically rely on a curriculum developed by the Falmouth Institute that builds on its knowledge of the law, logic, and history of Indian Country. Supplementing these training programs are events such as the Tribal Secretaries Conference that combine multiple related training sessions into several days. In recent years, the group has also started offering online training sessions to allow people to fit relevant professional development into their schedule without having to travel. Further, the Falmouth Institute has long offered on-site training sessions for tribes in cases where clients need many people to receive training or are looking for training that is tailored to a nation's unique circumstances. In these cases, Falmouth faculty travel to the community to provide the contracted workshop.

Beyond training programs (whether away from the reservation, on-site, or online), the Falmouth Institute also undertakes consulting projects at the request of Native communities. Again, we see this with the opening example of the Eastern Band of Cherokee Nation's decision to hire the Falmouth Institute for a membership audit. In explaining its consulting practice, the organization reiterates its long connection with the realities and practicalities of Indian Country:

> Whether it's widespread changes in your government operations or simply assistance in achieving a better indirect cost rate, Falmouth Consulting can provide the experience and expertise that will make it happen for you. We will discuss your objectives; review and assess your current situation; develop or revamp policy, procedures or systems; and help you implement change with your staff. (Falmouth 2012c)

The approach to consulting goes beyond technical knowledge; rather, the Falmouth Institute (2012a, 2012c) accentuates its specific "experience and expertise" with Native nations, and states that it will be deliberate in collecting and assessing data and collaborative in assisting with the implementation of changes. Again, Falmouth's approach to consulting privileges the use of "culturally relevant" knowledge to aid tribal nations, rather than advocating for specific outcomes.

Private-Specialist Category
The private-specialist sector of the field of tribal training is largely ori-

ented towards economic development and, more specifically, casino gaming. In this category, nine of the ten organizations work in the area of economic development. This reflects the reality that the household income of Native peoples on reservations is only 58 percent of the median household income for all Americans. Moreover, absolute and relative rates of poverty are equally high for Indigenous peoples (HPAIED 2007; Ogunwole 2006). Reacting to United States Supreme Court ruling in *California v. Cabazon Band of Mission Indians* (1987) that when states allow gaming, tribes are also legally permitted to participate in gaming, Congress passed the Indian Gaming Regulatory Act (IGRA), which defined classes of gaming and established a process requiring states and tribes to negotiate compacts under which gaming could occur. Subsequently, a tribal gaming industry has grown. According to the National Indian Gaming Commission (2012), the 421 Indian gaming facilities generated more than $27.2 billion in gross revenues in 2011, up from 215 facilities with $5.46 billion in revenues in 1995.[3] While the industry's revenues are highly concentrated, gaming has been a tool for job creation and economic development for a number of tribal nations. To deal with policy hurdles, capital needs, and project planning, tribal nations often turn to training organizations for assistance.

Mohegan Gaming Advisors (MGA) is a prime example of a private-specialist organization. Founded in 2011 as a subsidiary of the Mohegan Tribal Gaming Authority (MTGA), which is in turn overseen by the Mohegan Tribe, MGA's appeals to expertise are rooted in the Mohegan Tribe's experience operating its own casinos. The Mohegan Tribal Gaming Authority's (2012) "business model focuses on creating and operating world-class gaming/entertainment facilities. We understand that today's gaming guest is seeking a multi-dimensional 'entertainment experience.' ... Mohegan Sun, MTGA's flagship property, has captured all of these elements." More specifically, the MGA emphasizes both general gaming knowledge and an understanding of the particular dynamics of Indian gaming. Here MGA "is an ideal source of wisdom, strategy and solutions for Indian tribes that are considering entering the gaming business. We know what the process is like from start to finish—and we know how to work through the many challenges that lie ahead" (MTGA 2012). Hard-earned wisdom, strategy, and solutions drawn from years of experience running a pair of gaming facilities—the Mohegan Sun in Connecticut and the Mohegan Sun at Pocono Downs in Pennsylvania—serve as this group's distinctive calling card.

In terms of training services, MGA (2012c) aids clients by working to "develop and implement practical, real-world solutions to the problems [they] face. [MGA is] ready to help by serving as [their] management team or providing consulting services where needed." Whether casino marketing, operations, finance, human resources, or developing ancillary services, MGA can consult with tribal nations or become involved with project management. Again, these capacities are predicated upon MGA's long experience with gaming. The group's senior leadership team has decades of experience in corporate gaming, tribal gaming, or more often both (MGA 2012b). MGA has entered into a contract to facilitate the development of casinos with the Cowlitz Indian Tribe in Washington and the Menominee Indian Tribe in Wisconsin, as well as smaller-scale consulting projects with the Middletown Rancheria of Pomo Indians in California (Hallenbeck 2011; MGA 2012a). Importantly, this expertise has expanded to the wider gaming marketplace, with MGA leading development efforts to bid for a casino licence in Massachusetts and managing the Resort Casino in Atlantic City, New Jersey (Mohegan Sun 2012; Parmley 2012). MGA not only assumes leadership for the Mohegan Tribe's gaming efforts, it also uses its expertise to strengthen the effectiveness of other sovereign nations' casino operations.

Public-Specialist Category

Of the fifty-four training, technical assistance, and capacity-building organizations in the field, the largest number are public-specialist groups (46 percent, n=25). Unlike the public-generalist sector, where seven of the eight groups are affiliated with universities, public-specialist groups are more often owned by Native peoples (60 percent; fifteen of the twenty-five groups). Moreover, while the sector as a whole includes groups working on such diverse issues as dispute resolution, law enforcement, and tribal governance, each specific group works in a fairly circumscribed area, limiting the topics on which it provides training. Because of the robust linkages with Indigenous proprietors and intentionally limited claims-making about expertise, public-specialist groups represent a fascinating space in which to consider cultures of training and affirming sovereignty.

An intriguing public-specialist organization is the Native American Training Institute (NATI). NATI was created in 1995 as a collaboration between four tribal nations in North Dakota—the Standing Rock Sioux Tribe, the Three Affiliated Tribes, the Spirit Lake Sioux Tribe, and the Turtle Mountain Band of Chippewa—based on their shared concerns about Indian Child Welfare Act issues. Recognizing the need to train tribal leaders, state agents, service providers, and families, NATI (2012a) was established with a mission "to empower individuals, families, and the community to create a safe and healthy environment so children and families can achieve their highest potential." The Institute seeks to work across governmental jurisdictions to create "unique, culturally-relevant training" that can meet the needs of the substantial number of Indian foster children, foster families, and those who work with these issues. This is a critical contribution given the frequently tense relationship between tribal nations and state governments (Corntassel and Witmer 2011).[4]

NATI offers four major programs: healthy relationships for Native American youth; learning and healing from historical trauma; Native American foster parent training; and wraparound in Indian Country, which seeks to involve entire communities in aiding families in crisis (NATI 2012b). For each program, NATI offers formal training at regular intervals as well as offering curricular materials for sale. Throughout the year, NATI also organizes conferences related to Indian child welfare and healthy relationships, such as the annual Indian Child Welfare and Wellness Conference in North Dakota. In addition, NATI offers technical assistance in these areas, with a focus on strategic planning and implementing innovative systems of care (NATI 2012c). Across its work with Indigenous peoples, NATI is focused on creating community-based, Indigenously inflected systems that empower tribal nations and families.

The dynamism of NATI's training work coupled with focused intergovernmental collaboration can be seen in recent examples.

Between 2003 and 2007, NATI was part of the Medicine Moon Initiative, a partnership between federal agencies (specifically, the Department of Health and Human Services' Administration on Children, Youth, and Families) and the child welfare agencies from four tribal nations in North Dakota. The goal of the Medicine Moon Initiative was to improve outcomes for Native children in state and tribal foster care using the NATI's wraparound curriculum and knowledge. This approach sought "to reintroduce Indigenous cultural strengths and protective factors such as use of extended family and natural support systems; healing ceremonies and supports; and traditional values such as respect, relationships, and spirituality" (Aratani et al. 2007, 63). To address the real problem of Native families in crisis and children in crisis, the Medicine Moon Initiative identified Indigenous cultures as sources of potential solutions and elaborated a process for how these can be used to heal historical and contemporary traumas. Also, since 2009, NATI has partnered with the Tribal Law and Policy Institute (a public-specialist training group) and the Butler Institute for Families at the University of Denver to operate the National Child Welfare Resource Center for Tribes. The Resource Center is "the focal point for coordinated and culturally competent child welfare" training and technical assistance services related to programs, grants, and opportunities through the federal Administration on Children, Youth, and Families (National Child Welfare Resource Center for Tribes 2012). As in its training programs, NATI utilizes cultural knowledge and strength to revitalize Native families.

Discussion

The first part of the new millennium is marked by an ever growing scope and breadth of proactive endeavors by Native Americans, individually and collectively, to establish their own fabric of life by their own designs.... It is a drive for *self*-determination. (HPAIED 2007, 2, emphasis in original)

During this Self-Determination era in the United States, many Native nations are choosing to seek the expert aid of training, technical assistance, and capacity-building organizations. This paper has argued for the importance of looking beyond specific trees to envision the proverbial forest; that is, it is imperative to read particular organizations as part of a larger complex, dynamic field of professional practice. Recognizing the existence of a field and describing how it is structured are key contributions of this research. In assessing the field's terrain, one can divide the organizations into four broad categories based on their market orientation and breadth of services. I found the largest number of these training and consulting organizations to be public-specialist groups, followed by smaller numbers of private-generalist, private-specialist, and public-generalist. Because all training organizations confront the challenge of establishing their ability to work with tribal clients, each category can be seen as representing a distinctive culture or approach to training.

As the field expands, it is possible that training organizations may be imparting neo-liberal ideas and practices. For example, in recent years the Harvard Project on American Indian Economic Development has sought to expand beyond the United States to work with First Nations in Canada and Aboriginal peoples in Australia. Some academics in these countries critique the normative "Harvard Project model" for positing modes of development that inadequately reflect the needs and concerns of these Indigenous communities (Dowling 2005; Mowbray 2006; Sullivan 2006). Seeing the tremendous number of groups across sectors that purport to offer "culturally relevant" knowledge and training, we should ask what this means, how it works, and what visions of sovereignty are reflected in the practice of training. Beyond debating whether Indigenous sovereignty is best framed in terms of independence versus interdependence (Alfred 2007; Cattelino 2008; Champagne and Goldberg 2002), I acknowledge the importance of recognizing the diversity and specificity of Indigenous conceptions of sovereignty. Here we can see examples from specific nations, such as Kathryn Manuelito's (2008) education research that found students and schools contrasting a selfish, individualistic American conception of Self-Determination with an engaged, communal Ramah Navajo vision. Similar discussions are taking place around Indigenous conceptions of math and science (James 1996), program evaluation (Kastelic and Sahota 2012), and research methods

(Smith 2012). Understanding the implications of the burgeoning field of training and technical assistance necessitates grappling with what communities themselves envision Self-Determination and sovereignty as meaning.

In thinking comparatively about the consequences of the rise of tribal training, it is interesting to consider tribal nations' experiences with the Indian Reorganization Act (IRA) of 1934. A major element of President Franklin Delano Roosevelt's Indian New Deal, the IRA was a reversal of the allotment era of the late nineteenth century, which resulted in the dispossession of millions of acres of tribal land (Cornell 1988; Deloria and Lytle 1998). Although the IRA ostensibly enabled tribes to organize their own governments and create business corporations, pressures from government attorneys and anthropologists resulted in homogeneous constitutions that seldom reflected cultural distinctiveness. Among tribes, IRA constitutions were felt to be largely boilerplate (Deloria and Lytle 1998). A disconnection from tribal histories, cultures, and traditions generally resulted in the weak institutionalization of IRA governments (Champagne 2007). It seems reasonable to ask whether something similar might happen at the intersection of Self-Determination, neo-liberalism, and expert training where organizations profess technical expertise and a deep understanding of the issues facing tribal nations. The prospect of structural and ideological homogeneity in the contemporary moment is all the more concerning since tribal governments actively solicit the assistance of these organizations. Further research should be done in how tribal nations critically consume training services and advice from these experts, as well as how organizations from different sectors of the field approach tribal engagement. The field's diversity, the influence of Indigenous actors in training groups, and the sophistication of tribal nations at least suggests that this history will not be easily repeated.

Beyond these issues, future research should consider a pair of pertinent questions. First, how do tribal nations determine which tasks should be allocated to outside training groups rather than handled within the community? In a number of cases, tribes are establishing their own planning departments. While often created to address human resource or grant writing issues, in a number of cases the purview of these divisions has expanded considerably. For example, the Oneida Nation of Wisconsin has a planning department that undertakes needs assessments while engaging the community in an ongoing dialogue about how to meet future goals. Second, when tribes choose to use these organizations, how can they be critical consumers of training services? Here it is important for tribes to recognize the composition of the field and that different sectors have distinct approaches, but also that within or across categories more than one group might work on an issue. These decisions, concerned with education, meeting the needs of citizens, and sustaining the nation for future generations, are more than just present-day governmental calculations of efficiency; rather, they are decisions shaped by sacred responsibilities. In this way, posing critical questions to potential training organizations and consultants about their assumptions, curriculum design, and the meaning of "cultural relevance" should be encouraged. Furthermore, research into the impact of such training services is also required.

Appendix:
List of Tribal Training Organizations in the United States

American Indian Development Associates
American Indian Law Center
Arviso Business Consulting
Bill Helmich Associates
Blue Stone Strategy Group
Bluehouse Peacemaking Institute
Council Lodge Institute
Creating Stronger Nations
DCI America
Diné Policy Institute
Falmouth Institute
First Nations Development Institute
First Peoples Fund
Fox Valley Technical College Tribal Training
George Gaasvig Training
Guyaushk and Associates
Harvard Project on American Indian Economic Development
Indian Dispute Resolution Services
Indigenous Language Institute
Indigenous Peoples Council on Biocolonialism
J. Dalton Institute
Joseph Eve
Michigan State University Native American Institute
Mohegan Gaming Advisors

List of Tribal Training Organizations in the United States
Continued

Nakwatsvewat Institute

National Center for American Indian Enterprise Development

National Indian Child Welfare Association

National Indian Justice Center

Native American Management Services

Native American Public Health

Native American Resources

Native American Training Institute

Native Americans in Philanthropy

Native Wellness Institute

Osiyo Communications

Oweesta

Oyate Research and Training

Portland State University Institute for Tribal Government

Potlatch Fund

Raving Consulting

Sacred Circle

Southwest Business Development Consultants

Southwest Center for Law and Policy

Syracuse University Center for Indigenous Law, Governance, and Citizenship

Three Feathers Associates

Tribal Law and Policy Institute

University of Arizona American Indian Language Development Institute

University of Arizona Native Nations Institute

University of California, Los Angeles Tribal Learning Community and Educational Exchange

University of Montana American Indian Disability Technical Assistance Center

University of North Dakota Tribal Judicial Institute

University of Oklahoma American Indian Institute

Veriti Consulting

WhiteSand Consulting

Notes

1. Many thanks to Brian Calliou and the staff of the Aboriginal Leadership and Management Program at The Banff Centre for their generous invitation to participate in the Wise Practices in Indigenous Community Development Symposium, held in September 2012. Tom Biolsi, Brian Calliou, Duane Champagne, Jeff Corntassel, and Jessica Vasquez all offered excellent feedback during the process of researching and writing. Hailey Chalhoub and Kimberly Luciano have been diligent,

detail-oriented research assistants. An Ethnic Studies Research Grant from the University of California, Los Angeles' Institute of American Cultures helped to underwrite the early phases of this research. I am grateful to the many organizations, trainers, and tribal nations that shared their opinions.

2. Each of the four categories can be seen as an ideal-type of training. Max Weber (1978) explains ideal-types as a method for sociologists to study events and actions by formulating an intellectually coherent vision of how elements fit together and then comparing these with what takes place in the world.

3. The National Indian Gaming Commission is the body created by IGRA to administer and oversee gaming activities on Indian lands.

4. In one sign of NATI's wider influence, former executive director Jodi Gillette was appointed as President Barack Obama's Senior Policy Advisor for Native American Affairs in April 2012 (White House 2012).

References

Abbott, Andrew. 1988. *The System of Professions: An Essay on the Division of Expert Labor*. Chicago: University of Chicago Press.

Alfred, Taiaiake. 2007. "Sovereignty." In *Sovereignty Matters: Locations of Contestation and Possibility in Indigenous Struggles for Self-Determination*, edited by Joanne Barker, 33–50. Lincoln: University of Nebraska Press.

Aratani, Janice L. Cooper, Janice L., Sarah Dababnah, Jane Knitzer, and Rachel Masi. 2007. *Strengthening Policies to Support Children, Youth, and Families Who Experience Trauma*. National Center for Children in Poverty, Mailman School of Public Health, Columbia University, July 2007. http://kidslinkcares.com/wp-content/uploads/2012/03/Policy-Strenghening-NCCP-2007.pdf.

Associated Press. 2005. "Cherokees Begin Membership Audit to Cull Non-Indians." *State and Local Wire*, October 10, 2005.

Babb, Sarah L., and Marion Fourcade-Gourinchas. 2002. "The Rebirth of the Liberal Creed: Paths to Neoliberalism in Four Countries." *American Journal of Sociology* 108 (3): 533–79.

Beckfield, Jason, David Brady, and Wei Zhao. 2007. "The Consequences of Economic Globalization for Affluent Democracies." *Annual Review of Sociology* 33: 313–34.

Begay Jr., Manley. 1991. "Designing Native American Management and Leadership Training: Past Efforts, Present Endeavors, and Future Options." Harvard Project Report Series No. 91-3. Cambridge: John F. Kennedy School of Government, Harvard University. Available online: http://hpaied.org/images/resources/publibrary/PRS91-3.pdf

Bolton, Maggie. 2007. "Counting Llamas and Accounting for People: Livestock, Land and Citizens in Southern Bolivia." *Sociological Review* 55 (1): 5–21.

Brint, Steven G. 1994. *In an Age of Experts: The Changing Role of Professionals in Politics and Public Life*. Princeton: Princeton University Press.

Bunten, Alexis Celeste. 2010. "More Like Ourselves: Indigenous Capitalism Through Tourism." *American Indian Quarterly* 34 (3): 285–311.

Calliou, Brian. 2005. "The Culture of Leadership: North American Indigenous Leadership in a Changing Economy." In *Indigenous Peoples and the Modern State*, edited by Duane Champagne, Karen Jo Torjesen, and Susan Steiner, 47–68. Walnut Creek: AltaMira Press.

———. 2008. "The Significance of Building Leadership and Community Capacity to Implement Self-Government." In *Aboriginal Self-Government in Canada: Current Issues*, edited by Yale D. Belanger, 332–47. 3rd ed. Saskatoon: Purich Publishing.

Castile, George Pierre. 1999. *To Show Heart: Native American Self-Determination and Federal Indian Policy, 1960–1975*. Tucson: University of Arizona Press.

———. 2006. *Taking Charge: Native American Self-Determination and Federal Indian Policy, 1975–1993*. Tucson: University of Arizona Press.

Cattelino, Jessica R. 2008. *High Stakes: Florida Seminole Gaming and Sovereignty*. Durham: Duke University Press.

Champagne, Duane. 2007. *Social Change and Cultural Continuity Among Native Nations*. Lanham, MD: AltaMira Press.

Champagne, Duane, and Carole Goldberg. 2002. "Ramona Redeemed?: The Rise of Tribal Political Power in California." *Wicazo Sa Review* 17 (1): 43–63.

Collins, H. M., and Robert Evans. 2002. "The Third Wave of Science Studies: Studies of Expertise and Experience." *Social Studies of Science* 32 (2): 235–96.

Cornell, Stephen. 1988. *The Return of the Native: American Indian Political*

Christopher Wetzel

Resurgence. New York: Oxford University Press.

Cornell, Stephen, and Joseph P. Kalt, eds. 1992. *What Can Tribes Do?: Strategies and Institutions in American Indian Economic Development.* Los Angeles: UCLA American Indian Studies Center.

———. 1998. "Sovereignty and Nation Building: The Development Challenge in Indian Country Today." *American Indian Culture and Research Journal* 22 (4): 187–214.

———. 2000. "Where's the Glue? Institutional and Cultural Foundations of American Indian Economic Development." *Journal of Socio-Economics* 29: 443–70.

Corntassel, Jeff, and Richard C. Witmer II. 2011. *Forced Federalism: Contemporary Challenges to Indigenous Nationhood.* Norman: University of Oklahoma Press.

Deloria, Vine, Jr. 1969. *Custer Died for Your Sins: An Indian Manifesto.* Norman: University of Oklahoma Press.

Deloria, Vine, Jr., and Clifford M. Lytle. 1983. *American Indians, American Justice.* Austin: University of Texas Press.

———. 1998. *The Nations Within: The Past and Future of American Indian Sovereignty.* Austin: University of Texas Press.

Dowling, Christina. 2005. "The Applied Theory of First Nations Economic Development: A Critique." *Journal of Aboriginal Economic Development* 4 (2): 120–28.

Epstein, Steven. 1996. *Impure Science: AIDS, Activism, and the Politics of Knowledge.* Berkeley: University of California Press.

Esber, George S., Jr. 1992. "Shortcomings of the Indian Self-Determination Policy." In *State and Reservation: New Perspectives on Federal Indian Policy,* edited by George P. Castile and Robert L. Bee, 212–13. Tucson: University of Arizona Press.

Eyal, Gil. 2006. *The Disenchantment of the Orient: Expertise in Arab Affairs and the Israeli State.* Stanford: Stanford University Press.

Falmouth Institute. 2012a. "About Us." http://www.falmouthinstitute.com/about.html.

———. 2012b. "Calendar." http://falmouthinstitute.com/training/calendar.html.

———. 2012c. "Consulting." http://www.falmouthinstitute.com/consulting/index.html.

——. 2012d. "Faculty." http://www.falmouthinstitute.com/faculty.html.

Fixico, Donald L. 2000. *The Urban Indian Experience in America*. Albuquerque: University of New Mexico Press.

Fourcade-Gourinchas, Marion. 2006. "The Construction of a Global Profession: The Transnationalization of Economics." *American Journal of Sociology* 112 (1): 145–94.

Goldman, Alvin I. 2006. "Experts: Which Ones Should You Trust?" In *The Philosophy of Expertise*, edited by Evan Selinger and Robert P. Crease, 14–38. New York: Columbia University Press.

Hallenbeck, Brian. 2011. "Mohegans trumpet move into gambling management." theday.com, July 8. http://www.theday.com/article/20110708/BIZ02/307089957/1044.

Hpaied (Harvard Project on American Indian Economic Development). 2007. *The State of Native Nations: Conditions Under U.S. Policies of Self-Determination*. New York: Oxford University Press.

——. 2012a. "About Honoring Nations." http://hpaied.org/honoring-nations/about-honoring-nations.

——. 2012b. "Honoring Nations: To Apply." http://hpaied.org/honoring-nations/to-apply.

——. 2012c. "Overview." http://hpaied.org/about-hpaied/overview.

Harvey, David. 2007. *A Brief History of Neoliberalism*. New York: Oxford University Press.

Hilgartner, Stephen. 2000. *Science on Stage: Expert Advice as Public Drama*. Stanford, CA: Stanford University Press.

James, Keith. 1996. "Identity, Cultural Values, and American Indians' Perceptions of Science and Technology." *American Indian Culture and Research Journal* 30 (3); 45–58.

Johnson, Troy R. 2008. *The American Indian Occupation of Alcatraz: Red Power and Self-Determination*. Lincoln: University of Nebraska Press.

Jorgensen, Miriam, ed. 2007. *Rebuilding Native Nations: Strategies for Governance and Development*. New York: Oxford University Press.

——. September 2012. "Indigenous Business and Economic Development in the United States." Presentation at the Wise Practices in Indigenous Community Development Symposium, the Banff Centre.

Kastelic, Sarah, and Puneet Chawla Sahota. 2012. "Culturally Appropriate Evaluation of Tribally Based Suicide Prevention Programs: A Review of

Current Approaches." *Wicazo Sa Review* 27 (2): 99–127.

Manuelito, Kathryn. 2008. "The Role of Education in American Indian Self-Determination: Lessons from the Ramah Navajo Community School." *Anthropology and Education Quarterly* 36 (1): 73–87.

Mason, W. Dale. 2000. *Indian Gaming: Tribal Sovereignty and American Politics.* Norman: University of Oklahoma Press.

MGA (Mohegan Gaming Authority). 2012a. "Experience and Insight." http://mohegangamingadvisors.com/experience-insight.html.

——. 2012b. "Our Team." http://mohegangamingadvisors.com/our-team. html.

——. 2012c. "What We Do." http://mohegangamingadvisors.com/what-we-do.html.

Mohegan Sun. 2012. "About Mohegan Sun Palmer." http://mohegansun. com/sitelet/palmer/about-palmer.html.

MTGA (Mohegan Tribal Gaming Authority). 2012. "Our Model." http:// newsroom.mtga.com/corporate-development/our-model/.

Morris, C. Patrick. 1992. "Termination by Accountants: The Reagan Indian Policy." In *Native Americans and Public Policy,* edited by Fremont H. Lyden and Lyman H. Letger, 63–84. Pittsburgh: University of Pittsburgh Press.

Mowbray, Martin. 2006. "Localising Responsibility: The Application of the Harvard Project on American Indian Economic Development to Australia." *Australian Journal of Social Issues* 41 (1): 87–103.

Nagel, Joane. 1997. *American Indian Ethnic Renewal: Red Power and the Resurgence of Identity and Culture.* New York: Oxford University Press.

National Child Welfare Resource Center for Tribes. 2012. "About Us." http://www.nrc4tribes.org/about-us.cfm.

National Indian Gaming Commission. 2012. "Gaming Revenue Reports." http://www.nigc.gov/Gaming_Revenue_Reports.aspx.

NATI (Native American Training Institute). 2012a. "About Native American Training Institute." http://www.nativeinstitute.org/abouttheinstitute.htm.

——. 2012b. "NATI Training." http://www.nativeinstitute.org/training.htm.

——. 2012c. "Technical Assistance." http://www.nativeinstitute.org/ services.htm.

Nelson, Robert A., and Joseph F. Sheley. 1985. "Bureau of Indian Affairs Influence on Indian Self-Determination." In *American Indian Policy in the Twentieth Century,* edited by Vine Deloria Jr., 177–96. Norman:

University of Oklahoma Press.

Nesper, Larry. 2003. "Simulating Culture: Tourism and Identity in Lac du Flambeau's Wa-Swa-Gon Indian Bowl." *Ethnohistory* 50 (3): 447–72.

Ogunwole, Stella U. 2006. *We the People: American Indians and Alaska Natives in the United States.* United States Census Bureau. http://www. census.gov/prod/2006pubs/censr-28.pdf.

Ottmann, Jacqueline. 2005. *First Nations Leadership Development within a Saskatchewan Context.* PhD diss., University of Saskatchewan.

Parmley, Suzette. August 9, 2012. "Mohegan gaming authority extends reach with deal to manage Resorts in Atlantic City." philly.com. http:// articles.philly.com/2012-08-09/business/33101420_1_morris-bail-ey-mitchell-etess-mohegan-indian-reservation.

Reay, Mike. 2007. "Academic Knowledge and Expert Authority in American Economics." *Sociological Perspectives* 50 (1): 101–29.

Self-Governance Communication and Education. 2009. *Tribal Self-Governance: A Handbook for Tribal Governments.* http://www.tribalselfgov. org/____NEWSGCE/__documentsdownload/FINAL_COM-PLETE_BOOK_OTSG.pdf.

Smith, Linda Tuhiwai. 2012. *Decolonizing Methodologies: Research and Indigenous Peoples.* London: Zed Books.

Stark, Heidi Kiiwtinepinesiik, and David E. Wilkins. 2011. *American Indian Politics and the American Political System.* Lanham, MD: Rowan and Littlefield.

Sullivan, Patrick. 2006. "Indigenous Governance: The Harvard Project on Native American Economic Development and appropriate principles of governance for Aboriginal Australia." Research discussion paper 17, Australian Institute of Aboriginal and Torres Strait Islander Studies, Research Discussion Paper 17.

United States Commission on Civil Rights. 2003. "A Quiet Crisis: Federal Funding and Unmet Needs in Indian Country." http://www.usccr.gov/ pubs/na0703/na0204.pdf.

Walter, Maggie. 2010. "Market Forces and Indigenous Resistance Paradigms." *Social Movement Studies* 9 (2): 121–37.

Weber, Max. 1978. "Basic Sociological Terms." In *Economy and Society, Volume 1,* edited by Guenther Roth and Claus Wittich, 3–62. Berkeley: University of California Press.

Wetzel, Christopher. 2009. "Training, Technical Assistance, and Capacity Building with Tribal Nations Study." Unpublished Data. Various locations.

White House. April 27, 2012. "President Obama Announces Jodi Gillette as Senior Policy Advisor for Native American Affairs." Office of the Press Secretary. http://www.whitehouse.gov/the-press-office/2012/04/27/ president-obama-announces-jodi-gillette-senior-policy-advisor-native-ame.

Chapter 3

Deep Listening and Leadership: An Indigenous Model of Leadership and Community Development in Austraila

Laura Brearley

Introduction: Leaders as Deep Listeners

This chapter describes an organic model of community leadership that is underpinned by the Indigenous concept of Deep Listening. Within the chapter, stories and messages from community leaders provide living examples of how to incorporate Deep Listening into leadership practices. The concept of Deep Listening appears in many Aboriginal languages in Australia. For example, in the Ngangikurung-kurr language of the Daly River in the Northern Territory, the word for Deep Listening is *Dadirri*. In the Yorta Yorta language of the Murray River in Victoria, it is *Gulpa Ngawal*. For the Gunai/Kurnai, who reside near Gippsland in Victoria, it is *Molla Wariga*.

The Indigenous concept of Deep Listening describes a way of learning, working, and togetherness that is informed by the concepts of community and reciprocity. Leadership underpinned by Deep Listening involves listening respectfully, which can help build community. It draws on every sense and every part of our being. Deep Listening in community leadership involves taking the time to develop relationships and to listen respectfully and responsibly. It also means listening to and observing oneself (Atkinson 2001).

The chapter has been structured around seven dimensions of leadership, all of which are interconnected, as part of a model of Deep Listening and Leadership:

1. **Leaders as Collaborators:** Deep Listening in Relationship
2. **Leaders as Learners:** Deep Listening in Research
3. **Leaders as Facilitators:** Deep Listening in Community
4. **Leaders as Artists:** Deep Listening to Culture
5. **Leaders as Storytellers:** Deep Listening to Wisdom
6. **Leaders as Custodians:** Deep Listening to Country
7. **Leaders as Messengers:** Deep Listening to the Future

The Deep Listening and Leadership Model

The Deep Listening and Leadership Model has developed organically over ten years of experience within a project known as the Deep Listening Project. Linking Deep Listening and community leadership in this way foregrounds our interconnectedness and embeds leadership practice in relationships, respect, and reciprocity. The stories and insights gathered from project participants reveal how ancient Indigenous wisdom translates to leading-edge contemporary leadership practice. The examples of leadership practice included in this chapter have been drawn from the work of community leaders in Australia and Canada who participated in the Deep Listening Project.

The Deep Listening Project began at Australia's RMIT University in 2003 with a group of Indigenous researchers undertaking master's and PhD degrees. They were artists, musicians, educators, and community leaders. The initial group of researchers was called the Koori Cohort of Researchers. Over the years, the cohort expanded and corporate funding was secured to enable the project to extend its work in the public domain. This has included a range of Deep Listening events that were held at conferences, festivals, and exhibitions, as well as a cross-cultural exchange between community leaders in Australia and Canada.

The chapter begins with an introduction to the concept of Deep Listening.

The Deep Listening and Leadership Model

What is Deep Listening?

It was through the work of Aunty Miriam Rose Ungunmerr-Baumann, a Ngangikurungkurr elder from the Daly River in the Northern Territory in Australia, that the Koori Cohort of Researchers first heard about the concept of Deep Listening. Aunty Miriam describes it like this:

> In our Aboriginal way, we learn to listen from our earliest days. We could not live good and useful lives unless we listened. This was the normal way for us to learn—not by asking questions. We learnt by

watching and listening, waiting and then acting. Our people have passed on this way of listening for over 40,000 years.... (Brennan and Ungunmerr-Baumann 1989, 41)

Deep Listening is a concept that has much to teach us about effective community leadership. It is a process of becoming present to ourselves, to each other, and to the environment. Leaders who are Deep Listeners invite community members and colleagues to be fully present to each other and identify what is happening and emerging in the moment. It involves getting out of the way in order to open up a space in which genuine contact can be made. That space is a place of possibility, where current and emerging needs can be expressed and explored.

The core tenets of Deep Listening in community leadership are:

- Respect underpins our relationships with each other and with the land.
- Time is invested in relationships and the building of trust.
- Our understanding of ways of knowing is broadened and deepened.
- Creativity is embedded into the way we learn.
- A quality of care infuses our relationships and our work with each other.

Community development theorists from the Western tradition, such as Otto Scharmer and Karl Weick, advocate listening practices that align closely with the Indigenous concept of Deep Listening. When we are present, we are available to tune into other people and to our context. Otto Scharmer (2007) refers to this as "presencing"—a term that blends *presence* and *sensing*. It involves opening a space in which genuine contact can be made. The paradox is that the more we are present, the more we are able to get out of the way and become available for other people. Further, Scharmer's concept of Generative Listening aligns closely with Deep Listening. It invites community members and colleagues to be fully present to each other and identify what is happening and emerging in the moment.

Deep Listening in our leadership practice helps us pull out some threads and insights from the issues in which we feel caught. Organizational theorist Karl Weick's (2006) work on collective mindfulness aligns closely with the principles of Deep Listening. It involves developing the capacity to seek a complete and nuanced picture of any difficult situation. Reflecting on issues from different perspectives requires a degree of comfort with complexity and a reluctance to simplify. Community leaders who practise Deep Listening are aware of the complexities within a situation and the different perspectives from which one situation can be viewed.

The concept of respect is central to Deep Listening, and when applied to leadership practice it is about working with our commonalities and with our differences. Taking the time to invest in relationships is central to Deep Listening. The building of community is predicated on the development of mutual trust.

Leaders as Collaborators: Deep Listening in Relationship

Deep Listening
It is coming together, meeting to share our stories
Our connectedness to nature and each other
As part of the eternal cycle of life

(Couzens 2010)

My greatest teachers have been my students. Not long after my own doctoral completion, I was introduced to my first Indigenous doctoral student, Mark Rose. He was a community leader, a lecturer in the School of Management at RMIT University, and deeply committed to Indigenous education. The demands on Mark through his community service and his professional responsibilities were enormous. Over a period of eight years, his doctoral supervisors had not found a way of working with him that met his needs and where the listening and learning was a mutual exchange.

Mark was running out of time to complete his doctorate, and it looked as if he might not finish within the allotted time. Mark wanted the doctoral degree, recognizing its symbolic and practical power. He also wanted to contribute to the Indigenous community and be a role model for Indigenous youth. I felt enormous respect for his resilience and commitment.

When we were first introduced to each other, I had just completed an unusual PhD at RMIT's School of Management where I had explored multiple ways of knowing. A new wave of theory about issues of representation and an appreciation of voices that were marginalized (or muted) had informed my work. I knew I was on to something significant, but until I met Mark, I did not understand what it was. Mark and I were matched up as doctoral supervisor and candidate because the university wanted and needed him to succeed, but it had not been able to find a way to help him do so.

Mark told me stories of his Aboriginal father's abduction from the mission when he was eight years old, lured into the government car away from his family with a jar of lollipops. Meanwhile, his father, a deeply troubled man, spent his life passing as Spanish. Mark also told stories of his own long struggle to reclaim his identity and the process of making peace with his father. A deeply respected elder, Uncle Banjo Clarke, helped Mark with his unification with his Gunditjmara family in southwestern Victoria.

Mark and I found a way of working together that felt like a partnership while on a bridge that we could both cross. We bent and stretched and the trust between us grew. He taught me about the Indigenous Standpoint Theory of Professor Errol West (Japanangka), which reflected the multi-dimensional nature of experience through an integrated model of eight voices: cultural, spiritual, secular, intellectual, political, practical, personal, and public (Foley 2003). I shared with him the literature of multiple ways of knowing, narrative inquiry, and the theorization of creative forms of representation in research.

We struggled with questions of form and content while confronting some of the inherent absurdities of an educational system that is based on exclusion. We explored the ethical complexities and sensitivities of research. For example, "Who owns this knowledge? Who is it for? How might knowledge be shared and still protected? Who has the authority to determine this?" Together, we questioned the power relationships of the academic system and we challenged them.

Mark was successful and completed his doctoral degree. There was a big celebration on the night of his graduation. The senior elder, Aunty Joy Wandin Murphy, at his graduation ceremony, told me she could feel the ancestors very close and that they were dancing.

Word got around the Indigenous community of Mark's successful completion of his doctorate. Other Indigenous students heard that there was a way of doing research that made room for Indigenous voices and multiple ways of knowing. They wanted to join the research program and pursue postgraduate studies. This was the beginning of the Koori Cohort of Researchers, a community of scholars that began at RMIT University and later expanded to Monash University (both in Melbourne, Australia).

The model of listening and learning with respect that Mark and I developed during our work together formed the bedrock out of which the Deep Listening Project emerged. Mark is now a full professor at La Trobe University in Victoria, Australia. He is a community leader in the field of Indigenous education, whose national and international influence is predicated on his capacity to listen deeply and cultivate that capacity in others. Mark has been a pioneer in breaking down some of the dysfunctional elements in the power structure within the academy, and he has found his own voice and his own liberation within it:

> I seek liberations from many platforms. Liberation from the sanitised, jaundiced take on the invasion of this country, perpetuated to this day by successive education systems.... My ancestral spirits have called me. I stand as a testimonial to their power, influence and wisdom. For I am a Blackfella. (Rose 2003)

If it were not for Mark Rose, the Koori Cohort of Researchers and the Deep Listening Project would never have been born.

Leaders as Learners: Deep Listening in Research

Deep Listening has been a long tradition for thousands of generations of Aboriginal people in Australia. The immersing of all senses to observe, learn, create, share and grow throughout time is of vital importance to our cultural knowledge. Deep Listening opens up a space to think about inner experience. It means listening not only

with our ears. It's deep listening with our eyes, deep listening with
all the senses. (Treahna Hamm, email comm. with Kevin Argus)

On the day that Mark Rose handed in his PhD dissertation, he met a
women named Treahna Hamm at a public presentation he was giving.
He told her how he had incorporated Indigenous ways of knowing
into his research. Treahna contacted me the next day to inquire about
a similar program. I have always been drawn to artists, musicians, and
researchers who work on the edge of their own becoming. To me, their
work feels inspired, alive, and brave. Treahna is such a person. She is a
highly regarded Indigenous artist who works in many media areas and
who uses her art to facilitate cultural regeneration. Treahna played a significant role in establishing the Indigenous research student groups at
both RMIT University and Monash University. Together, Treahna and I
challenged the boundaries of knowledge within the university system.

Treahna was one of the first students in the Koori Cohort of
Researchers to collaborate with jazz musicians who were interested
in improvising with artworks and stories. She has been pivotal in
developing the framework for the Deep Listening Project by facilitating research-based cultural regeneration, language revival, and
cross-cultural exchange.

Treahna and I have now worked together in this way for many
years. We have co-facilitated Deep Listening Circles in the community and have made joint presentations in many different contexts. We
work together, both within and beyond the academic world, drawing
on the knowledge we have gained from our collaborative work. We
have also co-authored papers and book chapters. Some of Treahna's
stories from our most recent collaborative publication are found
below. Here she describes how Deep Listening has underpinned her
research and her artwork, as well as our relationship:

> My name is Treahna Hamm. I'm a Yorta Yorta woman. In my research
> and in my artwork I use the concept of Deep Listening as a way to
> bridge together my experiences creatively and culturally. In my
> PhD I looked at reconnecting with family through individual and
> community narratives.

When I first began my PhD, I met with Dr. Laura Brearley and I spoke about my connection to family, culture and land through my art. At the meeting, I highlighted the importance of the timing of my PhD and that it needed to be right culturally. I was determined to portray my connections using my own voice as an Indigenous woman. In previous study, my sense of identity had been diluted within the dominant discourse of mainstream study.

I felt a sense of urgency to gain knowledge and stories that were on the brink of extinction within the Victorian community. As I saw it, our old people were vitally important in saving cultural knowledge and continuing strong cultural links to our past. I could not put this aside. I hoped my study would affirm my deep connection to land, identity and community and to the stories of the Elders.

I felt that my PhD would give me the opportunity to save some of the Elders' stories within the community. Elders who attain and live their cultural knowledge and practices are integral to cultural survival. It is vital that their voices are heard in all realms of education, including the academic arena. We need to hear many voices in the space "in between." Healthy dialogue is the result. This space lies between Indigenous, European and multicultural communities where knowledge, culture and respect can merge and where understanding can be deepened.

Early on in my PhD, I remember showing Laura a series of my mother's maternal line which depicted six generations of women. This was Laura's introduction to the members of my family who had shaped my Indigenous identity. It was important for me to share these inter-generational stories with Laura at the very beginning of my PhD.

To undertake my research, I adopted the Indigenous principle of Deep Listening "Dadirri." Gulpa Ngawal is the Yorta Yorta equivalent. The experience of my research has given me the ability to explore my role in life as an Indigenous woman. Through the artworks I made in my PhD research, I wanted to regenerate culture. I learned from the Elders and from myself. My aim for my PhD was to experience cultural growth and development. This was indeed my experience.

The bond that Laura and I shared created a system of connection with community. The Koori Cohort created something new in a University system, a safe space in which to learn, create and write. It was not only about an individual narrative but a community narrative with the Koori Cohort of Researchers.

Laura and I worked as equals with no subordination in our role as student and supervisor. Through our conversations, both University requirements and Aboriginal responsibilities could be intertwined. There was a depth of understanding, mutual respect and a support for each other in our roles. It was a successful partnership which led to the establishment of a strong group able to express themselves at local, national and international events. (Brearley and Hamm 2013)

Emerging from our own work, Treahna and I identified some principles and practices for working effectively in a cross-cultural context. We developed and applied a framework of practice that was trans-disciplinary and culturally situated, and integrated the principles of Deep Listening. Its purpose has been to:

- incorporate Indigenous ways of knowing into research projects;
- provide a developmental infrastructure for staff and candidates that facilitates ways of working between Indigenous and non-Indigenous knowledge systems in a creative research context;
- create a cross-institutional community of staff, candidates, and members of the Indigenous community interested in research; and
- support the development of Indigenous researchers.

The five key aspects of our research model that may be helpful for others in a similar context are:

1. **Facilitate Mutual Exchange:** This is achieved by framing the relationship between the supervisor and the candidate as a collaboration. You must determine what you have to share as the foundational structure of the doctoral work. The candidate and the supervisor must invite each other into their cultural and creative

worlds to share songs, stories, images, and poetry that are related to the conversation.

2. **Value Whole Life Experience:** There must be a recognition of the value of creative and cultural lived experience that Indigenous candidates bring to the academic world. The Indigenous candidates' cultural practices, the richness of their knowledge base, and the significance of the research they are undertaking must be appreciated and valued by the academy.

3. **Create Multi-Layered Systems of Support:** A community must be fostered where Indigenous and non-Indigenous students and staff who are interested in exploring innovative approaches meet to advance research. These meetings should occur regularly in both formal and informal settings. Systems of collaborative support, including advocates, should be developed within the larger system. A strong group must be created that has a collective voice that cannot be ignored and that can prove itself deserving of respect and systemic support.

4. **Work Between Knowledge Systems:** One must be open to naming and questioning the assumptions held about different forms of knowledge. There should be a willingness to explore what is meant by concepts such as scholarship, creativity, and research. Approaches to assessment and research methods that examine the underpinning principles, criteria, and language have to be advanced.

5. **Develop Collaborative Frameworks of Learning:** Systems of support that encompass collaborative frameworks of learning and partnership models of scholarship need to be initiated, promoting opportunities across disciplines and cultures for ongoing dialogue with people who are genuinely excited about each other's work. There must be a willingness to question and move beyond the systemic power relationships endorsed by the current university structure. (Brearley and Hamm 2013)

The key to the kind of work that Treahna and I have undertaken is the building of a collaborative relationship underpinned by Deep

Listening—at the heart of which is mutual respect and trust.

Leaders as Facilitators: Deep Listening in Community

Deep Listening
Blackfellas have been doing it for hundreds and hundreds
    of generations
Deep Listening is what we are doing here
Just listening to each other
Listening to the country
Listening to each other
And understanding each other's journey.

(Clarke 2009)

After Treahna completed her doctoral studies, we continued to
co-facilitate Deep Listening events within the community. One of
these events was a cross-cultural Deep Listening Circle held in Melbourne in 2012. It was hosted by a collective of African storytelling
women now living in Australia. In this Circle, we facilitated a ritual
that explored our interconnections. The ritual generated a number of
messages from the participants that was distilled into poetic form:

Everything lies within the Circle
All connected

Stand up, speak up
Make contact

Making space for doubt
And yet still connecting

Acting as if
There were no boundaries between us

Sharing cultures
Looking through the eyes of others

Seeing ourselves reflected there
Interdependent

I see you
I know you in me

The following week, Treahna and I facilitated another cross-cultural Deep Listening Circle in Melbourne to bless a warehouse that was being dedicated as an Aboriginal Arts Hub. At this Deep Listening Circle, participants were invited to write messages about what community meant to them. Participants tied their messages onto a large 2.6-metre diameter wooden circle that had been prepared by Swinburne University design students. The circle was then rolled through the streets of Melbourne to the warehouse. The messages included:

We are all connected
Community is a net

Community is belonging
Community is a place to be

Community is people of all ages
Community is all families, all cultures

Community is storytelling, connecting, listening, healing
Community is inviting new stories of new members

Community is mutual memories
Community is people getting together and making things happen

Community is inclusion
Community is trust

Community is being able to be ourselves
Community is embracing ourselves through each other

Both African and Chinese cultures were strongly represented in these Deep Listening Circles. The research we have undertaken indicates that both of these cultures share traditions closely related to Indigenous Deep Listening.

From the African tradition, researcher Jon Roar Bjørkvold (1992) describes a Swahili word, *Sikia*, which in a way resonates with the concept of Deep Listening. He translates it as "integrated sensing." *Sikia* refers to a single complex experience in which one simultaneously sees and hears, pays attention to, notices, understands, and perceives. He argues that it is a Western construct to encourage specialization and the division of sensation into collections of isolated skills that can then be mapped and studied one by one rather than as a collective. African thought, he claims, makes no clear-cut distinction between subject and object, mind and body, or self and world. In the African paradigm, life-force, sound, and word are identical.

According to the Taoist Chinese Buddhist tradition, the concept of Deep Listening can be represented by the Chinese characters for Listen and Respect. These characters incorporate the ideas of Heaven, People, Earth, Ear, Eye, Heart, Respect, Authority, Ten, One, and the relationships between all of them.

Traditional Chinese characters have been passed down through the ages and each character has a story with multiple layers of meaning. The story in each character only reveals itself if you are looking for it, and there are many interpretations to each story. According to the Tao, the layers of meaning in this combination of characters that represent Deep Listening involve:

Knowing our position in relation to Heaven and Earth
Listening in the context of surroundings—
    Land, People, Heaven and Earth
Oneness of mind and heart

Being connected to all things
Relationality to the Land
Understanding relationality

Giving your undivided attention
Giving yourself wholeheartedly
Involving total dedication

Jing	Ting	
Respect	Listen	
敬	聽	(Ching Tan and William Wu, pers. comm.)

The ongoing exchange of stories, messages, and shared experiences with our Canadian friends continues to inform and enrich us. We have explored the concept of Deep Listening in both Australia and Canada with respected community leaders Bob and Audrey Breaker. Bob Breaker, a former Siksika Nation chief, shared with us that in his Blackfoot language and culture the concept of Deep Listening also existed. In his tradition, there are different layers of Deep Listening:

Istsiwakakkit: Listen to me
Sopoyaapistsiyiita: Listen carefully
Niitaapsopoyaapistsiyiita: Really listen carefully

He described a fourth even deeper layer, which involved listening to those who have passed on. Access to this level of Deep Listening brings guidance with it as well as enormous responsibility.

Audrey Breaker described a related Cree concept of *Meyopimatsi-win,* "living in harmony," and a Blackfoot concept *Mokakoyis,* "dwelling in wisdom" (Audrey Breaker and Bob Breaker, pers. comm.). The concepts reveal the links between language, land, knowledge, and how to live.

Treahna has also undertaken research with linguists with expertise in the Sanskrit and Dravidian languages, such as Tamil, Malayalam, and Telegu. She has been told of three words that relate to her understanding of Deep Listening:

Manna sakshee: Witness of your heart
Oolmanathu: Inner heart
Nal mannam ode kathukarathu: Learning with good heart
(Treahna Hamm, pers. comm. with Kevin Argus)

Through these cross-cultural connections and her own deep links to culture, Treahna recognizes the ways in which we are all connected:

By connecting to our stories
We are stabilised

If we are disconnected
We are cut off from love and life

We need to value our shared humanity
Before any real connection can begin

We look up at the sky and we see the clouds
We see the blue gaps in between

The gaps matter
They link the clouds together

The shapes we see in the clouds may differ
But the sky and the clouds connect us all

(Hamm 2009)

A key skill in fostering a sense of connection and interconnectedness in community is the capacity to listen deeply, especially to what lies in the spaces in between.

Leaders as Artists: Deep Listening to Culture

Deep Listening—it's feeling the words
Feeling the pictures
Feeling the conversations

Particularly as I get older
I learn to trust my intuition and instincts
I feel—and that's my guide

(Weightman 2009)

Artists and musicians in the Deep Listening Project interweave songs, stories, and multimedia in ways that celebrate and regenerate Indigenous culture. Within the Project, Indigenous and non-Indigenous artists, musicians, and researchers come together in different configurations to improvise, record, and perform in different community contexts.

In 2011, the Project facilitated a Deep Listening Stream at a conference for Indigenous community leaders called the Deadly in Gippsland (DIG), held in regional Victoria, Australia. The purpose of the Deep Listening Stream was to provide a space to facilitate connections, reflections, and creative responses on the conference themes:

- Sustainable Futures
- Working Together
- Health and Well-Being

The Stream provided an alternative space to enrich the exploration of the conference themes through creative ways of engaging with people and ideas.

The Deep Listening Stream included performances and improvisations by the Deep Listening Band, a songwriting workshop, and the performance of an "end of conference song" written by conference delegates. The conference was subsequently awarded a National Local Government Award for promoting reconciliation through Deep Listening in Action.

At the conference, a Deep Listening Room was created to provide an alternative space for people to meet, share stories, and explore the conference themes. In the Deep Listening Room, mandalas of fabric, natural objects, and quotes served as focal points (like campfires) for ongoing Deep Listening Circles. Tables of arts and crafts materials and natural objects were provided for participants to create a contribution to the conversation. An artist-in-residence explored the interface between art, music, and cultural knowledge, and responded to the content of conference presentations through his artwork.

As part of the Deep Listening Stream, a distillation of key ideas from workshops, accompanied by photos of activities from the conference, was presented to conference delegates on day two of the conference. What emerged was a collective snapshot of what the current issues were and what community leaders were committed to.

We are committed to...

Getting connected
Building community confidence

Embracing an Aboriginal perspective
Promoting Aboriginal culture

Keeping kids off the street
Stopping men from going into prison

Getting beyond being reactive
Talking about problems

Breaking the cycle of disadvantage
Educating, engaging

Helping steer the future in a positive way
Working in a framework of respect, culture, empowerment

Acknowledging the possibilities of change in people
Prisoners gaining skills, building better lives

Men standing up to say no to violence
Helping women perpetrators get their lives back

Learning from, learning with
Discovering purpose in life

Being patient and flexible
Listening deeply   (DIG Conference 2012)

The artists and musicians in the Deep Listening Stream of the conference were able to distill and creatively reflect back to the community what its leaders were working towards. The shared recognition of the collective strength of the community and its strong links to culture was best expressed in the lyrics of the collective song that was written and performed at the conference by participants led by Monica Weightman, a Murri song woman.

Dooyedang: The Deadly in Gippsland Song

1. Uncle Albert—can you tell us Timeless stories of this land?
   Uncle Albert—he did tell us Take the watch from our hands
   Enter the smoke Bathe in the love of our ancestors
   Cleanse your spirit

Chorus: Dooyedang   Carry us home
           Singing and dancing   Your songs
           Dooyedang   Please make us strong
           Singing your songs   The Dooyedang
           Deadly in Gippsland / Dooyedang (*repeat*)

2. Booran and Tuk, the pelican, musk duck
   And the dancing of Djeetgun and Yeering
   Nuntim on Dooyedang
   To the wetlands we come
   Dancing in the stories
   Of the old ones

Repeat Chorus

The collectively created song seamlessly wove together commitment to culture, language regeneration, respect for elders, and the land. The creative process of composing and performing it and having it witnessed by the community reflected the strength and power of leaders as artists.

Leaders as Storytellers: Deep Listening to Wisdom

Deep Listening happens on many levels
It's about walking on the land
Softly quietly
And listening to the stories around the campfire

Listening to the Elders
Listening to the teachers
Respect for Elders and respect for all people
And giving everyone the time
Deep Listening is about not judging people too quickly
We've got to listen to the wind in the trees
Listen to the birds
It's the feeling of a gift—a gift always comes back

(Murray 2009)

In 2008, members of the Koori Cohort of Researchers visited The Banff Centre in Alberta to perform and present at the Art of Management Conference. This was the beginning of the Creative Cross-Cultural Exchange within the Deep Listening Project, bringing together people from both sides of the Pacific to engage in Deep Listening events.

In Banff, we had the privilege of meeting Elder Tom Crane Bear, Brian Calliou, Don McIntyre, and other staff and friends of the Indigenous Leadership and Management Program at The Banff Centre. We were welcomed into The Banff Centre tipi for smoking ceremonies and we were also invited to a powwow at the nearby Morley First Nation. In Banff, we shared many stories, and thus created opportunities for collaboration. These events built relationships and generated creative forms that transcended the boundaries of disciplines, genres, and cultures.

Following this, a group of artists, researchers, and community leaders from the Indigenous Leadership and Management Program were invited to Australia. Their visit included participation in the World Indigenous People's Conference in Education that took place in Melbourne in 2008. A joint exhibition of artworks from the Creative Cross-Cultural Exchange was held at the Koorie Heritage Trust, and a collaborative CD of songs and stories was recorded at the RMIT studios.

The Canadian visitors were invited into our homes and important connections with local elders were made, including a sacred naming ceremony where Elder Tom Crane Bear (senior Siksika elder) presented Uncle Albert Mullett (senior Gunnai elder) with his grandfather's name. The Deep Listening Community had built international, intergenerational, and interdisciplinary relationships and had become a family. The exchange of stories and ideas between Canada and Australia within the Deep Listening Project has been ongoing since that time.

The storytelling medium has been documented in a number of ways. For example, a film crew has been following the Cross-Cultural Exchange since it began, and it continues to make short films documenting the collaboration and the stories that are shared. Our filmmaker, Kimba Thompson, who completed her Master of Arts in storytelling and multimedia in 2010, says this about stories:

Storytelling is crucial to our individual, communal, and cultural
identity. Story is learning, celebrating, healing, and remembering.
It can mark a life, enrich individual emotional and cultural development, and assist in making sense of our world. (Thompson 2010)

Ron Murray is a Wamba Wamba man who has been a member of
the Deep Listening Community since its inception. He is a storyteller,
didgeridoo player, wood sculptor, and community leader. In 2010, he
completed a Master of Arts in which storytelling practice was a central feature. This is what he says about the importance of storytelling:

Lake Boga is my traditional area and my totem is the red-tail black
cockatoo. I find it easy to tell stories. It's important to keep the art
of storytelling alive. In my work, I aim to foster a sense of pride in
Aboriginal people and to develop a sense of understanding and recognition of our history. I'm not really doing a lot of things differently
from the old people. They would have taught the same. They would
have talked about the environment, the family and important people.

Stories are powerful things. If you look at our old storytellers,
they were our educators. They made the links with the past. They sat
around camp fires, and told stories. If you listen to the creation story
of my mother's people, it goes for an hour and a half, and the more
I listen to it, the more lessons I hear in it. There can be thousands of
layers to a story.

I hope that my work makes a contribution to increasing an understanding of our community and what living a good life might mean.
What I am trying to achieve in my work is to have people, both black
and white, feeling proud of Aboriginal people. (Murray 2010)

In her artwork and filmmaking practice, Kimba works collaboratively with communities, using stories and new media to interpret,
express, and celebrate culture. She recognizes the links between
storytelling and healing. In her research, she writes,

It is very important for Indigenous people to tell their stories. Our
people have many scars. The scars are layered like in a scar tree.

The scars are emotional, physical and even traditional. Stories open wounds that allow the process of the healing to begin. They celebrate our being, identity, culture and land. (Thompson 2010)

Elder Tom Crane Bear has also been very generous with sharing his knowledge through stories. Elder Tom is a teacher and spiritual leader from the Siksika Nation in Canada. He is a pipe carrier and has been inducted into the Spiritual Indigenous Elders Circle of the World. Elder Tom has been to Australia twice as part of the Deep Listening Project's Cross-Cultural Exchange. Both times, we have invited Elder Tom into the studio to record stories and songs. On his most recent visit, he spoke about the importance of storytelling:

Our culture begins with storytelling
Stories can teach you

Storytelling used to happen in the early evening
All of us children, we never made a sound

Me, my brother and my young cousin
We were raised by our grandmother

We'd go to bed early just as the sun went down
She'd say "Don't make a noise"

She would cover the windows
We had beds in the house but we didn't sleep on them

We never used the beds
That was the European way

We'd sleep on the floor in the corner
In a nice bed made out for you

The children would listen to the stories
It was part of our culture

We were taught the meanings of things
We would talk our language

The Elders would talk about days gone by
How things were run

It was a clan system
So many clans living out on the prairies

They would sleep out there
Camping together with all their relations

At a certain time of the year
They would gather together

They would make a plan
Of what they should do for the summer

Some of them would go berry picking
The young people would go hunting on horseback

Our Elders taught us about the past
This is how we learned

I look back to the days of my grandmother
Like all the people from the plains, she could ride horses

She was one of the women who signed the Treaty in 1877
As I grew older, I began to understand the stories she told me

Sometimes, we get into trouble
We think "Oh never mind those stories, I'll make my own trail"
If we listen carefully to the Elders, Deep Listening
We can work out that they were right

Stories are our culture
They develop you into a good man or a good woman.

(Crane Bear 2012)

Community leaders such as Ron Murray, Kimba Thompson, and Elder Tom Crane Bear recognize the value of storytelling in supporting the development of good men and women as well as in sharing wisdom. Whether telling contemporary stories through new media or sharing traditional stories around a fire, the storytellers in the Deep Listening Community recognize the crucial role stories play in guiding us and teaching us how to listen. If we listen deeply enough, stories can transform and heal us. This rich source of knowledge is a well from which leaders can draw, enabling them to pass on wisdom to future generations.

Leaders as Custodians: Deep Listening to Country

Country for us is also centrally about identity. Our lands, our seas underpin who we are. Where we come from. Who our ancestors are. What it means to be from that place from that country. How others see and view us. How others identify us. How we feel about each other. How we feel about our families and ourselves. Country to us is fundamentally about our survival as peoples. (Dodson 2007)

The Australian Indigenous concept of *country* is not just about the land, the sea, and the sky. It includes all living things and the stories, songs, dances, and responsibilities that go with sustaining an environment in which everything is interconnected. The cultural regeneration and creative language revival work within the Deep Listening Project reflect the seamless links between country, culture, language, identity, song, story, and dance. This strength-based regeneration work is taking place not only in the Deep Listening Project but also in many Indigenous communities in Australia and around the world. Through organizations such as the Victorian Aboriginal Corporation for Languages (VACL), language revival processes are now incorporating songs, stories, poetry, theatre, and the visual arts. Indigenous researchers, community members, linguists, and artists are working collaboratively to undertake language revival processes, creating and disseminating resources, soundscapes, and art forms.

Rather than approaching the reclamation process from the deficit model of lost community memory and limited historical records, a descriptive approach to linguistics is now emerging that involves collaborative work between elders, linguists, and community members to develop new models of Indigenous "languages-in-progress."

Vicki Couzens is a high-profile Aboriginal artist and a leader in the field of creative regeneration and language revival. She completed her

Master of Arts degree in 2010 and is now undertaking a PhD in this field. Vicki has been a key player in the revival of possum skin cloak making and has worked with many community members to pass on this art form. She has participated in many Deep Listening events and projects, including live performances, the ABC radio program *Listening to Country*, and an audio CD, *On Country*. On this CD, Vicki demonstrates the strength of her leadership qualities and her understanding of what it means to be a custodian of Country. She says:

Strong People, Strong Culture, Strong Country
In speaking our language we awaken the Spirit

The Land resonates in response
In our dancing, in our songs and our stories

We make ourselves stronger and then the Land is strengthened
When the Land is strong, so are the People

Language, story, song and dance resonate with Country and place
The voice of the Land is heard in our language and songs

Our stories are the body of the Land
The rhythm and heartbeat of the Land is felt in the dance

In revitalising language and culture
We gain a sense of peace and strength in knowing who
    we are and where we belong

As Aboriginal people, identity and belonging
Are central to who we are and to our well-being

Our culture is the context through which we relate to
    the environment
Each other and to the world

Language revival involves exploring unseen, intangible things
Our spiritual connection to Country and the notion
    of belonging and place

The links between song and dance, words and intonation,
    resonance and vibration

The connectedness of Spirit to the Land

The Dreaming from which we all came to Be

(Couzens 2011)

When there was a successful National Native Title[1] decision made in favour of the traditional owners of Gunditjmara country in 2007, Vicki Couzens was chosen by the community to do the Acknowledgement of Country at the beginning of the ceremony. The following is an excerpt from her Acknowledgement:

Teen ngeeye Meerreeng
Here is our Country

Ngeeye Meerreeng peeneeyt teenay
Our Country is strong here

Laka Meerreeng
Talk the Country

Leerpeen Meerreeng
Sing the Country

Karweeyn Meerreeng
Dance the Country

Karman kanoo Meerreeng
Paint up the Country

Yana poorrpa Meerreeng
Travel through the Country

Mayapa Meerreeng peeneeyt
Make the Country strong

Mayapa maar peeneeyt
Make the people strong   (Couzens 2007)

Vicki Couzens has undertaken linguistic work at the Victorian Aboriginal Corporation for Languages (VACL), an organization that shows strong leadership in the field of cultural and linguistic regeneration. Like Vicki, Paul Paton is a significant community leader and is the executive officer of the VACL. On the Deep Listening CD *On Country*, Paul recorded the following message that reveals his understanding of the interconnectedness of language with Country and culture. He said:

Language is your identity
It tells you who you are

Your place in the world
The rules to live your life by

It tells you
About the seasons

When to gather your food
How to listen

It tells you your stories
Of kinship and community

Language needs a place to live
It lives in daily use

As soon as you say one word
You've moved into a different culture

Reviving language helps people
Reclaim who they are

Language is culture
Culture is everything

(Paton 2011)

From the other side of the Pacific Ocean, Elder Tom Crane Bear also has messages about the importance of our role as custodians of the land. Here are some ideas he shared about the importance of caring for the land and our interconnectedness with it. I have represented his words in poetic text:

A lot of people don't realize how important the land is
We all come from the land
Water sustains our lives
The animals and the fish
So much of our body is fluid

It's important that we look after the ecosystem
The undergrowth of the forest
Everything is connected and doing its work
If the system breaks we all get sick

The trees purify the air that we breathe
The rocks purify the water that we drink
The trees drink that water
And give us branches and leaves

People see money in the forest
So they cut the trees down
It used to be so pretty going through British Columbia to Vancouver
Now we see bare spots on the mountain

They will be dirt one day
We have to watch out
In 1945 an old man told my Dad
The white man has dropped a bomb
The explosion has been so powerful
It has made a hole in the seven blankets that cover the earth
Since then the hole in the seven blankets has got bigger

Summer is different now
We have longer summers and shorter winters
The ice will melt and disease will come
We are not looking after the planet well enough
A little baby crying is sending a message to you
But it's up to you to understand the message
You have to be alert to try and understand what that baby needs
All humans have a message for each other

The Earth is sending a message too
We know about the Creator who made everything
The planets and the sun
Everything is holy   (Elder Tom Crane Bear, pers. comm.)

More leaders who listen to the messages the Earth is sending and who are willing to take responsibility as custodians of Country in its deepest sense are needed.

Leaders as Messengers: Deep Listening to the Future

Deep Listening is about hearing the sounds that
haven't been made yet. (McIntyre 2012)

The international cross-cultural exchange of messages continues in the Deep Listening Project through ongoing visits, dialogue, and Deep Listening events. As part of the Project, we facilitated a Shearwater Festival on Phillip Island in Victoria, Australia, to celebrate the return of the short-tailed shearwater birds on their migration from the North Pacific in November 2012. One million short-tailed shearwaters live on Phillip Island, and five hundred thousand of them have their rookeries at Cape Woolamai, part of the Phillip Island Nature Park. It is an experience of wonder, watching them return to land as the sky becomes black with birds.

The shearwaters are messengers about the health of our oceans. If there is a drop in the numbers of krill on which they feed in the North Pacific Ocean, the numbers of birds that make it back to Australia drops significantly. Two years ago, there was a "crash" in the krill stock and a million dead shearwaters were washed up on Australian shores due to insufficient fuel in their systems to make it home safely. These birds have deep cultural significance for the local Boonwurrung people, having brought the community together for thousands of years for feasts, gatherings, and ceremonies. The birds migrate fifteen thousand kilometres each year, flying from Australia up the west coast of Canada to the Bering Sea off Alaska. In one year they can fly up to fifty thousand kilometres, and in a lifetime they can fly farther than from here to the moon.

The Shearwater Festival honours the birds for their cultural significance and their resilience and as symbols of global interconnectedness. The Festival is held under the auspices of the Victorian Aboriginal Corporation for Languages and adheres to the principles of Deep Listening. It is designed to bring the community together to promote cross-cultural understanding, cultural regeneration, and environmental awareness.

Boonwurrung linguists have worked with Aboriginal community members, local artists, photographers, poets, musicians, and school-children to introduce creative language revival practices into the Festival. The Festival includes art displays, concerts, environmental talks, and guided walks to see the shearwaters taking off from and returning to the rookeries at Cape Woolamai. With The Banff Centre's support, Elder Tom Crane Bear, Brian Calliou, and Don McIntyre flew to Australia in 2012 to participate in the inaugural Shearwater Festival and the two-week Creative Cross-Cultural Exchange that accompanied it.

An International Message Exchange between schoolchildren and artists along the birds' flight path began in 2012. France Trepanier, a high-profile Mohawk/Québécoise artist and researcher, has been participating in the exchange between schoolchildren on Phillip Island and on Vancouver Island, where she lives. France has received and passed into safe hands a message written by a nine-year-old girl on Phillip Island. The message was tied with a ribbon around the neck of a small knitted shearwater bird that was made by an artist from the Country Women's Association on Phillip Island and hand-delivered to France. The message read:

> To Children in Alaska
> Please look after the shearwaters and look after
>   our oceans for the shearwaters.
> Take good care of them and give them love.
> Make sure they come home safely.

Other children on the Island have also sent messages to children in Alaska, talking about the birds. These were hand-delivered to teachers in Alaska by the education ranger at the Phillip Island Nature Park, Graeme Burgan, at a Marine Educators Conference in Anchorage.

As part of the message exchange taking place between Australia and Canada, France Trepanier and I have recorded and distilled our conversations. We have noticed a shift in our communities towards an expanded awareness of shared concerns that transcend national borders. The experience of dispossession and the interlinked environmental, political, socio-cultural, and economic crises now have global implications.

How do our histories connect us?
We breathe the same air
We drink the same water

Shifting our notion of the Land
To one based on Respect
Is like learning to speak a new language

Exploitation brings wealth
And wealth brings security
The system functions on that formula

There's another wheel of fear
Fear is a powerful tool used against the people
The wheels go round and round

It's a false equation
We have to unhook these things
And stop making people afraid

If we engage in that framework
We are stuck in a dichotomy of opposites and arguing against
We need to look at the epistemology of the conversation

Art has a way of doing this
Interconnectedness is complex
Art helps take the complex and make it understandable

The conversations we need to be having are about
Sustainability and security
Shared connections

Identifying what matters
In the rich soil of convergence
And interconnectedness

This is how our histories
And our futures
Connect us all

(France Trepanier, pers. comm.)

Over the course of the Cross-Cultural Exchange, Don (AhnAhn-sisi) McIntyre, an Ojibwa storyteller, researcher, lawyer, and artist, has gifted us with messages and stories from his tradition. He speaks engagingly about the challenges we face and the process of transforming ourselves through the course of our lives. Here are some of Don's ideas that I have distilled from conversations we had during an artist's residency he undertook at The Banff Centre:

The smoke of the fire dances in spirals
That's how life works
Things need to change
They must

We start as blank canvases
And transform along the way
If we're stuck
We need to move forward

Moth is the transformer
The dark transformer
The Moth Medicine is helping us all to move through

We are at our most present in crisis
There is a point where it stops being about us
All Medicines have positive and negative aspects
The Moth and the Butterfly, the Raven and the Eagle
They all have the potential to transform

In the Shadowlands

There are no secrets
Time and space don't work in the same way
Everything plays back into the spiral

Our work here is connected to a much larger project
We are all part of it
Our community includes the Creator
We are in the protective arms of the Creator

(Don McIntyre, pers. comm.)

Elder Tom Crane Bear, France Trepanier, and Don McIntyre all pass on messages that reveal the qualities of care, generosity, and responsibility that are the hallmarks of community leadership. As Elder Tom puts it, "This is our work."

I learned from the Elders
They taught me there are four things we have to practise
Honesty, Trust, Love, and Kindness
For each other and for the land too
This is what the Creator wants you to see

We are created in order to be available to other human beings
To share our wisdom
To guide young people through life
This is our work.   (Elder Tom Crane Bear, pers. comm.)

Conclusion

Brian Calliou, program director of Indigenous Leadership and Management at The Banff Centre, recognizes the leadership qualities of members of the Koori Cohort of Researchers. In conversation with Kimba Thompson in the *Gulpa Ngawal* film, he said:

I've noticed with the Koori Cohort what strong community leaders they are, leading revitalization of culture, collecting stories, and bringing them back to life, recovering them, finding them in archives or learning them from the Elders, recording them, reinterpreting them, and bringing them back to life.

I think this Deep Listening Project and the processes and the magic that is coming out can really inform the big world out there. There's the leadership, management, and organizational design community out there that is hungry for these new cutting-edge processes. (Calliou 2009)

The sense of interconnectedness we experience in the Deep Listening Project is a source of strength that sustains our leadership and creative practice. Deep Listening provides a framework for passing on learning, supporting the development of new leaders, and creating sustainable communities. In Margaret Wheatley's (2006) words, frameworks of this kind enable people to learn from each other, find support, create solutions, and discover new capabilities from a web of relationships.

The issues we face today are too complex and multi-layered for an individual leader to solve, no matter how charismatic or skilled he or she may be. We need each other. We need leaders as Collaborators, Learners, Facilitators, Artists, Storytellers, Custodians, and Messengers who listen deeply to the wisdom of the past, are fully present in the moment, and are awake to the emerging future.

Acknowledgements

I would like to express my profound appreciation to the people in the Deep Listening Community from Australia and Canada whose messages, stories, and artworks have been included in this paper and whose work has informed and enriched it. Special thanks go to Aunty Miriam Rose Ungunmerr, Aunty Dr. Doris Paton, Uncle Herb Patten, Aunty Carolyn Briggs, Aunty Fay Stewart-Muir, Uncle Albert Mullett, Elder Tom Crane Bear, Brian Calliou, Cora Voyageur, Don McIntyre, France Trepanier, Jeff Melanson, Bob Breaker, Audrey Breaker, Professor Mark Rose, Ron Murray, Treahna Hamm, Vicki Couzens, Paul Paton, Maree Clarke, Lou Bennett, Andrea James, Anthony (ToK) Norris, Monica Weightman, Steve Sedergreen, Mike Jordan, Andy Baylor, Kimba Thompson, Rob Hely, Rob Bundle, Christina Eira, Daniel Browning, Sarah James, Marcia Howard, Frances Ford, Stillwater Storytelling Community, Dori Tunstall, Siegi Edward, Michael Hall, Ching Tan, William Wu, Graeme Burgan, Jenny Churchill, Terry

Melvin, Victorian Aboriginal Corporation for Languages, Koorie Heritage Trust, SILCAR, RMIT University, Monash University, Swinburne University, Phillip Island Nature Park, Wellington Shire, Bass Coast Shire, Boonwurrung Arts Hub Community, Janice Tanton, and Stonnington City Council.

Notes

1. The Federal Court of Australia made a consent determination on March 30, 2007, recognising the Gunditjmara Traditional Owners non-exclusive native title rights and interests over the majority of almost 140,000 hectares of vacant Crown land, national parks, reserves, rivers, creeks and sea north-west of Warrnambool in Victoria's western district (Ngootyoong Gunditj, Ngootyoong Mara 2012).

References

Atkinson, Judy. 2001. "Privileging Indigenous research methodologies." *National Indigenous Researchers Forum*. Melbourne: University of Melbourne.

Bjørkvold, Jon Roar. 1992. *The Muse Within: Creativity and Communication, Song and Play from Childhood through Maturity*. New York: HarperCollins.

Brearley, Laura, and Treahna Hamm. 2013. "Spaces between Indigenous and Non-Indigenous Knowledge Systems: Deep listening to Research in a Creative Form." In *Of Other Thoughts: Non-Traditional Approaches to the Doctorate. A Guidebook for Candidates and Supervisors*, edited by Tina Engels-Schwarzpaul and Michael A. Peters, 259–78. Rotterdam: Sense Publishers. In Press.

Brennan, Frank, and Miriam Rose Ungunmerr-Baumann. 1989. "Reverencing the Earth in the Australian Dreaming." *The Way* 29 (1): 38–45.

Calliou, Brian. 2009. *Gulpa Ngawal: The Indigenous Deep Listening Project*. In conversation with Kimba Thompson, Multi-Media Production, Sistagirl Productions/RMIT University.

Clarke, Maree. 2009. *Gulpa Ngawal: The Indigenous Deep Listening Project*. In conversation with Kimba Thompson, Multi-Media Production, Sistagirl Productions/RMIT University.

Crane Bear, Elder Tom. 2012. *Deep Listening Circle*. RMIT Recording Studios, production engineered by Anthony (ToK) Norris. Melbourne.

Couzens, Vicki Louise. 2010. "Land, Language and Identity: Reclamation, Regeneration and Revitalisation of our Aboriginal Identity and

Culture." Master's thesis, RMIT University, Melbourne. http://researchbank.rmit.edu.au/view/rmit:10223.

——. 2011. "Strong People." In *On Country: Songs, Stories and Soundscapes with the Deep Listening Band*. Audio CD, track 12.

DIG (Deadly in Gippsland) Conference. 2012. Deep Listening Stream conference notes, edited by Laura Brearley.

Dodson, Michael. 2007. "Indigenous Protected Areas in Australia." In *United Nations International Expert Group Meeting on Indigenous Peoples and Protection of the Environment*. Khabarovsk: Russian Federation.

Foley, D. 2003. "Indigenous Epistemology and Indigenous Standpoint Theory." *Social Alternatives* 22 (1): 44–52.

Hamm, Treahna. 2009. "Reconnecting with Family: Exploring Individual and Community Stories of Aboriginal Identity through Narrative and Artwork." Unpublished PhD thesis, RMIT University, Melbourne.

McIntyre, Don. 2012. *Deep Listening Circle*. RMIT Recording Studios, production engineered by Anthony (ToK) Norris. Melbourne.

Murray, Ron. 2009. *Gulpa Ngawal: The Indigenous Deep Listening Project*. In conversation with Kimba Thompson, Multi-Media Production, Sistagirl Productions/RMIT University.

——. 2010. *Analysis of Professional Practice of Being an Indigenous Cultural Awareness Trainer*. Master's thesis, RMIT University, Melbourne. http://researchbank.rmit.edu.au/eserv/rmit:6755/Murray.pdf.

Ngootyoong Gunditj, Ngootyoong Mara. 2012. "South West Management Plan Fact Sheet." Accessed March 14, 2014. http://www.google.com.au/url?sa=t&rct=j&q=&esrc=s&source=web&cd=1&ved=0CCoQFjAA&url=http%3A%2F%2Fparkweb.vic.gov.au%2F__data%2Fassets%2Fpdf_file%2F0018%2F523026%2FFS-Gunditjmara-Native-Title-Determination-Feb-2012.pdf&ei=I9swU4jgOomFkwXmjIDQAw&usg=AFQjCNHHsLm8iVXPO5AwrL7ufVxXoaQRpA&bvm=bv.63587204,d.dGI.

Paton, Paul. 2011. "Culture is Everything." In *On Country: Songs, Stories and Soundscapes with the Deep Listening Band*. Audio CD, track 4.

Rose, Mark. 2003. "Bridging the Gap: The Decolonisation of a Master of Business Administration Degree by Tactical and Pedagogical Alignment with the Capacity Building Needs of the Aboriginal and Torres Strait Islander Community." Unpublished PhD thesis, RMIT University, Melbourne.

Scharmer, Otto. 2007. *Theory U: Leading from the Future as it Emerges.* San Francisco: Berrett-Koehler.

Thompson, Kimba. 2010. *Sista Girl: An Indigenous Woman's Perspective on Creative Artist, Curator and Director in the Koori Community.* Unpublished master's thesis, RMIT University, Melbourne.

Weick, Karl E. 2006. "Faith, Evidence and Action: Better Guesses in an Unknowable World." *Organization Studies* 27: 1723–36.

Weightman, Monica. 2009. *Gulpa Ngawal: The Indigenous Deep Listening Project.* In conversation with Kimba Thompson, Multi-Media Production, Sistagirl Productions/RMIT University.

Wheatley, Margaret. 2006. "Relationships: The Basic Building Blocks of Life." Margaret Wheatley's personal website. http://www.margaretwheatley.com/articles/relationships.html.

Further Information on the Deep Listening Project

Website: *http://www.deeplistening21.com.au*

Short film about Deep Listening in Action at the Deadly in Gippsland Conference: *http://vimeo.com/36995984*

Short film about the Shearwater Project: *https://vimeo.com/58521654*

Short film about rolling circle through Melbourne for Deep Listening Circle: *http://youtu.be/dwSoNtrn7gE*

More information about the Indigenous Deep Listening Project at RMIT University: *http://rmit.net.au/browse;ID=vldmuvmeiy5gz*

Music of the Deep Listening Band and interviews with Vicki Couzens, Lou Bennett, and Aunty Doris Paton are featured in a program "Listening to Country" on ABC Radio National's *Awaye*. *http://www.abc.net.au/radionational/programs/awaye/saturday-11-february-2012/3816462*

The Deep Listening Band has produced two CDs: *Gulpa Ngawal: Indigenous Deep Listening*, 2009; and *On Country: Songs, Stories and Soundscapes with the Deep Listening Band*, 2011. The *Gulpa Ngawal* CD features the creative cross-cultural exchange with Indigenous musicians and elders in Canada; it can be heard at *http://www.rmit.edu.au/browse;ID=erudytqwirao*. The CD *On Country* features living examples of creative language revival and cultural regeneration.

Chapter 4

Restorying the Leadership Role: Indigenous Women in Politics and Business in Canada

Cora Voyageur

Introduction: The Colonial Context

Being Indigenous in Canada has never been easy—especially for the women. Since the earliest European contact, Indigenous women have been placed in a precarious and subordinate position by foreign and, later, domestic governments. Foreign imperialist governments emphasized racial bias and differential values to rationalize their belief in European superiority over Indigenous populations (Memmi 2000) and in the subordination of women vis-à-vis men (Anderson 1991). Domestic governments quickly took up the repressive laws of the mother country and imposed rules that garnered women few, if any, political rights, and little economic power or social standing. As a result of these hegemonic views, the role and rights of Indigenous women were altered and limited by the colonizer's Eurocentric beliefs and practices.

Colonization had a detrimental effect on Indigenous women when gender relations within the Indigenous community began to mirror those of the colonizer. The newcomers' governing principles and accompanying church doctrine were based on patriarchy (Barman 2010). This was illustrated by the early Jesuit missionary Paul Le Jeune who introduced the hierarchical principles of patriarchy in interpersonal relations to the Montagnais-Naskapi in eastern Canada in the 1600s (Anderson 1991).

According to those principles, European females were chattels of their fathers and later of their husbands, if they were to marry. Socially, their place was in the home, where they concerned themselves exclusively with household and family matters (Carter 1997). Housebound, they could not define themselves or become involved in outside pursuits. This was a far cry from the position of Indigenous women who had always played an important and highly visible role in their society. They were integral to community activities, as shown by the matriarchal social system of the Iroquois Confederacy, where women played a vital role in economic and political decisions (Anderson 2000). For example, women controlled the community's land holdings and surplus foods, and thus its wealth (Black et al. 1988). Further, women controlled the community's governance by selecting and deposing its leaders (Williams 1990).

Although the settler government began drafting Indigenous-related policies shortly after its establishment, the Europeans' deeply entrenched beliefs manifested themselves in one document above all: the Indian Act of 1876.[1] Indigenous women saw the prominent role they played in their community diminish as their subordination was codified in the federal statute, which favoured Indigenous men over women. They too had become the property of their husbands and fathers—just like their settler sisters.

Examples of male bias in the Indian Act include women losing their Indian status[2] through marriage to non-Indian men, while Indian men were free to marry non-Indian women and still remain Status Indians[3] (Voyageur 2010). Women's input into the governance of their community was further hampered when the Indian Act made political involvement the exclusive right of men. Indigenous women were not *officially*[4] allowed to exercise their franchise or stand for elected political office in reserve politics. These rules would remain in place for almost one hundred years, until Indigenous women began to push back against oppression and exert their rights.

The Indian Act was amended in 1951 to allow First Nations women to participate in band politics. Section 76(1) stated:

A member of a band who is of the full age of twenty-one years and is ordinarily resident on the reserve is qualified to vote for a person nominated to be chief of the band, and where the reserve for voting purposes consists of one section, to vote for persons nominated as councillors. (Government of Canada 1951)

Thus, First Nations women were reinstated in their role as political participants and were henceforth officially able to guide the governance of their communities.

Indigenous Women's Agency and Leadership

Indigenous women were no longer relying on others to determine their future. Their initiatives had them blazing new trails in territory that would have been unthinkable under the patriarchal and colonial authority of yesteryear. In this chapter, I will give the reader a glimpse into the world of Indigenous women leaders in Canada who work to advance themselves, their families, and their communities. Through achievements in education, political involvement, and entrepreneurship, Indigenous women are changing their social, economic, and political positions in their communities and in mainstream society. We will look at Indigenous women's involvement in post-secondary education and see the effect that gaining educational credentials has had on their political and entrepreneurial pursuits. I draw information from my recent research studies that explored two little-examined aspects of Canadian Indigenous women's experience. The first is the rise of female elected chiefs in Canada's First Nations community and their experiences in that role.[5] The second is Indigenous women's experience with entrepreneurship and self-employment.[6]

Indigenous women are entering educational, political, and business domains in increasing numbers. Indigenous women are leading the charge into post-secondary education, where they outnumber Indigenous men at a rate of approximately three to one. One explanation for this situation is that Indigenous men can more easily obtain well-paying jobs without higher education than Indigenous women can (Howe 2002). This means that women must increase their human capital in order to earn higher wages and obtain jobs that allow them to support themselves and their families. This is due in part to the large number of single-parent households in the Indigenous community—most of which are headed by women. In short, a woman must be better educated in order to support her family alone.

The fact that women are gaining educational credentials is having a direct impact on their involvement in their communities. Politically, they are competing for, and winning, the highest elected political position in the First Nations community—that of chief. In economic terms, they are entering the world of commerce and are starting businesses, large and small, at a rate higher than that of Indigenous men and mainstream society (Aboriginal Business Canada 2003).

I explore the emergence of Indigenous women leaders in these three domains and offer some explanations for these recent occurrences. I begin with Indigenous women's involvement with post-secondary education in Canada.

Education in the Indigenous Community

Education is a prime determinant of social standing and well-being. Educated people are more likely to be employed, are healthier, and live longer (Voyageur 2011). Sociologists differentiate between formal and informal education; they define formal education as "the social institution through which society provides its members with important knowledge, including basic facts, job skills and cultural values" (Gerber and Macionis 2000, 103). On the other hand, informal education is acquired outside the classroom. It is the lessons one might learn in the home, in the community, and from family members or peers.

Indigenous people, and specifically women, have recently embraced education, viewing it as a way to improve their life chances, status, and standard of living. They do this despite the negative experiences that Indigenous people have had with education in the past; in the Government of Canada's ill-fated Indian residential schools, assimilation, not education, was the goal. In the past, Indigenous people also encountered barriers when pursuing higher education, because many of their communities had limited access to the type of academic preparation required to gain entry to post-secondary institutions. Reserve schools typically offered only kindergarten to grade eight. Given that few reserves had a high school, those entering grade nine had to leave home in their early teens to continue their education. Many returned to their home communities after dropping out of school, and thus not obtaining their high school diploma.

Currently, Indigenous people have lower education attainment levels than those in mainstream society, with 42 percent of mainstream society members over the age of fifteen having some form of post-secondary education, compared with 28 percent in the Indigenous community (Statistics Canada 2008). While Indigenous people lag behind mainstream society vis-à-vis educational attainment, they recognize society's need for an educated workforce and are gaining credentials at a rate never seen before in the community. The way in which First Nations people have embraced education is nothing short of remarkable. For example, only fifty years ago there were about two hundred First Nations students enrolled in Canadian colleges and universities. By 2004, that number had increased to about twenty-five thousand (Indian and Northern Affairs 2006).[7]

Indigenous students are now enrolling in and graduating from many disciplines. The diversity of study is beneficial to the Indigenous community and a departure from earlier post-secondary enrollment, which was heavily concentrated in the social work and education fields. In the 2003–4[8] academic year, 3,584 Indigenous students completed post-secondary studies in Canadian institutions. Of these, 60 percent received non-university certificates or diplomas while 40 percent received undergraduate or graduate degrees from universities (Indian and Northern Affairs 2006). The majority of Aboriginal post-secondary students are enrolled in undergraduate studies, but there are increasing numbers completing both graduate and professional programs such as law, medicine, pharmacy, and dentistry. Some of these educated Indigenous people choose to return to their communities, thus becoming a valuable local human resource. The following sections highlight the impact of education on Indigenous women involved in political and business leadership.

Indigenous Women Practising Political Leadership

When local First Nations people get together, the discussion eventually turns to leadership and politics. When I refer to political leadership in the First Nations community, I mean the work of the elected chief and council, who govern pursuant to Indian Act legislation (Imai 2002, 119). These elected community representatives are the government of the First Nation community. They make decisions that affect band members' lives, speak on behalf of the community, and have the power and authority to allocate scarce resources. They are the link between Indian Affairs and Northern Development Canada and the community. This governing system can be likened to the mayor and councillors of a municipality.

Women have always played a role in politics in the Indigenous community. Sometimes the involvement was overt, sometimes covert. Rebecca Tsosie (2010, 32) states, "There is historical documented instances of women assuming military leadership roles, political leadership roles and economic leadership roles that may not have been the norm for all women in the tribe but were sanctioned for these individuals." Yet, prior to the 1951 amendments to the Indian Act, only men could vote in reserve elections and serve as elected political representatives on Indian reserves in Canada.[9]

In the past, political involvement by Indigenous women on the reserve was practised by stealth. An opportunity that inadvertently presented itself for women to organize politically came with the creation of the Native Homemakers' Association. In 1937, the Department of Indian Affairs encouraged women to form local chapters of the Native Homemakers' Association on reserves across Canada, where they would regularly gather to acquire information about greater home efficiency. Little did the department know that these seemingly harmless women's meetings served as forums whereby they could organize dissent and strategize for changes to their social, political, and economic conditions. Thus, First Nations women were primed for official political involvement when legislative changes finally came in 1952.

Elsie Marie Knott was elected chief by the Mississaugas of Mud Lake at Curve Lake, Ontario, in 1952. It is uncertain whether she knew that, by being elected, she was making history: she became Canada's first female Indian Act chief. Although she did not believe she would win, Knott would go on to win eight campaigns in all and serve as the community's chief for sixteen years.

The past twenty years have seen a rapid increase in the number of women being elected to the role of chief in Canada's First Nations community. With approximately 109 female chiefs elected across Canada, they now mirror the percentage of female Members of Parliament in the federal government. In addition, there are approximately 800 female band councillors across Canada.

Women Chiefs

It took a long struggle for First Nations women to become formal political leaders. They have emerged from purely domestic roles to share in leading the rebuilding of their communities. Women are now chiefs of more than a hundred of Canada's 625 reserve communities. The number of elected female chiefs has more than doubled in the past twenty years.[10]

For these women, the climb to the reserve's highest-ranking elected political office was slow and steady. In the recent past, most had been low- to mid-level band administrators in the reserve community. It was from this vantage point that they were able to become familiar with the issues on the reserve and learn the policies and procedures needed to operate the community.[11] One woman stated, "I was the band manager for more than a decade. I did not see many changes in the community since I left that position. I did not want to go back to being the band manager again, so I decided to be 'boss' instead" (Voyageur 2002, int. 24). Another said, "Everyone who knows the reserve community knows that women work to keep the community together. We work in the offices, agencies, and schools. There is a lack of recognition for all that we do" (Voyageur 2002, int. 21). Yet another spoke about the community's resistance to a female chief by saying that it was going against "tradition." She commented, "At the very beginning, one of the old hereditary chiefs told my cousin that I would not last on the job because it was for men. That was back in 1994. I outlasted his prediction" (Voyageur 2004, int. 23).

Despite the recent increase in the number of women being elected as chiefs, "gender relations are clearly at work in the First Nations community as the band members continue to have differing expectations of male and female chiefs" (Voyageur 2008, 100). One female chief said, "People expect you to be more compassionate and listen to them. I was the first chief to visit in their homes and to go out into the community to see and hear for myself what their issues were. Many people were very surprised by my visit" (Voyageur 2004, int. 7). The female chiefs described themselves as resourceful and their transformational leadership style as being more conducive to solving community problems. They cited their work as community administrators as good training for their present position because it exposed them to the information and people necessary to bring about community change. They learned what worked and what did not. More importantly, they learned whom and what to avoid if they wanted a successful resolution to any situation. Subjectively, they saw themselves as being better listeners, more objective, more "hands-on," and more willing to see all points of view. They believed that this made their approach to finding solutions different from a man's method of problem solving. They also viewed themselves as less ego-driven and more willing to tackle mundane tasks than male chiefs.

The women also felt that, to be elected, they required more skills and had to make more of an effort than men. Some bands are governed by charismatic men who dominate by sheer force of personality (Bigfoot et al. 2007). One woman commented, "Yes, our society is male dominated. Women have a very different perspective when it comes to our family, community, and well-being. Women take on the responsibility for feeding our children. Men appear to be more corruptible and lose sight of the issues in the community" (Voyageur 2003, int. 7). None of the women interviewed felt they were charismatic leaders.

Unlike men, women are expected to maintain their domestic roles within the household after they are elected. One chief commented that her husband seemed resentful that she was spending so much time away from home (Voyageur 2001, int. 17). Thus, she was not receiving the support from her spouse that many married men receive from their wives when they are chiefs. In addition, those with children living at home found it difficult to juggle all that was expected of them. Balancing the demands of home and family and the job of chief was overwhelming for most of them. One chief stated:

It's different when you are a man. You have a wife. She is there to cook and clean. A man comes home, he puts down his briefcase, and his wife brings him some tea. He gets to relax. Even if he is unmarried, he generally has a mother or sisters who "take care of him." That would be the day that my brother would come over and clean my house because I had been at meetings all week! (Voyageur 2004, int. 28)

According to feminist scholar Gayatri Spivak (1987), women are to be controlled. In the case of some of the women chiefs, attempts were made to control them with intimidation and threats of physical violence. One of the most startling findings in the research was that many women said they had feared for their physical safety since taking office. Some women had received threats of violence, and some had even been assaulted by community members. Many said they had been intimidated, both overtly and covertly, including reports of verbal abuse and threats of physical violence. One chief stated that someone tried to run her down when she was walking along a road on her reserve (Voyageur 2002, int. 9), while another spoke of her home being vandalized (Voyageur 2001, int. 3), and yet another said a note telling her to "back off" was left on her doorstep, with a bullet on it (Voyageur 2004, int. 4). Even on council, males treated their female colleagues differently and used intimidation tactics to try to bully them into submission. One woman said, "Some of these men on council get so mad when you do not go along with them. Sometimes they bang on the table. I was pretty scared when this big hulking man was looking down at me trying to get me to change my mind. I didn't change it" (Voyageur 2001, int. 41). This woman stood her ground. Many of these women bring change and new ideas to the community and practise courageous leadership under such circumstances.

The women leaders felt they brought a larger skill set (formal education, community knowledge, agency work, and communication skills) to their position of chief than their male counterparts. Women transferred to the political sphere the skills they had learned as heads of households, such as budgeting, organizing, prioritizing, and resolving disputes rooted in differing agendas. The women were still responsible for their family's well-being but had also taken on the responsibility for the governance and well-being of the community. They were not always embraced as leaders by those who clung to the colonial notion that women do not belong in public affairs.

One way that these women leaders gained the confidence needed to become involved in the public affairs of their communities was through their formal educational attainment.

Formal Education

Indigenous women chiefs in these studies were well educated by both Canadian mainstream standards (42 percent have some form of post-secondary education) and Aboriginal standards (28 percent have some form of post-secondary education). The First Nations women chiefs' formal education ranged from less than grade twelve to university graduate degrees. Most women (65 percent) had some form of post-secondary education, such as training in business administration, political science, community development, or law (Statistics Canada 2008).

An advanced education means that the women had exposure to the world outside the reserve.[12] They would have been exposed to new ideas and new ways of doing things, which in turn made them more innovative in finding solutions. In addition, they could draw on the social and political networks that they built up during their post-secondary careers to help them handle some of the community's concerns. They had learned a variety of skills during their time at school that were useful when leading the community.

The women's educational attainment helped them get where they wanted to go. Education opens up a person's world, and these women had had an array of experiences and been exposed to new ideas and innovations while obtaining their education. This exposure also gave them confidence. In addition, pursuing and completing post-secondary studies show the women's commitment to completing a task. The investment that they made in themselves helped them to obtain their goal of self-sufficiency and financial security for themselves while at the same time giving them tools to lead their community to a healthier and more prosperous place. When asked whether they believed their academic training had helped them in their role as chief, 52 percent said yes. While they were post-secondary students, they had acquired other skills as well, such as meeting deadlines, multi-tasking, and setting priorities. They also learned to organize, analyze data, communicate results, think critically, and be persistent.

However, many noted that the formal credentials they acquired in mainstream society did not necessarily ensure success and support in the community. As one woman put it, "The credentials are more for the outside world; non-Indians seem to respect you more if you have an education." Some believed, as many educated Indigenous people do, that they had to prove themselves to the community and win the people's trust. They thought they had to prove that they had not "sold out" to mainstream society, that their hearts and minds were still in the community, and that they had legitimacy (Voyageur 2008).

Informal Education

While formal education was important in preparing the women for life, an equally significant factor was the informal teaching they received during their primary socialization process.[13] This family-based learning practice includes learning cognitive skills, self-control, moral standards, appropriate attitudes and motivations, and an understanding of their societal roles and expectations. Informal education also teaches the language, customs, and traditions of their people, which they can use to guide them throughout their lives (Gerber and Macionis 2000).

Women in the Indigenous community are taught to be caregivers and about the importance of family and community. They are also instructed on the value of modesty and self-respect, and instructed not to do anything that might bring shame or embarrassment on the family. The socialization process is particularly important for a female born into, and growing up in, a political or business family in the community, since they occupy a high-status position. This was even more reason for them to act in a dignified manner, to respect themselves and others, and to look out for their own well-being, as well as the well-being of their families and their communities.

One aspect of informal education is political connection. The vast majority of these Indigenous women chiefs (75 percent) said they came from families that were involved in politics. A review of the relatives holding political office shows that about 60 percent were chiefs and 15 percent were band councillors. When asked whether they felt their relatives had influenced their decision to go into politics and the types of decisions they made while in office, almost three-quarters of the women said yes (Voyageur 2008).

Another aspect of informal education is the influence of role models. The female chiefs said they were influenced by their memories of how their relatives had dealt with community issues in the past and by the involvement of these relatives in improving the community. Many had served as role models for these female chiefs; and it was beneficial for these chiefs to be able to seek advice from them. They understood the struggles that their relatives went through, because they had observed them first-hand. They saw how they made decisions and how their decisions affected the community. They saw their relatives as proud and dignified people who dealt fairly and respectfully with others. Their relatives were concerned about the land and resources, and the women who had grown up in this environment benefited from seeing how matters were addressed and resolved.

They witnessed the respect their family members garnered in their communities. As leaders, they were expected to do the same. They commented that these relatives taught them to keep abreast of what was going on in government and in the community. Information and knowledge were viewed as positive. They were taught to file away information for a later date when it might be useful. They said they also learned about politics at an early age, and this acculturated and socialized them into the political realm of reserve life. Many felt they had been groomed, however unknowingly at the time, for their present positions. For these women, their informal socialization lasted into adulthood, when they could draw on the wisdom of their relatives and gain confidence in their own decision-making abilities (Voyageur 2008).

Business Ownership by Indigenous Women

The past two decades have seen tremendous growth in self-employment in Canadian society, and this phenomenon has spilled over into the Aboriginal business community. Aboriginal Business Canada states that there are now more than twenty-seven thousand businesses owned and operated by Indigenous people in Canada. Aboriginal entrepreneurship has increased more than 30 percent since 1996 (Aboriginal Business 2003). Metis people have the highest proportion of entrepreneurs among the Aboriginal groups.

Although Indigenous business ownership is dispersed into virtually every sector of the economy, more than two-thirds of Aboriginal businesses fall under four categories: professional (scientific, technical, education, health, and social) at 23 percent; retail/wholesale at 12 percent; primary natural resources at 17 percent; and construction at 17 percent (Statistics Canada 2009). However, there is a trend towards more diversity in Aboriginal entrepreneurship, the "Other" category increasing from 11 percent to 18 percent in a mere five years.

Indigenous entrepreneurship is increasing at a much higher rate—nine times faster—than that of the non-Indigenous community. Indigenous business owners are found in all parts of Canada, including urban, rural, and remote locations. The vast majority of Aboriginal businesses (80 percent) serve local markets (Aboriginal Business 2003).

Aboriginal business ventures in rural and reserve areas allow Aboriginal people to remain in their home communities while creating job opportunities for themselves and others. They have a chance to earn a living for themselves and their families while transferring their skills and knowledge to other community members. Indigenous entrepreneurship shows a continued contribution to Alberta's growth and development in particular. Many Indigenous business owners want to prosper from the exploitation of the rich natural resources of this province—just as the non-Indigenous do.

Indigenous Women and Entrepreneurship

The Indigenous female entrepreneurs who participated in this project were a diverse group. They differed in terms of Indigenous affiliation, age, business location, length of time they owned their company, and the types of businesses they ran. They also differed in the reasons for starting their own company. Some went into business so they could earn a living after a divorce or because their previous employer passed them over for a promotion. The business owners represented a wide range of occupations, from herbalist to computer programmer. However, they were similar in many respects.

These Indigenous women entrepreneurs dealt with an array of issues both in starting their companies and in maintaining a steady client base after the business was established. Most of the women juggled motherhood, family, and domestic responsibilities while running their company. It was not an easy chore for most, who tried to find a workable balance between the demands of their company and their own family obligations, as well as their own needs as individuals.

Personal skill acquisition was an issue for many of them. As one woman said, "You don't know what you don't know" (Voyageur 2009, int. 17). Many commented that they did not realize how much was involved in running a business until they were self-employed and well into a project. For example, being and staying organized was challenging, with most saying they were rarely up to date with their paperwork at the beginning.

The women are contributing to the economies of their communities by providing goods and services. They are also supporting their communities by providing jobs to others. These women are keeping alive the entrepreneurial spirit of their ancestors, who travelled across the continent to trade with other Indigenous peoples. They are also continuing in the footsteps of the Indigenous peoples who provided goods and services to the fur traders in the early days of Canada. For many of these women, the business world they stepped into was a foreign world, but they were able to adapt and thrive.

The academic discourse has shown that Indigenous people have been active in the economy for a very long time (Friesen 1987; Miller 1989). Arthur Ray (1974) documented the central role played by Indigenous people as trappers and traders from the mid-1700s. To begin with, they played an enormous role in European explorations and in the fur trade. Frank Tough (1992) found that in northern Manitoba, in the post-treaty period, many Indigenous people voluntarily left the fur trade to pursue wage labour in lumbering and fishing, and they geared their diversified economy to seasonal changes. Tough (1996) found that Indigenous peoples' participation in the wage labour market occurred as early as the mid-nineteenth century. He further noted that wage labour was only one component of a complex regional economy, which included market and domestic production components.

Rolf Knight's (1996) study *Indians at Work* indicates that Indigenous peoples in British Columbia, and elsewhere in Canada, have a long history as both wage workers and independent producers who quickly adjusted to the industrial world. Knight argues that the farming, trapping, and other methods of independent production undertaken by Indigenous peoples were an integral part of the Canadian capitalist economy (212).

Frank Tough (1996) found that Indigenous people successfully integrated into the capitalist labour economy in northern Manitoba despite government policies that hampered their initiatives. Local Indians were active participants in the logging and commercial industries. Indian agents and missionaries commented on the prosperity displayed by the Indians, saying that they were able to purchase sewing machines, buggies, threshing machines, and other consumer goods with their earnings (Voyageur 2009, int. 23). These modern-day female entrepreneurs have shown that they, like their ancestors, are no strangers to business and enterprise.

These women were happy that they made the choice to start their own businesses. Most of all, the women liked the freedom they had in being their own boss. "Nobody can tell me to do something I don't want to do. Sure, there are some things I like doing more than others, but I can hire someone to do those things for me," commented one business owner (Voyageur 2009, int. 19). The flexibility is also a benefit. As one respondent put it, "I can take a day off if the jobs are not all stacked up" (Voyageur 2009, int. 7). Perhaps one of the most important factors to the women was that they could control the amount of work they chose to do. As a respondent said, "If things are too busy, I am in a position right now that I can pass the work on to someone else. That wasn't always the case. When I first started, I was afraid to turn down work in case they [clients] did not come back" (Voyageur 2009, int. 42). Coupled with controlling the *amount* of work they did was controlling the *types* of work that the women chose to take: "When I worked for my old boss, I had to do some pretty tedious jobs and jobs that I didn't particularly like. I have more control over that now. If I really don't like a particular project, I will simply turn it down" (Voyageur 2009, int. 21).

The women liked that they made more money as business owners than they would have if they worked for someone else. They had an opportunity to earn more money if they worked more hours or took on additional work. This was not the case when they were salaried employees. The employer made more money, but they earned the same salary regardless of how much they produced. "When the boss took on more work, I had to work harder and faster. I didn't earn any more money—he did," said one respondent (Voyageur 2009, int. 39).

The entrepreneurial leaders were able to create jobs and employ family members. This was a motivation for some of the women. One businesswoman stated, "I wanted to help people in the community earn money and support their families. It makes me feel good to know that I help people feed their kids" (Voyageur 2009, int. 19). Another said, "I employ both of my children. One has kids and this gives her a bit of extra money to buy the things she needs for them. The other one is in post-secondary and he earns his spending money by working for me" (Voyageur 2009, int. 47).

More than 80 percent of the women employed others. Most of their employees were either relatives or other Aboriginal people. Most of these women-led businesses had at least one other employee. All the female entrepreneurs took their commitment to the business seriously and wanted to continue their success. Most worked hard at their business by trying to remain current with new technologies and innovations in their industry. All stated that customer service was important to remaining in business. "Building a relationship with the client is what it is all about. You want to be sure that you have them come back," commented a business owner (Voyageur 2009, int. 17). "This is my job. It is my livelihood, so I have to take good care of it," stated another (Voyageur 2009, int. 21).

The women liked to see the results of hard work. It made them feel good to see something they had initiated come to fruition. One participant commented, "I can be creative in what I do and how I solve problems. I can try new things and see if they work. Sometimes when you are working for someone else, they aren't prepared to take a chance on trying something new" (Voyageur 2009, int. 33).

For the most part, the women derived a tremendous amount of satisfaction from their work and from their product or service. They felt they were helping themselves by using their skills or ingenuity to solve problems or satisfy customers. They were proud that they could create jobs and help others earn a living.

Formal Education

The female entrepreneurs in this study were better educated than the average Indigenous person in the community. Slightly more than 70 percent had some form of post-secondary education, compared with approximately 28 percent of the overall Aboriginal community (Statistics Canada 2008). Twenty-six percent of these women had a university degree, compared with only about 8 percent of the Aboriginal community overall.

The formal education of the female entrepreneurs in this study ranged from less than grade nine to university graduate degrees; 92 percent had completed grade twelve. The younger women generally had higher levels of education, with 90 percent having some form of post-secondary education, followed by 70 percent of the older women and 60 percent of the middle-aged.

A great number of these entrepreneurial women were highly skilled individuals who ran knowledge-based businesses such as computer programming, environmental consulting, filmmaking, and graphic design. They obtained their skills through post-secondary training. They were able to become part of the knowledge economy and to compete in mainstream society and provide services to the public.

The typical Indigenous woman entrepreneur in this study located her business in an urban area and started a business within her area of expertise. For example, most had worked in the industrial sector in which they started their business, and few ventured into uncharted waters. As a result of working in a particular area, they were able to easily indentify the un-serviced niches in the market. One woman stated, "I had worked in the business for a number of years and I always thought that there was a gap in service" (Voyageur 2009, int. 37). They were able to capitalize on these openings because they had skills, knowledge, and experience in a specialized field.

Informal Education

The vast majority of female entrepreneurs, almost two-thirds, said they came from families that ran businesses. Of those who came from business families, almost three-quarters had a male relative who was a business person. This included many whose father ran a company. The male relatives were more likely to run trucking, logging, welding, or construction companies. The female relatives ran bussing companies, restaurants, taxi companies, or craft companies. Many of the respondents commented that both their parents worked in a family-owned business.

When asked whether they thought their relatives had influenced their decision to go into business, 54 percent of the respondents said yes. Those who came from business families were much more influenced by their business-owner relatives, at 84 percent. One woman stated, "I grew up in a business family. I saw my mother and father work together in the family business. There were some freedoms but also some uncertainty. They were my role models in starting my own business" (Voyageur 2009, int. 23). Another said, "My family helps me make decisions. They are in business too, so they know what I am going through" (Voyageur 2009, int. 45).

Rationale for Starting a Business

The women started their businesses for a number of reasons. For example, one woman had a sick child and needed flexibility to take care of her when the illness flared up. The largest number of women started their businesses when they were downsized from their jobs. Others purchased their current business from their previous employer when he or she retired. These women said they were fortunate because they already knew the operations of the business and did not have to build a clientele. Some found themselves out of work for one reason or another. In some cases, their previous employer deemed their job redundant and they suddenly found themselves out of a job. Others were unhappy with either their employer or their work environment. For example, some were denied raises or promotions; this upset them and they decided to strike out on their own. Yet others found themselves without support for themselves and their children when their marriage broke down or their spouse passed away. This forced these women to evaluate the merits of working for others, and perhaps earning a lower wage, or taking the risk of working for themselves. An assessment of the pros and cons of working for themselves versus working for others determined that self-employment was the better option for them. These individuals had only their own resources to rely upon. "If I failed, it was on my shoulders. I didn't have a second wage or a spouse's income to rely on. I had to make it work," recalled one divorced woman(Voyageur 2009, int. 14). Thus, they were very motivated to work hard and succeed.

Types of Businesses

The businesses run by these Indigenous women entrepreneurs ranged from service-based businesses such as hairdressing and dog grooming to knowledge-based businesses such as environmental consulting and contract research. These were primarily urban-based businesses, with thirty-one of fifty, or 62 percent, being located in cities. Rural businesses made up fourteen of fifty businesses in the study, with the remaining five businesses being in remote communities. The rural enterprises were more likely to be retail businesses such as gas bars or convenience stores (Voyageur 2008).

Individual urban enterprises included business consultant, artisan, artist, photographer, event planner, facilitator, employment agent, consignment store owner, and filmmaker. Rural businesses included operating a bus company, brush clearing, research, and running a campground. Remote businesses included operating a taxi service, a convenience store, and a pool hall, as well as recreational guiding. Some businesses lend themselves more readily to any location, such as artisan, cleaner, and consultant, which all operated in remote, rural, and urban locations.

The entrepreneurial women in this study ran successful businesses that were sustainable. The businesses had been in operation between six months and forty-four years, with an average of eight years. The longest-running businesses were service businesses and artisans. These businesses were located in urban areas, which housed both the oldest venture (established in 1964) and the most recent (established in 2008). The rapid increase in knowledge-based businesses can be explained by the higher levels of educational attainment of Aboriginal women in Canada compared with Aboriginal men. The oldest business in a rural setting was established in 1987 and the most recent in 2008, while remote communities saw the most recent additions. The most established of the remote enterprises was founded in 1999 and the newest was started in 2008. The most common business was business consulting, followed by artisan and facilitator. The estimated business income ranged from a low of $4,000 per year (part-time worker) to a high of more than $3 million per year, with an average of $75,000. The top-earning companies were operated by women of all ages (Voyageur 2008).

Indigenous women business owners are helping rebuild the economy. When purchases are made from Indigenous businesses, money is recirculating within the community, where it has the potential to benefit more community members. These businesses create jobs and transfer skills and knowledge to their employees. They are allowing employees to earn a living and support their families.

Conclusion

The Indigenous world is transforming, with changes occurring on the educational, economic, and political fronts. The once-marginalized women have moved front and centre. They are regaining their traditional place in the public sphere in politics and business, with the help of both formal and informal knowledge. They are assuming positions of authority in Indigenous and mainstream societies. This newly regained authority goes against the colonial ideals that marginalized them as Indigenous people and as women. These same ideals meant that they were expected to be silent, remain in the home, and concern themselves only with family and their spouse, deferring all decision making to men.

Ironically, the stereotyping of women's roles, as found in the colonial mindset, is serving as one rationale for women to be elected as leaders and to start their own businesses. Both groups of women are taking up the traditional female role of caregiver within the community. As elected chiefs, they are able to help build healthy communities through an emphasis on social programming. The ethos of the community is more than just bricks and mortar; it lies in the sense of community and security in relationships. As business owners, the women in the study were able to demonstrate their abilities, provide needed goods and services, exert their independence, and create employment opportunities for themselves and others.

The First Nations female chiefs were able to negotiate their way through the unique situations within the community. The women had a sense of duty to family and community, since many of the community's men leave in search of work and the women are left to tend to day-to-day life and take care of the children. This gave them an opportunity to stay close to their support networks and families. They were able to draw support from these contacts. Their large extended families served as emotional and political support for them. They relied heavily on their families for advice, since most came from political families where there was a wealth of experience in dealing with complex issues. Furthermore, they coped with the demands of their jobs by surrounding themselves with supportive friends and family and like-minded politicians.

Whether running a community or managing a business, these women put their values into action. Sometimes there was a conflict between the centrality of the family in the Indigenous community and the demands of work. This situation was softened by the fact that there was little delineation between work and home life. They could rely on family members with political or business experience for advice and guidance in their decision making.

The expectations of the First Nations community leader are changing. Currently, there is an emphasis on community healing as a means of counteracting the ravages of the residential school system, which has had a lasting impact on the community, especially in the form of social pathologies. There is a good fit with the organizational and household skills traditionally used by women to meet the needs of the family. The women in the study were accustomed to managing a large family, multi-tasking, and compromising to work towards the best outcome.

Education, both formal and informal, played a big role in the workplace experience of these women. Regarding formal education, the women were able to draw on skills gained in post-secondary institutions to help them solve problems and deal with challenging situations with confidence. The social and professional networks built up in post-secondary institutions were important when resource people were needed to deal with community issues. The informal teachings from family helped the women make decisions, and the family served as social and emotional support. They learned the book smarts from the post-secondary institutions, but they learned the heart smarts from their families.

Indigenous women are now more directly involved in their world. They have more power and authority than they had in the past, and they are not waiting for permission to act. This new attitude allows them to bring positive change to themselves, their families, and their communities through employment, programs, and services. They are serving as role models to the youth and are giving them hope. They also serve as ambassadors to the non-Indigenous community, since success in politics and business can open many doors for future interaction.

Women are moving into leadership positions in the Indigenous community. They are resuming their roles as caregivers, but are doing so in a modern context by providing employment, programs, goods, and services. The status and visibility of female leaders serves as a catalyst, persuading the uninvolved individual to become engaged and perhaps bringing more women into education, politics, and business.

Notes

1. The 1876 Indian Act was a compilation of policies pertaining to the Indigenous peoples in Canada and governed virtually every aspect of Indian life from cradle to grave.
2. An Indian was defined as any male person of Indian blood reputed to belong to a particular band; any child of such a person; and any woman lawfully married to such a person.

3. Statute of Canada, 1880, c. 28, section 12 states, "Any Indian woman marrying any other than an Indian or a non-treaty Indian shall cease to be an Indian in any respect within the meaning of this act, except that she shall be entitled to share equally with the members of the band to which she formerly belonged in the annual or semi-annual distribution of their annuities, interest moneys [sic] and rents; but this income may be commuted to her at any time at ten years' purchase with the consent of the band."

4. Women were valued as advisers and confidantes away from the gaze of the Indian Agent.

5. The data gathering (n=64) began in 2001 and culminated in a monograph (Voyageur 2008).

6. The data from that study was disseminated through a discussion paper that will soon be published in an academic journal.

7. The financial aid given to First Nations students has been capped for the past number of years by the government. This has occurred at a time when tuition and book costs have increased.

8. This is the most recent information available. There have been many changes in the types of information being collected in Canada under the Conservative government that was elected in 2006. There is usually a two-year lag between data collection and the report's release date.

9. The selection of leadership was also administered under the Indian Act. Section 61 states, "With regard to Councils and Chiefs: At the election of a chief or chiefs, or the granting of any ordinary consent required of a band of Indians under this Act, those entitled to vote at the council or meeting thereof shall be the male members of the band of the full age of twenty-one years; and the vote of a majority of such members at a council or meeting of the band summoned according to their rules, and held in the presence of the Superintendent-General or an agent acting under his instructions, shall be sufficient to determine such election, or grant such consent" (Venne 1981, 338).

10. According to Marie Frawley-Henry of the Assembly for First Nations Women's Secretariat, there are 109 women chiefs in Canada. This means that approximately 17 percent of Canada's elected chiefs are women. For more information, see Voyageur 2008.

11. In 2001, I initiated the first systematic academic study of women chiefs

in Canada. For this groundbreaking research, I conducted interviews in person or on the phone with sixty-four of the then ninety women chiefs to gather information about their experiences. I used a semi-structured interview schedule to gather information about their lives, experiences, political preparation, and struggles. This section of the chapter is informed by that data.

12. There are a few post-secondary educational institutions on the reserve, but most First Nations people pursuing an advanced education must leave the reserve.

13. Primary socialization is the development of language and individual identity.

References

Aboriginal Business Canada. 2003. *Aboriginal Entrepreneurs in Canada: Alberta*. Retrieved December 21, 2006, http:..strategis.gc.ca/epic/internet/inabc-eac.nsf/en/abo0425e.html.

Anderson, Karen. 1991. *Chain Her by One Foot: The Subjugation of Native Women in Seventeenth-Century New France*. London: Routledge.

Anderson, Kim. 2000. *A Recognition of Being: Reconstructing Native Womanhood*. Toronto: Sumach/Canadian Scholars' Press.

Barman, Jeanne. 2010. "Indigenous Women and Feminism on the Cusp of Contact." In *Indigenous Women and Feminism: Politics, Activism, Culture*, edited by Cheryl Suzack, Shari Huhndorf, Jeanne Perreault, and Jean Barman, 92–108. Vancouver: University of British Columbia Press.

Bigfoot, Dolores S., Deborah Jones-Saunty, Clara Sue Kidwell, and Diane J. Willis. 2007. "Feminist Leadership among American Indian Women." In *Women and Leadership: Transforming Visions* and Diverse Voices, edited by Jean Lau Chin, Bernice Lott, Joy K. Rice, and Janis Sanchez-Hucles, 314–29. Malden, MA: Blackwell Publishing.

Black, Naomi, Paula Bourne, Gail Cuthbert Brandt, Beth Light, Wendy Mitchinson, and Alison Prentice. 1988. *Canadian Women: A History*. Toronto: Harcourt Brace Jovanovich.

Carter, S. 1997. *Capturing Women: The Manipulation of Cultural Imagery in Canada's Prairie West*. Montreal: McGill-Queen's University Press.

Elias, Peter Douglas. 1990. "Wage Labour, Aboriginal Relations, and the Cree of the Churchill River Basin, Saskatchewan." Native Studies

Review 6: 43–64.

Friesen, Gerald. 1987. *The Canadian Prairies: A History*. Toronto: University of Toronto Press.

Gerber, Linda, and John J. Macionis. 2000. *Sociology: Third Canadian Edition*. Scarborough: Prentice Hall Allyn and Bacon Canada.

Government of Canada. 1951. *The Indian Act (Chapter 29)*. Ottawa: Department of Citizenship and Immigration.

Howe, Eric. 2002. "Education and Lifetime Earnings for Aboriginal People in Saskatchewan." Discussion Paper 2002-1 ISSN 0831-439X. Saskatoon: University of Saskatchewan.

Imai, Shin. 2002. *The 2002 Annotated Indian Act and Aboriginal Constitutional Provisions*. Toronto: Carswell.

Indian and Northern Affairs. 2006. *Basic Departmental Data, 2003*. Catalogue No. R12-7/2003E. Ottawa: Indian and Northern Affairs Canada, First Nations and Northern Statistics Section.

Knight, Rolf. 1996. *Indians at Work: An Informal History of Native Indian Labour in British Columbia, 1858–1930*. Vancouver: New Star Books.

Memmi, Albert. 2000. *Racism*. Minneapolis: University of Minnesota Press.

Miller, J. R. 1989. *Skyscrapers Hide the Heavens: A History of Indian–White Relations in Canada*. Toronto: University of Toronto Press.

Ray, A. J. 1974. *Indians in the Fur Trade: Their Role as Trappers, Hunters, and Middlemen in the Lands Southwest of Hudson's Bay, 1600–1870*. Toronto: University of Toronto Press.

Spivak, Gayatri. 1987. *In Other Worlds: Essays in Cultural Politics*. New York: Methuen.

Statistics Canada. 2008. *2006 Census of Canada: Analysis Series—Aboriginal Peoples of Canada, A Demographic Profile*. Catalogue No. 96F0030XIE20010007. Ottawa: Statistics Canada.

——. 2009. "Labour Force Activity (8), Aboriginal Identity (8B), Age Groups (13A), Sex (3), and Area of Residence (6A) for the Population 15 Years and Over of Canada." Provinces and Territories, 2001 and 2006 Censuses—20% Sample.

Tough, Frank. 1992. "Regional Analysis of Indian Aggregate Income, Northern Manitoba." Native Studies Review 12: 40–66.

———. 1996. *As Their Natural Resources Fail: Native People and the Economic History of Northern Manitoba, 1870–1930*. Vancouver: University of British Columbia Press.

Tsosie, Rebecca. 2010. "Native Women and Leadership: An Ethics of Culture and Relationship." In *Indigenous Women and Feminism: Politics, Activism, Culture*, edited by Jean Barman, Shari Huhndorf, Jeanne Perreault, and Cheryl Suzack, 29–42. Vancouver: University of British Columbia Press.

Venne, Sharon H. 1981. *Indian Acts and Amendments, 1869–1975: An Annotated Collection*. Saskatoon: Native Law Centre.

Voyageur, Cora J. 2001. "Women Chiefs Study." Unpublished data, Calgary.

———. 2002. "Women Chiefs Study." Unpublished data, Calgary.

———. 2003. "Women Chiefs Study." Unpublished data, Calgary.

———. 2004. "Women Chiefs Study." Unpublished data, Calgary.

———. 2008. *Firekeepers of the 21st Century: Female First Nations Chiefs in Canada*. Montreal: McGill–Queen's University Press.

———. 2009. "Not Just Small Change: Indigenous Women and Entrepreneurship in Alberta." Unpublished data, University of Calgary.

———. 2010. "Contemporary First Nations Women's Issues." *Visions of the Heart: Canadian Aboriginal Issues*, edited by David A. Long and Olive Dickason, 213–37. 3rd ed. Toronto: Oxford University Press.

———. 2011. "Female First Nations Chiefs and the Colonial Legacy." *American Indian Culture and Research Journal* 35 (3): 59–78.

Williams, Robert A., Jr. 1990. "Gendered Checks and Balances: Understanding the Legacy of White Patriarchy in an American Indian Cultural Context." *Georgia Law Review* 24: 1019–44.

Chapter 5

Exploring Australian Indigenous Artistic Leadership[1]

Michelle Evans

Introduction

To my mind, you cannot speak about the need for leadership in our communities without being prepared to take on responsibility yourself.... Nor can anyone afford to call themselves a leader unless they truly have the interests of our community at heart. (Huggins 2004, 5)

Leadership is an iconic idea. When asked to think about leadership, you are likely to have many images or thoughts fill your mind. You may think about your parents or elders; for some it is Martin Luther King Jr. or Nelson Mandela; or it may be the idea of a boss or CEO. The ideas most associated with leadership are that leaders are male, that they are great orators, and that leadership is about inspiring people with a vision that is big enough to bring many together in a united action (Jackson and Parry 2008). However, in leadership studies, scholars do not always agree on a single, unified definition of what leadership is. In fact some scholars say that when we study leadership, get up close and personal with it, it disappears or is difficult to capture (Alvesson and Sveningsson 2003). Leadership is a contested concept. The leadership studies field encourages us to explore by listening and noticing when, where, how, and why leadership arises. I have chosen to study Indigenous artists and arts managers as leaders. This chapter reports some of the findings about where leadership springs from for these Indigenous arts leaders.

I will explore how Indigenous artists and artistic practices offer significant lessons about the phenomenon of "leadership," and provide rich, descriptive, and theoretical opportunities for us. In studying the term "leadership" as it makes sense to Indigenous artists and arts managers in Australia, this chapter will unfold in three parts. The first part will explore the supporting influences on Indigenous artistic leadership, and the second will explore influences that undermine Indigenous artistic leadership. In the first section, I describe three themes that one can term as generally supporting influences on artistic leadership. These are family and childhood stories, connecting to culture, and artistic mastery. Through them, Indigenous arts leaders make sense of their connection to the arts and more broadly to Indigenous culture. These sets of influences highlight important life stories and how they contribute to the construction of artist and leader identities. The second section explores three disruptive or undermining influences on artistic leadership. These include the pressures that Indigenous artists experience in regard to their egos; the entrenched power relations in the Indigenous arts sector, narrated as "playing the game"; and the ubiquitous pressure of managerial responsibility and its impact on creativity. In the third part, I will bring in theoretical arguments to assert the value of studying artists as a site of knowing about leadership.

This chapter is written from the insights found in my doctoral study, entitled *Be:Longing—Enacting Indigenous Arts Leadership* (Evans 2012). The dissertation focused on the nexus between Indigenous arts and leadership. It produced important findings about how the layers of community influence, cultural authorization, and generational responsibility influence and contextualize the leadership enacted by Indigenous artists. It is these layers, or tensions, that make up the landscape or territories of Indigenous arts leadership. Shaded by tensions of identity politics and lateral violence, and hemmed in by discourses of managerialism, Indigenous arts leaders enact what it means to belong.

Based on interviews with twenty-nine Australian Indigenous artists and arts managers (from now on referred to as "Indigenous arts leaders"), the study builds a platform for the voices of the participants to be front and centre. The study used a three-tiered analysis process. After identifying themes across the interviews, this study upholds important narratives and then analyzes the power dimensions by conducting a discourse analysis. It presents these narratives and explores the supporting influences and pressures experienced by Indigenous arts leaders as the work to enact leadership.

This chapter has also been written within an Australian context and from an Indigenous point of view. Australia, invaded by the English in 1788 when Captain Arthur Phillip took possession of New South Wales, was declared a land belonging to no one under the doctrine of *terra nullius* (Langton and Perkins 2008). What followed was nearly two centuries of conflict, the spread of introduced disease, and successive policies aimed at assimilating Indigenous peoples into the general population. As the settlers removed Australian Indigenous people from their lands and children from their families, they dispossessed Indigenous people of their traditional cultural homelands. After generations of cultural genocide and the stolen generations, Australian Indigenous people continue to experience racial discrimination directly, institutionally, and economically. Sadly, these colonial legacies are ever present in contemporary Australia. Compounding these colonial legacies are the daily politics over land ownership, identity, Indigenous peoples' inherent right to self-determine their own lives, and the Australian government's management of Aboriginal people in Australia.

For Australian Indigenous arts leaders, historic trauma is a key tension in their work. It drives their desire to highlight cultural connections and revive language and culture through their art practice. By listening to how creative practitioners speak about their practice— how it is informed by family relationships, cultural connections, and creative traditions—we can learn about the complex cultural navigation that artists are engaged in on a daily basis. Further, exploring the undermining impediments to leadership, as experienced by Indigenous arts leaders, provides us with salient ways to understand the pressures inherent in Indigenous leadership and in leadership more broadly.

Strengthening Influences on Indigenous Artistic Leadership

Indigenous arts leaders spoke of strong childhood and family memories and how they were able to connect these stories to their contemporary practice of art making and leadership. Their first memory of the arts linked these stories to their artistic voice and purpose. These stories helped the Indigenous artists and arts managers to link early conceptualizations of self and how their self aligns to artistic expression.

Indigenous arts leaders connected present-day artistic leadership with the influence of their place in the family structure or connected it to the role art began to play in their lives from an early time. Importantly, Indigenous arts leaders spoke at length about how they connected their life stories to a larger cultural narrative of Indigenous Australia. These connective themes act as a supporting influence in their artistic leadership.

Finally, Indigenous arts leaders connected support for their artistic leadership with their mastery of their art form. Telling stories about productions and projects, participants asserted positive self-regard in these moments. For example, choosing to wait for better performance opportunities rather than taking up offers to perform at lesser standards illustrated their commitment to a quality project. Furthermore, identity narratives were attached to early memories nested in the understanding of self in relation to family and culture.

Family and Childhood Stories

Stories were gathered from each Indigenous arts leader about their first memory of the arts or of exposure to the arts. Some Indigenous arts leaders were aware of "the arts" as a category they might use to describe their own childhood art making. However, many spoke about drawing or expression that was yet to be linguistically connected to the category of "the arts." Some of the most powerful narratives describe an almost pre-verbal connection.

For example, r e a[2] (pers. comm.) talks through making connections between these early memories and what she does now as her profession:

> Because I still hadn't really kind of processed that stuff about what art was, what an artist was. And you know, I guess I saw them as pic-

tures. But I didn't really have that kind of, you know, connection yet
to that. I think for me the drawing stuff was really like a—I guess
kind of like a meditation. Like a kind of spirit thing. Like a—I was
a very deep-thinking child. I was very much like an introvert, that
you could probably say.

r e a connects spirituality and art making, describing how she
would be fully engaged with her artistic expression, almost like a
meditation. For Sam Cook,[3] (pers. comm.) her first memory of the
arts takes her right back to being a toddler on the floor at home:

I stored a lot of memory through imagery, a visual memory, a
photographic memory, of a lot of the childhood, over and above
documenting it in the obvious ways. So yeah, there's—I remember
tracing shapes on floors and the colours of the browns. In those
photos I'm wearing one of those cloth nappies, so you can imagine
how old I was then. I was a baby still.

Sam continues to connect her preference to communicate visually
with childhood memories:

It actually came more natural for me to tell someone how I felt by
creating a picture around it. So I don't necessarily know if there's any
of those left, but there were drawings I did. If I had something to tell,
they weren't the best images of individuals, but I'd characterize them
around a drawing, so I communicated quite early in just visual art.

What comes naturally for artists is the visual representation of
their interpretation of the world. These rich works allow outsiders
to glimpse the complex inner world of the artist's mind. Further,
connecting the artistic expression of the inner child, who is relatively
free from the "reality" of the adult world, is not limited by educational
systems (Aronica and Robinson 2009).

Participants also spoke of how their childhoods and position in
the family shaped their artistic voice. For r e a, artistic expression
through photography acts to cohesively meld history, identity, and

connection to family. In the following excerpt, r e a (pers. comm.) speaks about stepping up into a kind of co-parenting role. Responsibility was placed upon the young r e a to hold on to the memories, history, and identity of the family. This narrative is about the importance of capturing these memories and history:

> I already, along the way, picked up this practice of photography. Because I actually was introduced to photos by my mother. She's not a photographer. But she collected our family visual history through photography. So she just used to get photos all the time. So you know, it was kind of—By the time I was about nine, she started to pull out this—I always describe it as a biscuit tin with roses all over it, red roses, and she just slowly started to reveal these sepia tone and black-and-white photos. So that—I just was completely mesmerized with these photos. I think that stayed with me. And then I started to pick up the camera, in my early teens, and started to document—I thought, I started—I got this sense of responsibility. Because I was the eldest. Primarily grew up in a single-parent family, because my parents got divorced when I was about six or seven. So my childhood was pretty much gone by that time. I mean, I had to step into this kind of co-parent role.

Visual representations of relational cultural connections inhabited that biscuit tin. Today, r e a explores identity construction, representations of memory, and the repercussions of colonization in her new media work. Reproduced through r e a's childhood narratives, these stories and memories signal the sense of responsibility Indigenous artists have to represent Indigenous experience.

Artistic director Stephen Page[4] (pers. comm.) describes the tensions he experienced when shifting from inhabiting his original place in the birth order to the place he occupies in his family in more contemporary times. This shift has occurred in relation to his professional role and success. In the presence of his family, Stephen experiences moments when he is "quiet as hell." He also experiences moments where his family notices his achievements, and where his success disrupts his birth order position:

Even though he's my older brother, he's like my younger brother in this world, so my ego seems to be much [more] of a leader than he is in that situation, and it's probably because I've always been his boss... and I've directed him in shows. When we're home and family, I'm quiet as hell, like. Everyone knows what I do in the family and they're so overwhelmed and proud of what I do. Yet they're so—I have half the family just adore and learn and when I'm with them they will communicate a language with me, which is about who we are as people.

Stephen describes how his family dynamics are intertwined and interact with his professional work as an artistic director and choreographer. For Stephen, different spaces require different leaders; at work he steps up and at home he steps into the younger brother role. Families and the community at large notice the success of Indigenous artists. Success does bring with it increased social capital as well as increased expectations to give back to the community. Families are places where participants noticed these changes. There is a tension for Indigenous artists between belonging in ways they always have and not belonging in those ways anymore. The feeling of not belonging is exacerbated when family members enact jealousy.

Connecting to Culture

Indigenous arts leaders demonstrated a serious deliberation in their choice of narratives that connected their personal cultural identity to broader Indigenous narratives. The story work Indigenous artists practise connects them (and their audiences) to a larger understanding of who they are. These narratives strengthen Indigenous artistic practice and demonstrate leadership:

> I thought to myself, who's going to want to listen to me talk for seventy minutes, it's ridiculous... but even then I thought—see, I didn't see the big picture of, um, this is a huge story, this is part of a huge story in our nation's history. All that time ago I was coming to the realization it's taken all this time to get the apology and you know, so once I realized it was part of a big story, I started to respect it as that. (Deborah Cheetham, pers. comm.)[5]

Indigenous artists often produce and reproduce Indigenous knowledge and cultural connection through visual language. Billy Missi[6] (pers. comm.) explores how his art practice connects to larger cultural narratives: "So that is the reason why I really looked at that [the natural environment]. Because by that time, I didn't look at the other artists. They were always wanting to do the major stories and the sacred stories too. But I think there was a gap coming on about recording that environment for the other generations to come." Billy's art practice presents another dimension of his connection to the seasons, the animals and plants, the sea and land. His work displays how Billy places himself in relation to the larger ecosystem. Billy Missi has lived a culturally rich life. Raised inside Torres Strait Islander culture, Billy demonstrates how his artistic practice is an extension and expression of his cultural knowledge. The purpose of Billy's work is to tell the stories of the environment and ecosystem.

Time spent in Indigenous community settings re-energizes Indigenous artists in their art practice. Community provides inspiration for Tammy Anderson,[7] (pers. comm.), who states:

> As an artist I think we're sponges. We go out there and absorb into us, into our soul.... You go in and you feel, you know, it sucks into you and you come home and your heart's heavy and you see your visuals and you remember stories and things stick in your head. I even dream about stuff—it's quite, um, it's really hard to disconnect from things sometimes. The way for me to do it is to write it down. Share a story, talk about those experiences. Stay in contact with, you know, communities.

Stories and visuals soak into artists' souls. Tammy Anderson described the act of sharing stories as a spiritual experience. Unable to disconnect, haunted in her dreams by the power of their stories, Tammy adds these community members and these stories to her relational web or broader constellation of story work. For Tammy Anderson, sharing her own life story and experiences of violence opens the door for others to share with her. Tammy's story acts like a door opening on some of the darker incidents women experience. Tammy listens and absorbs those stories, often of heartbreak. She creates a container for those women and honours them by showing how she found a way to live with those difficult experiences and transform her life.

Connecting to culture is about upholding Indigenous knowledge as well as speaking back to powerful historical narratives that have sought to disconnect Aboriginal people from their culture. Indigenous artists powerfully engage with these grand narratives as a platform upon which to present their achievements, give voice to their communities and cultures, and project a future-focused leadership.

Artistic Mastery

Mastering an artistic discipline takes years of dedication. Indigenous artists construct narratives to describe their artistic vision and practices. These narratives are important signifiers that foreground Indigenous artistic mastery. Narratives of artistic mastery describe how artistic practice creates engagements with others that provide the opportunity to enact Indigenous arts leadership. Indigenous artists do become synonymous with the content of their work. Creating artistic work from these personal provocations often results in artistic work that is autobiographical. Indigenous artists draw upon resonant personal narratives that often connect to broader cultural narratives, as described above.

Most Indigenous artists move in and out of feeling confident in their voice. Some argue that this is a result of working in a sector where criticism is a fixture (Cameron 2003). Negotiating the impact criticism has, through its value judgements, on their artistic practice is an important competency for Indigenous artists. Despite these potentially damaging experiences, participants spoke of being in the artistic domain as an overwhelmingly positive experience. For example, Noel Tovey[8] (pers. comm.) demonstrates a high level of passion for his practice when sharing his artistic ideas:

> So I had this wonderful idea. I have to say in my own mind it's one of the greatest moments of satisfaction with your art. What I did was, I had the entire cast walk up the ramp and take all their tops off with their backs to the audience so they were only in either

white trousers or white skirts. The stage manager stepped through them without anyone noticing with a bowl of white spiritual ochre and I had them smear their bodies with ochre. Then, one by one, then I had the Tiwi Islands songs of the dead chanted, which I have a recording of, from under the platform. Then I had smoke billowing out with a red spotlight on it so it looked like the entire cast were on this cloud of blood.

Savouring each descriptive element of the scene, Noel confidently indicates how deeply satisfying his practice makes him feel. His artistic practice, propelled from deep within his vivid imagination, is physically applied and shared.

There is a need for these artist leaders to prove that their success is not just chance; it is a result of hard work and long hours of practice. Bindi Cole[9] (pers. comm.) recalls a time when she felt a great deal of satisfaction from having others watch her perform her artistic mastery:

I brought my lights in and I brought in the system and in this full day I had to do ten shoots, ten individual shoots in different locations. So where I feel good is where they see that. They don't just see me hanging around taking photos for all the lead-up. They see that there must be years and years that I have devoted to becoming good at this, and then they see the outcome of the photos and they feel good about those photos. And they see that it's not just an off-chance thing. I'm not just picking up a camera and going, I think I'll take a shot now with you, but I'd actually devoted years and years of my life to becoming that person that can walk into that space and—and will set my lights up, have an assistant, and tell them to stand a particular way and look a particular—and make them look good. It's not just chance.

Striving for artistic excellence requires commitment to your craft. Indigenous arts leaders spoke about how they maintain control over their artistic practice through the standard of work produced. In the following excerpt, William Barton[10] (pers. comm.) describes his decision-making process and what weighs into a decision to take up a paid opportunity to perform:

It was more about me not saying yes to just the mediocre gigs or the gigs where, if you do too many of them, that's what they expect your standard to be. You've got a higher standard of musicality, but then, when it comes to the standard of the bank account, you've got to really aim high and—aim high as your talent allows you to. And so that's basically what I did. So I believed, I believed in myself, and, and I guess my team of people around me, to sort of get to where I am now, you know. And as the old saying goes, it doesn't happen overnight, but it will happen.

William values his artistic autonomy. There is tension between the reality of making a living and his commitment to artistic excellence and autonomy. The choice, in this example, is framed as strategic: it strengthens his reputation and brand. William performs the choice of investing in his artistic excellence rather than the financial short-term outcome.

Artistic mastery is one way that Indigenous artists enact leadership. The artistic presentation space is a creative platform over which Indigenous artists can assert some level of ownership. Indigenous arts leadership is created through the presentation of artistic talent. How the presentation is met and experienced by audiences adds another dimension. In the intersection between presentation and audience lie both the opportunity to celebrate and the power to criticize. How individual Indigenous artists receive and interpret what arises from this intersectional space is important to Indigenous arts leadership, because it not only signifies the personal preparation for feedback but indicates the readiness of the audience to interact with Indigenous stories and voice.

Impediments to Indigenous Artistic Leadership

Three areas of tension and challenge for Indigenous arts leaders emerged from the research. They are, first, their own ego needs; second, entrenched power relations in the Indigenous arts sector; and third, managerialism. Efforts to enhance voice and power are important. However, there are points where the expression of a vulnerable self presents a danger to Indigenous artists from others who wish to manipulate ego sensitivities. Indigenous artists also spoke of how power manifests in the idea of "playing the game." Whether subject to or objectified by "the game," Indigenous artists express the inevitability of their participation in "the game" as they struggle with it. The third major source of perceived tension is the language, responsibilities, and requirements of management.

Ego

Indigenous artists communicate grand ideas and complex cultural representations through their finely honed artistic mastery. It is important for Indigenous artists to have healthy egos. However, being publicly celebrated can bring ego tensions for artists, and there are particular Indigenous community values that tend to frown upon Indigenous artists seen to be egotistical. Stephen Page (pers. comm.) describes the experience of being publicly celebrated:

> Well, for me it was all a new experience. And I wasn't, um, well, my ego was celebrated and my ego was living a Western mainstream almost rock star–type lifestyle, um, you know—partying, travelling around the world, meeting influential people, meeting greed. I mean, that's what I was doing; I was meeting the form of greed in an artistic way.

Stephen experiences external adulation as well as the influence of "greed." This "rock star–type lifestyle" enhances Stephen's ego and leads to choices that feed this experience. Stephen further analyzes his success:

> We talk about being in a time in life where development of colleges like that gave you the advantage to, um, celebrate your imagination or celebrate this desire that you had in you to be a performer or to be—People were saying to me, "Why was it dance?" and I don't know. I mean, it was just something that I was attracted to, I did it sort of naturally around the house, we never had any formal training....And we had no living language ... or song or dance that we could rely on. So what was the spirit there that drew us to that energy?

Stephen sifts through his memories for answers to the question, why did he choose dance? The question throws up a dilemma for Stephen. He focuses on the context that led him to success, looking outside himself to understand why. Was it his training? Was it his "strong" cultural background? Stephen is rendered more fragile by looking for external attributions for his success, because it leads him to look beyond the consistent hard work he put in for over twenty years.

William Barton (pers. comm.) describes how he separates himself from what he calls brand William Barton. "I'm a brand of my own lifestyle, yes [laughter]." William explores the difference between himself and his brand:

> Well, brand, like people know you as a certain—when they see you walking around the street—like the people who see you on stage, and they'll see you walking the street, they'll more or less recognize you from something that they've seen you in on TV or in a concert or something. And so you're almost always on duty as yourself, but that's your brand name—not your brand name, but your brand or your persona and personality.

William is describing this idea of his brand as consisting of images of what others respond to from his artistic presentations coupled with the projection of who others think he is or what others think he stands for. William has a well-versed life story that he shares regularly in the public domain as well as in more private domains. It is a consistently produced narrative from which others can extract value.

To build a social and relational following for themselves and their work, Indigenous artists use the language of brand. Anita Heiss[11] (pers. comm.) explores the way she has built her brand:

> My brand as Anita Heiss is a writer and social commenter. She's professional and delivers. That's who I want to be known as and that's why I get invited, because I deliver and I'm professional and I can—I can project to a different audience and I can use books and I've got an opinion on everything. It doesn't mean I'll actually

publicize it. But I can use literature as a tool for getting whatever the topic is—Stolen Generations, reconciliation, you know, history, and literacy, whatever.

Anita (pers. comm.) determinedly states her brand characteristics: she delivers on time, is professional, communicates to diverse audiences, and speaks across a range of topics. Anita also identifies the trade-off she makes in relation to building her brand:

> I'm Indigenous, therefore I'm an Indigenous writer. I don't have a problem with the whole thing. I've been called a lot worse things than that. But then I decided that what I needed to separate in a way was this notion of that's all I can do. So I changed the phrase on the website to "Anita Heiss is a writer of Indigenous stories" or "is a well-known author of Indigenous literature." Which leaves it a little bit more open. Because what I don't want to get boxed into—and it's not that I'm getting boxed into an Indigenous category—I'm now having a change in direction in terms of my writing because I'm getting boxed into the chick lit category.... So I thought, right, I need to do some essays and now I need to [do] some memoir so that I'm not boxed into that, so that I can be seen as someone who writes Indigenous literature across genres.

Anita expresses a common issue raised by Indigenous artists, that of finding herself bound to the categorization "Indigenous artist" when she would prefer to be known as a writer. Anita explores the tangle of roles and positions she inhabits and the complication that branding brings. Being branded as a "chick lit" author seems more limiting than liberating.

Leaders have a healthy dose of narcissism, as discovered in a study of their ambitions and visions for their careers (Pullen and Rhodes 2008). However, it is important to draw attention to instances of vulnerability that may indicate a personal history of rejection that now seeks affirmation. The ego integrates conscious and unconscious thoughts, experiences, ideas, and fantasies that provide a powerful source for Indigenous artists to draw upon in their creative practice.

The commodification of the self through self-branding and the external influences that demand performances of an Indigenous self invite careful analysis and consideration.

Power Relations in the Indigenous Arts Sector

Indigenous artists gain status through their artistic contributions and are able to act with power and some self-determination. However, it was the feeling of disempowerment and being rendered an "object" in the "game" of the Indigenous arts sector that was a recurrent theme in the interviews. Stephen Page (pers. comm.) shares feeling high levels of confidence in his artistic mastery and his ability to play the game. Yet at the same time, he is challenged by thoughts that he arrived in his coveted position not necessarily on his own merits.

> Yes I was confident, yes I was cocky—I was all those things. But then I played a game with Sydney Dance that because I was going back to the college and I was teaching and choreographing, so that became my playground to choreograph and experiment because they all knew I was at Sydney Dance. And then there was the black politics; there was peer pressure from the students that graduated well that were in my year who still had to complete another two years. See, I only got a diploma, I only did three years—not even that, I think I did two and a half years and then I went to Sydney Dance, so. And then they were all saying it was because I had the fairest skin and if I had blacker skin... and I must admit there were much better dancers than me.

Stephen feels empowered by his ability to work across mainstream and Indigenous organizations. Yet he also feels disempowered by the attention his skin colour captures and that this attention interrupts his sense of confidence. The attention Stephen and other fairer-skinned Indigenous artists receive, especially when their skin colour is raised as a topic of curiosity, can cause a range of responses, including anger, self-loathing, grief, and exhaustion: "I thought, I'm a fraud, I'm doing no good." These responses interrupt and sometimes overwhelm the empowering experiences.

Brenda Croft[12] (pers. comm.) explains the power struggle she has experienced while "playing the game" in non-Indigenous organizations:

> I was like, "Excuse me, can you just stop patronizing me and guess what, I don't work for you anymore, this show is going there because it's a really good show." I got over there and I found that all the wall text had been rewritten, my text. I mean, I curated this show, I'm a curator. You wouldn't do this to another curator just because she's Aboriginal. I got this email back from the [institution]: "Oh we reworded it because it was for an international audience." I thought this just underlined exactly why I left.

Brenda described being subjected to institutional power games. Authorship issues cause high levels of tension for all artists. Unable to assert control over the rewritten wall text, Brenda, curator of the exhibition and custodian of Indigenous and professional knowledge informing the interpretation of the work, expresses her disempowerment. She finds herself pitted against colleagues, having her intellectual property appropriated by the institution and denied voice at the opening of her exhibition.

On the other hand, Deborah Cheetham (pers. comm.) describes herself as a "control freak":

> I am a control freak. The things that I can do, I know I can do well. So if I'm wanting to do something relating in that area but I'm going to want to sort of manage it, I don't suffer fools. I don't expect anyone to deliver any more than I give, but you know, if it's a project that's got my name on it, I want it to be the best, right. So generally the only way to make that happen is if you do it yourself. Because you know what I mean, this is really hard, particularly if you work with friends, it's because you could lose friendships.

Deborah acknowledges how hard it is to forsake friendships for control. Deborah owns her power; she can "deliver the goods," yet there are consequences to living up to these demanding expectations. The invisible power relations that underpin the work of Indigenous artists interrupt the positive and empowering work they contribute to the broader Australian community. Many times these powerful forces have become internalized, causing emotional distress to individuals in their pursuit of artistic excellence.

Managerial Narratives

The language of business and the imperatives of business do take up space in the domain of the Indigenous artist. Individual responses differ as to whether the language of business seeks to confine and control artistic independence or whether the language is a vehicle that can be mobilized towards creating artistic independence. Either way, there is an important tension evoked through the engagement in managing or strategizing about the business side of being an Indigenous artist (Loustel, Overall, and Wuttunee 2007).

Indigenous artists spoke about learning the business side of being an Indigenous artist and how it supports as well as interrupts their artistic practice. Troy-Anthony Bayliss[13] (pers. comm.) shares how he pragmatically supplements his artistic career by working in arts management:

> So then I'd get jobs, which meant I wasn't being an artist then necessarily. But those particular jobs were really valuable...So even though those jobs kept me away from, you know, being really productive as an artist, ultimately, you know, it, it just informed a whole lot of things for me in terms of how the, how the world operates and, um, I think there are not a lot of artists who get that type of opportunity. So I think the bright light is that it's really prepared me now to be a much better communicator and to be more strategic and businesslike in my practice.

Artist leaders apply managerial concepts such as strategy and productivity to their artistic practice. Indeed, "the words that make the worlds of the powerful can be used as tools for mobilisation and resistance. It is, after all, in the very ambiguity of development buzzwords that scope exists for enlarging their application to encompass more transformative agendas" (Cornwall 2010, 13).

It could be argued that one of the most marshalled buzzwords over the past few decades has been *partnership*. Rising to prominence in the 1990s, partnerships between public, private, and community-based sectors have become a model taken up within the arts sector. Managing these cross-sector partnerships requires expertise and time as well as a mutual commitment to serve public-, private-, and community-sector interests. Billy Missi (pers. comm.) describes his work as including complex partnership brokering:

> So me, as a front man, I've got to follow up … working directly with the economic development officer from TSRA [Torres Strait Regional Authority] to get someone to come and do a feasibility [study]. Also we partnershipped [sic] with the state development at that time, with the John Hughes Foundation. So I sort of did all that thing on my own.

Artist leaders, along with the management task, have to juggle the sometimes conflicting requirements of the regional authority, a government department, and a philanthropic foundation. Artists may defer their own artistic practice in the short term to ensure the establishment of a project such as an arts centre. Indigenous leadership requires an ongoing negotiation between Indigenous culture, business imperatives, and managerial processes. These tensions are dynamic features of leadership in the Indigenous arts sector.

Connecting Indigenous Arts and Leadership

Over the years, scholars have shown how, through studying the practice of artists, we can learn about creativity, power, and influence (Foucault 2009; Csikszentmihalyi 1996; Gosling and Sutherland 2010). In the management literature, studying artists and art has long held interest because of the possibility of grasping the conditions needed to foster innovation and creativity (Langer 2005; Ladkin and Taylor 2010). By placing the voices and narratives of Indigenous arts leaders up front, we can see that these strengthening influences and competing impediments are clearly inherent in their practice of leadership.

There is great value in looking to Indigenous arts leaders for new understandings about Indigenous leadership and leadership more generally. An Indigenous world view, or ontology, is predicated on the construction of reality through a system of relationships by means of which knowledge is transmitted (Meyer 2001; Wilson 2008). Indigenous arts leaders embody this world view; their artistic practice is a way that we, the audience, can come to understand their priorities in making artistic work that is deeply informed by the way they see the world, and by the positioning of their art within their context— family, community, and culture.

Leadership is a malleable lexicon, socially constructed among those negotiating the idea and experience of leadership (Bolden et al. 2011). Understanding leadership in the context of Indigenous culture and community has been an interest of many Indigenous and non-Indigenous scholars (Begay Jr. 1991; Ottmann 2005; Calliou 2005; Skuthorpe and Sveiby 2006; Grint and Warner 2006; White 2010). The research generally finds that Indigenous leadership enacts and supports values not usually represented in conventional leadership literature. Indigenous leaders describe the experience of leadership as having to negotiate complex tensions in their context, such as having to navigate stakeholder tensions from both inside and outside Indigenous culture (Sanders 2007).

Artists have been viewed by society as craftspeople or master technicians as often as they have been thought of as geniuses, philosophers, and those uniquely spiritually enlightened. Individual artists produce cultural outcomes, products, and experiences for society to consume, consider, and reject. They act as tricksters, critics, mirrors, clowns, and romantics to the world in which we all live by disengaging and re-imaging culture and society. They practise leadership through their individual embodied knowledge system; they interpret versions of the world for us all to see, hear, touch, taste, and smell. These sensory experiences are the gifts from the artist, offerings from their mind and spirit, independent of the transactional or transformational meaning they may have for audiences (Zangwill 1999).

In studying leadership, I am interested in upholding evidence of the invisible dynamisms that impact on the way leadership can be performed and experienced (Ladkin 2010). Indigenous arts leaders perform novel as well as critical ways of viewing and creating new visions for the world (McIntyre 2009). Interacting with artists' representations of their "world views" influences the way we view our own world, as they can unveil truths in ways that resonate. These sometimes visible, sometimes invisible, strategic impacts employed by artists or enacted by works of art are powerful forms of influence (Foucault 2009). Influence is a key feature of leadership (Avolio, Walumbwa, and Weber 2009; Crossman and Crossman 2011). However, it is important to note that "influence" is not the property of an individual, but a feature of a socially constructed, relational system or world (Uhl-Bien 2006). Therefore, a leader or arts leader influences through their networks and practices, which are embedded within social structures.

Indigenous leadership, founded on an Indigenous world view, can be understood by looking at ways in which Indigenous people produce knowledge. Two features of an Indigenous way of viewing the world that are different from Western viewpoints are the way Indigenous people construct time, and the nature of multi-generational relational connection and its role in knowledge exchange. Indigenous knowledge is cyclical by nature rather than linear (Agrawal 1995; Fixico 2003; Little Bear 2004; Nakata 2007). Rather than establishing a linear chain of events, this deep concept of time, sometimes referred to as the "eternal now," emphasizes the present moment as an encapsulation of how the past influences, as well as how the future is evoked and made. Indigenous researchers such as Karen Martin (2007, 19) awaken Indigenous futures in their work: "This [work] is the tracks we leave for our young ones, of the present and of the future."

Indigenous artists build knowledge by connecting the past, present, and future into the significance of their creative investigations. Like a tuning fork, the artist's body transmits the act of creation, engaging the mind to interpret sensory inputs through voice or the creation of objects via the hands, feet, and body. Artistic practice is performative. Artists' bodies are central to the birth of artistic expression and, therefore, the historic, social, economic, cultural, and sexual layers embodied by artists inscribe their practice with contextual complexity. The performativity of the practice is contextualized through the artist—their identity, place, history, and imagination. "Collective social memories both reflect and reinforce particular beliefs and understandings.... Individual memories that cumulatively feed and shape the social memory are linked to social and cultural position and context" (Casey 2004, xvi–xvii).

Multi-generational relational connections and knowledge exchange is an important feature of Indigenous knowledge systems. In particular, identity is a central concern for Indigenous artists. As much as Indigenous artists' bodies are sites of ancestrally passed-down cultural knowledge and values, they are also places of competing and powerful cultural, post-colonial, and identity narratives (Moreton-Robinson 2003; Dudgeon 2007). Australian Indigenous writer Larissa Behrendt (2009, 74) describes how the past impacted upon the process of writing her novel *Home*:

> In writing my novel, I used the historical record. I looked at historical events and figures, and I wove them into the story. I blended that with what I knew of my family history, from the stories I had heard from many Aboriginal people about their experiences and the experiences of their families, and I also went back and reread the stories in *Bringing Them Home*.[14] I merged all of these voices to capture the struggle to deal with removal [of children] from family and the long journey home.

Behrendt describes how she drew not only upon her personal and family narratives but upon those of a broader Indigenous experience of being removed from family and the ensuing journey home. Indigenous artists bring forward their own voice and those of other Indigenous peoples, countering the tradition of being rendered voiceless by the colonizing project. Their connection to (and disconnections from) the land, flora, and fauna of Australia is indivisible from their understanding of self (Kwaymullina 2005), which makes them distinct from non-Indigenous Australians. It is this fundamentally different way of understanding how the world is ordered and relates to self that produces some profoundly different ways of expressing self through artistic practice. First, it upholds how Indigenous artists create social space for their own and other Indigenous voices and ideas to be heard. Second, it upholds Indigenous embodied identities as both historic and dynamic (Butler and Reddy 2004). Third, it upholds how Indigenous artists and peoples occupy a series of contexts that overlap in the contemporary time but draw upon the past, imagine futures, and problematize the present. Indigenous artistic works open up these three important gateways: space, body, and time.

There are a number of concerns that might be voiced about introducing leadership to Indigenous arts practice, or in connecting the two. The first is that these artists are doing art, not leadership. My research showed that there is not a clear dividing line between innovative artistic practice and leadership. The focus of the work involved mapping across what are blurred domains of influence. Another concern that might be raised is that a leadership framework has been imposed inappropriately on the participants and their activities. Care has been taken to listen to Indigenous artists and arts managers and collaboratively discuss aspects of their practice and work that might be considered leadership according to common understandings. As other leadership researchers have pointed out, sometimes leadership is not a useful descriptor for the range of activities that influential individuals get involved in (Gosling and Sutherland 2010). At the same time, introducing frames and ideas of leadership has helped Indigenous arts leaders to recognize aspects of their practice as leadership (Evans 2012). They practise leadership when they take action to bring about change in the world through their ideas. Their works have a clear impact on society and provide diverse lenses through which all of us can view the world. There is something to learn from the intersecting cultural, creative, and leadership contexts in which Indigenous arts leaders in Australia work.

Conclusion: The Contribution on the Value of Indigenous Artistic Leadership

In this chapter, I have explored how the enactment of leadership by Indigenous arts leaders offers rich material for building theoretical conceptualizations about what Indigenous arts leadership can bring to the Indigenous leadership field and, more broadly, the leadership studies field. Further, I have explored the ways in which Indigenous artistic leadership is influenced by both supporting and undermining narratives carried by individual Indigenous artists. Practising artistic leadership is informed by these sets of influences that arise from and mesh with individuals' identities. Indigenous artists construct artistic identities in concert with their context and their worlds, such as family, culture, and community. Narratives show how Indigenous artists take responsibility for their family, culture, and history through their artistic practice. Their stories are embodied, visual, aesthetic, spiritual, and symbolic. Their stories act like passports for audiences seeking to access new domains of knowledge about Indigenous ways of experiencing, seeing, and imagining the world.

However, Indigenous arts leaders spoke about difficult disempowering experiences such as "playing the game," or how they felt that they had been "played by the game." These stories feature a game-like environment with sometimes known, other times unknown, rules and risks. As in any business, there are winners and losers, and the stakes are high.

Managerial concepts and language abound in the field of Indigenous art. Narratives of management and business come through in this study. Managerial language tends to act in two main ways: pragmatically, as a business application, and yet also as an interruption to creativity. Business and management mediate the economic exchange of artistic products and of running an arts organization. Managerial discourse manifests itself when artists speak about protection, policy, and protocols. Indigenous artists speak of the pressure they feel to be good managers and yet how this sometimes compromises their creativity. Indigenous arts leaders spoke of feeling bound by the tentacles of procedure, funding requirements, and arts bureaucracy.

Indigenous arts leaders find themselves captured in the tricky negotiation between Indigenous culture, business imperatives, and managerial processes. They negotiate this overlapping space in order to stay successful. Each Indigenous arts leader finds his or her own way of being emissary and interpreter. While some try to ensure their voice is untouched by these pressures, others are more ready to interpret and adapt into non-Indigenous contexts.

Looking at these contextual tensions that Indigenous arts leaders face when they prepare to make leadership contributions, we can understand that there is much to navigate and consider when leading. Western conceptions of leadership understand it to be a process of influence between an individual leader and her or his followers. Historically, leadership has often been visualized as a triangle created by the efforts of leaders and followers working towards a common goal (Bennis 2007). While the field of leadership studies agrees on some broad parameters, it has not produced a single, widely accepted definition (Bolden et al. 2011). What the field does seem to agree on is that leadership is never a neutral act; it is a co-produced practice experienced by both leaders and followers (Baggaley et al. 2011; Godsoe, Ospina, and Schall 2001; Sinclair 1998). It is in our relationships that we construct the phenomenon of leadership.

Understanding leadership as a socially constructed or relational concept rather than as a set of attributes and competencies powerfully aligns with an Indigenous epistemology or way of seeing the world. Leadership is about "invent[ing] the future whil[st] dealing with the past" (Wheatley 2005). It requires people who can move between and speak across world views (Drath 2001). Exploring leadership with Indigenous arts leaders requires invoking and reflecting on the discourse selectively and mindfully.

We need to change our assumptions about where we are most likely to find evidence about leadership. Indigenous arts leaders are a rich source of new insights about leadership, and they are one of many new places we might find powerful contexts for leadership. As Don McIntyre (2009, 7) says, "Aboriginal leaders, like Aboriginal artists, are showing how they see the contemporary world and are creating visions for the future."

Indigenous arts leaders have complex experiences through which they produce powerful cultural symbols, which help us to unravel the layers of knowledge in pursuit of meaning for our own lives.

Rather than evoking ideas of leaders and followers, Indigenous arts leadership pays attention to the emotional, historical, socio-economic, and cultural contexts that we both embody and experience. Indigenous arts leaders create leadership contributions, or demonstrate leadership practices, that are underpinned by complex navigations of inter- and intra-personal meaning-making (Ford, Harding, and Learmouth 2008).

Indigenous artists are the navigators and leaders of the twenty-first century. They see and feel the world and interpret it in novel ways. They traverse time and space through their bodily and cognitive engagement with both. They connect the past, present, and future through practices and outcomes of their work, sharing with us visions of their world(s). They are the cultural producers, the content makers, the cultural movers and shakers of our world. We can learn more about leadership by studying their practice and the context they practise within.

Acknowledgements

My thanks and gratitude to the generosity of the participants in the study; I came to the idea of linking leadership with the work you all do by working with you. I would specifically like to personally thank the following participants, whose words appear in this chapter: r e a, Sam Cook, Stephen Page, Deborah Cheetham, Billy Missi (sadly passed away in 2012), Tammy Anderson, Noel Tovey, Bindi Cole, William Barton, Anita Heiss, Brenda Croft, and Troy-Anthony Bayliss. To Billy Missi's family and friends, I convey my deepest condolences. Billy was a true leader and a great artist. I dedicate this chapter to his memory.

Notes

1. Paper commissioned by the Indigenous Leadership and Management Program for a collected set of papers arising from the 2012 Wise Practices in Community Development Symposium at The Banff Centre, Alberta, Canada.
2. The artist known as r e a is a descendant of the Gamillaroi and Wailwan nations. r e a is one of Australia's best-known digital media artists.

3. Sam Cook, a Nyikina woman, is an artistic director, visual artist, social commentator, musician, writer, and publisher.
4. Stephen Page is the artistic director of Bangarra Dance Theatre, Australia's only major Indigenous performing arts organization. Stephen has been at the helm of Bangarra since 1991.
5. Deborah Cheetham, a Yorta Yorta woman, is a soprano, actor, playwright, and composer.
6. Printmaker Billy Missi is an award-winning artist from the Western Torres Strait (sadly passed away in 2012; please see acknowledgement at the end of the article).
7. Tammy Anderson, a Palawa woman, is a performer, musician, director, teacher, and playwright.
8. Noel Tovey is often cited as one of the fathers of Indigenous performing arts in Australia. He has worked as an actor, writer, director, and gallery owner over his sixty-year career.
9. Bindi Cole, a Wathaurung woman, is an award-winning photographer based in Melbourne.
10. William Barton, a Kalkadoon man, is internationally regarded as a virtuosic didgeridoo artist with an extensive performing, recording, and touring career.
11. Dr. Anita Heiss, a Wiradjuri woman, is the author of Indigenous literature ranging from chick lit to non-fiction, poetry, social commentary, and historical fiction.
12. Dr. Brenda Croft, a Gurindji/Malngin/Mudpurra woman, is a visual artist, curator, artistic director, and academic.
13. Troy-Anthony Bayliss is an artist, curator, writer, and doctoral candidate.
14. *Bringing Them Home* is a report commissioned by the Commonwealth of Australia in 1995 to investigate and publicly record the stories of Aboriginal and Torres Strait Islander people who had been forcibly removed from their families, now known as the Stolen Generations.

References

Agrawal, Arun. 1995. "Dismantling the Divide between Indigenous and Scientific Knowledge." *Development and Change* 26 (3): 413–39.
Alvesson, Mats, and Stefan Sveningsson. 2003. "The Great Disappearing Act: Difficulties in Doing 'Leadership.'" *Leadership Quarterly* 14 (3): 359–81.

Aronica, Lou, and Ken Robinson. 2009. *The Element: How Finding Your Passion Changes Everything.* New York: Viking Penguin.

Avolio, Bruce, Fred Walumbwa, and Todd J. Weber. 2009. "Leadership: Current Theories, Research, and Future Directions." *Annual Review of Psychology* 60: 421–49.

Baggaley, Sarah, Maggie Carson, Elaine Haycock-Stuart, and Susanne Kean. 2011. "Followers and the Co-Construction of Leadership." *Journal of Nursing Management* 19 (4): 507–16.

Begay, Manley A., Jr. 1991. "Designing Native American Management and Leadership Training: Past Efforts, Present Endeavors and Future Options." Report for Harvard Project on American Indian Economic Development. Cambridge: Harvard University.

Behrendt, Larissa. 2009. "Home: The Importance of Place to the Dispossessed." *South Atlantic Quarterly* 108 (1): 71–85.

Bennis, Warren. 2007. "The Challenges of Leadership in the Modern World." *American Psychologist* 62 (1): 2–5.

Bolden, Richard, Beverley Hawkins, Jonathan Gosling, and Scott Taylor, eds. 2011. *Exploring Leadership: Individual, Organizational, and Societal Perspectives.* Oxford: Oxford University Press.

Butler, Judith, and Vasu Reddy. 2004. "Troubling Genders, Subverting Identities: Interview with Judith Butler." *Agenda—Empowering Women for Gender Equity* 18 (62): 115–23.

Calliou, Brian. 2005. "The Culture of Leadership: North American Indigenous Leadership in a Changing Economy." In *Indigenous Peoples and the Modern State*, edited by Duane Champagne, Karen Jo Torjesen, and Susan Steiner, 47–68. Walnut Creek: AltaMira Press.

Cameron, S. 2003. "Criticism in the Arts." In *A Handbook of Cultural Economics*, edited by Ruth Towse, 161–65. Cheltenham, U.K.: Edward Elgar Publishing.

Casey, Maryrose. 2004. *Creating Frames: Contemporary Indigenous Theatre 1967–1990.* St. Lucia: University of Queensland Press.

Cornwall, Andrea. 2010. "Introductory overview – buzzwords and fuzzwords: deconstructing development discourse." In *Deconstructing development discourse: Buzzwords and fuzzwords,* edited by Andrea Cornwall and Deborah Eade, 1–18. Warwickshire, UK: Practical Action Publishing Ltd in association with Oxfam GB.

Crossman, Brian, and Joanna Crossman. 2011. "Conceptualizing Follower-
ship—A Review of the Literature." *Leadership* 7 (4): 481–97.

Csikszentmihalyi, Mihaly. 1996. *Creativity: Flow and the Psychology of Discovery and Invention.* New York: Harper Perennial.

Drath, Wilfred. 2001. *The Deep Blue Sea: Rethinking the Source of Leadership.*
San Francisco: Jossey-Bass.

Dudgeon, Patricia. 2007. *Mothers of Sin: Indigenous Women's Perceptions of
their Identity and Sexuality/Gender.* Perth: Murdoch University.

Evans, Michelle. 2012. *Be:Longing—Enacting Indigenous Arts Leadership.*
Melbourne: University of Melbourne.

Fixico, Donald L. 2003. *The American Indian Mind in a Linear World:
American Indian Studies and Traditional Knowledge.* London:
Routledge.

Ford, Jackie, Nancy Harding, and Mark Learmouth. 2008. *Leadership as
Identity.* Hampshire, U.K.: Palgrave Macmillan.

Foucault, Michel. 2009. *Manet and the Object of Painting.* London:
Tate Publishing.

Godsoe, Bethany, Sonia Ospina, and Ellen Schall. 2001. "Co-producing
Knowledge: Practitioners and Scholars Working Together to Understand Leadership." Paper presented at the International Leadership Association Conference, New York University Robert F. Wagner Graduate
School of Public Service, New York.

Gosling, Jonathan, and Ian Sutherland. 2010. "Cultural Leadership: Mobilizing Culture from Affordances to Dwelling." *Journal of Arts Management, Law and Society* 40 (1): 6–26.

Grint, Keith, and Linda Sue Warner. 2006. "American Indian Ways of Leading and Knowing." *Leadership* 2 (2): 225–44.

Huggins, Jackie. 2004. "Indigenous Women and Leadership." *Indigenous
Law Bulletin* 6 (1): 5–7.

Jackson, Brad, and Ken Parry. 2008. *A Very Short, Fairly Interesting and
Reasonably Cheap Book About Leadership.* London: Sage Publications.

Kwaymullina, Ambelin. 2005. "Seeing the Light: Aboriginal Law, Learning
and Sustainable Living on Country." *Insights—Indigenous Law Bulletin*
6 (11): 12–15.

Ladkin, Donna. 2010. *Rethinking Leadership: A New Look at Old Leadership
Questions.* Cheltenham, U.K.: Edward Elgar Publishing.

Ladkin, Donna, and Steven S. Taylor. 2010. "Leadership as Art: Variations on a Theme." *Leadership* 6 (3): 235–41.

Langer, Ellen J. 2005. *On Becoming an Artist: Reinventing Yourself Through Mindful Creativity*. New York: Random House.

Langton, Marcia, and Rachel Perkins. 2008. *First Australians: An Illustrated History*. Carlton, Australia: Miegunyah Press.

Little Bear, Leroy. 2004. "Aboriginal Paradigms: Implications for Relationships to Land and Treaty Making." In *Advancing Aboriginal Claims: Visions/Strategies/Directions*, edited by Kerry Wilkins, 26–38. Saskatoon: Purich Publishing.

Loustel, Mary Jane, Dan Overall, and Wanda Wuttunee. 2007. "Indigenous Values and Contemporary Management Approaches." *Journal of Aboriginal Economic Development* 5 (2): 20–30.

Martin, Karen. 2007. "Ma(r)king Tracks and Reconceptualising Aboriginal Early Childhood Education: An Aboriginal Australian Perspective." *Childrenz Issues* 11 (1): 15–20.

McIntyre, Don. 2009. "The Art of Leadership and Leadership of Art." *Buffalo Mountain Drum* 2009–2010: 6–7.

Meyer, Manulani Aluli. 2001. "Our Own Liberation: Reflections on Hawaiian Epistemology." *Contemporary Pacific* 13 (1): 124–48.

Moreton-Robinson, Aileen. 2003. "I Still Call Australia Home: Indigenous Belonging and Place in a White Postcolonizing Society." In *Uprootings/Regroundings: Questions of Home and Migration*, edited by Sarah Ahmed, Claudia Castaneda, Anne-Marie Fortier, and Mimi Sheller, 23–41. Oxford: Berg.

Nakata, Martin. 2007. *Disciplining the Savages—Savaging the Disciplines*. Canberra: Aboriginal Studies Press.

Ottmann, Jacqueline. 2005. "First Nations Leadership Development within a Saskatchewan Context." PhD diss., University of Saskatchewan.

Pullen, Alison, and Carl Rhodes. 2008. "It's All About Me! Gendered Narcissism and Leaders' Identity Work." *Leadership* 4 (1): 5–25.

Sanders, Will. 2007. "The Ins and Outs of Australian Indigenous Leadership." Paper presented at the Understanding Public Leadership in Australia Workshop, Australian National University, Canberra.

Sinclair, Amanda. 1998. *Doing Leadership Differently*. Carlton, Australia: Melbourne University Press.

Skuthorpe, Tex, and Karl-Erik Sveiby. 2006. *Treading Lightly: The Hidden Wisdom of the World's Oldest People*. Sydney: Allen & Unwin.

Uhl-Bien, Mary. 2006. "Relational Leadership Theory: Exploring the Social Processes of Leadership and Organizing." *Leadership Quarterly* 17 (6): 654–76.

Wheatley, Margaret. 2005. *Finding Our Way: Leadership for an Uncertain Time*. San Francisco: Berrett-Koehler Publishers.

White, Nereda. 2010. "Indigenous Australian Women's Leadership: Stayin' Strong Against the Post-Colonial Tide." *International Journal of Leadership in Education* 13 (1): 7–25.

Wilson, Shawn. 2008. *Research is Ceremony: Indigenous Research Methods*. Black Point, NS: Fernwood Publishing.

Zangwill, Nick. 1999. "Art Identity." *Dialogue* 38 (2): 335–48.

Chapter 6

Four Contemporary Tensions in Indigenous Nation Building: Challenges for Leadership in the United States

Miriam Jorgensen[1]

In 1992, the American Indian Studies Center at the University of California, Los Angeles published *What Can Tribes Do? Strategies and Institutions in American Indian Economic Development*, the first book produced by the Harvard Project on American Indian Economic Development. The book did not enjoy a splashy launch. There was no Harvard Kennedy School–sponsored signing party. It was not featured at book tables at American Indian Studies or American Studies conferences—fields which, at the time, were more concerned with Indigenous history and anthropology than with tribes' contemporary politics and economics. It was not reviewed in political science or policy journals, disciplines in which Indigenous issues were considered arcane and institutional theories were still edgy.

But *What Can Tribes Do?* was a sleeper hit. A small grant funded the distribution of a single copy to every tribe in the United States. As time went on, questions and stories began to filter back. What was this Harvard study? Tribal planners, program directors, elected leaders, and even United States government officials began to call the Harvard Project, asking for more information. One tribal leader from a remote Alaskan village reported finding the book at the tribal office after he was elected. Out of curiosity and a degree of desperation, he read it cover to cover. Now well thumbed, marked up, and riddled with Post-it Notes, the book had become his guide to imagining a new future for his nation.

For many readers, the most striking piece in the collection was the introductory chapter by Harvard Project co-founders Stephen Cornell and Joseph Kalt (1992). Although its title ia a metaphor derived from the still-nascent Indian gaming industry, the essay "Reloading the Dice: Improving the Chances for Economic Development on American Indian Reservations" did not point to casinos (or any other industry) as the key opportunity for tribes. Instead, it identified political and organizational factors as crucial to tribal progress (economic and otherwise). A tribe taking charge of its own affairs, being accountable to citizens and partners, and backstopping active self-determination with capable and legitimate governing institutions—these were the real underpinnings of tribal economic and community development. Cornell and Kalt called the process by which a Native nation enhances its own foundational capacity for effective self-governance "nation building." Subsequent research and writing, undertaken primarily by affiliates of the Harvard Project and its sister organization, the Native Nations Institute at the University of Arizona, clarified the fundamentals of Indigenous nation building, as summarized here:[2]

1. **Sovereignty Matters.** When Native nations make their own decisions about what development approaches to take, they consistently outperform external decision makers—on matters as diverse as law enforcement, natural resource management, economic development, health care, and social service provision (Cornell et al. 2013; Krepps 1992; Caves and Krepps 1994; Begay et al. 2001; see also Berry 2009; Dixon et al. 1998; Champagne and Goldberg 2012).

2. **Institutions Matter** and 3. **Culture Matters.** Assertions of self-governing power are solidified when a nation backs them up with capable and legitimate governing institutions. On the one hand, this involves adopting a stable rule of law and protecting the rule of law with efficient administrative procedures, fair and independent mechanisms for dispute resolution, and systems that separate politics from day-to-day business and program management (Cornell and Kalt 1998; Jorgensen 2000, 2004; Jorgensen and Taylor 2000;

see also Hoberg et al. 2008). On the other hand, the constitutional and statutory laws, governing mechanisms, and policies and procedures a nation adopts must be its *own*; a fit with the nation's contemporary culture helps ensure that citizens respect government and that governing institutions provide a real foundation on which development success can be built (Jorgensen 2000; Cornell and Kalt 1993, 1995, 1997, 2000; see also Trosper 1995).

4. **Strategic Thinking Matters.** When a tribe's leaders and citizens shift their focus from the short term to the long term, they are able to shift from responding to crisis to gaining some control over the future; from acting on what can be funded to evaluating each opportunity for its fit with the nation's vision; and from fixing isolated problems to addressing interconnected community concerns. This strategic orientation puts them on track towards the future they desire (Cornell and Kalt 2007; see also Zaferatos 2004).[3]

5. **Leadership Matters.** When Native nation leaders—whether elected, community, or spiritual—introduce new knowledge, challenge assumptions, convince people that things can be different, propose change, and mobilize the community to take action, they make nation building possible. When they abide by the rules and policies of a changed system, enlivening new institutions by their example, they sustain nation building through its vulnerable stages. Conversely, nation building cannot succeed if a tribe's leaders behave as if they are exempt from the nation's rules (Begay et al. 2007; Cornell et al. 2007a; Cornell and Kalt 2007).

These were fairly startling and provocative ideas when first proposed, and they remained so as more research was conducted and the "what matters" list solidified.[4] But today, the initial findings are twenty years old; the youngest findings among the five core claims were published at least ten years ago. Are they still relevant? Are they still useful? Given the academic world's standard that research findings more than five years old are stale, can they safely be ignored? Since so many Native nations are now on their own nation-building paths, haven't these ideas run their course?

In order, my answers to these questions are yes, yes, no, and no. It is *because* so many Indigenous nations are engaged in nation building that the ideas have current value. These tribes and First Nations are encountering second-generation governance problems—tensions in their work on nation building—whose resolution requires a closer examination of the principles, or that point to the need for new information concerning implementation.

This paper examines four such tensions or contemporary problems in nation building. With regard to self-determination, it examines the push for complete administrative autonomy. With regard to effective institutions, it probes the meaning of separating politics from business. With regard to legitimate institutions, it explores the boundaries of cultural match. With regard to strategic thinking, it wrestles with a common divergence between popular politics and seventh-generation thinking. It concludes by pointing again to the critical role of public-spirited, nation-building leaders who can help their nations move beyond these challenges.

Does Exercising "Practical Self-Rule" Imply an All-Or-Nothing Approach?

In taking seriously the advice that practical sovereignty matters for improved social and economic outcomes, it is not uncommon for Native nation leaders to say, "Well, that means we need to do everything ourselves." This can make sense in view of the initial research findings, which identified the benefits of moving from federal program management to tribal management: employees become accountable to the nation rather than an outside government, Native nation priorities move to the fore, tribal citizens report that services and programs are more accessible and responsive, and together these advantages lead to better program outcomes.

But in contemporary practice, the prescription is more complicated. One reason for this is that many tribes and First Nations have already picked the low-hanging fruit. Under statutory and administrative rules developed from the 1970s to the 1990s, a number of North American Indigenous nations have taken control of programs and services once administered by the United States or Canadian government.[5] These transfers may not have been easy or risk free or entirely advantageous for Native nations, but at least the processes were relatively clear. Once a tribe or First Nation exhausts these opportunities, however, it can expand jurisdiction *only by creating new methods* for the reclamation of authority. It must imagine the means of reclamation, strategize the process, and then implement both the takeover and ongoing management.

In some cases, this approach involves a longer time horizon and, rather than a "work around," a "work toward"[6]—a compromise position in which a Native nation exercises partial control. It is a strategy not for circumventing a jurisdictional challenge but for facing it head-on and eventually gaining more complete jurisdiction. It is a next step from which a tribe can work toward greater authority.

An example of this choice for partial authority is the Apsáalooke (Crow) Nation's decision to use the State of Montana's filing system for registering liens against personal property. Earlier, the tribe had created its own secured transactions code, specifying the rules for using personal property as loan collateral. In Indian Country, where land ownership arrangements limit the usefulness of real property as collateral, secured transactions rules can spur small business development and strengthen tribal economies. By providing the option to secure transactions under tribal rather than state law, a tribal code also makes tribal government more relevant in citizens' lives. Apsáalooke Nation leaders recognized these advantages in passing their own code. But they also recognized that their government lacked the capacity to implement it. Tribal administrators knew they were not yet in a position to manage the complex filing system necessary to register and track collateral. The tribal government also needed to establish a record of fair dealing in loan disputes in order to assure the lending market of its objectivity. Until these additional tasks (creating new administrative systems, proving the trustworthiness of tribal processes for loan adjudication) were accomplished, the Apsáalooke Nation needed a system for filing liens. It opted to enter into a compact with the state of Montana to use the state system. In part, the agreement reads:

> Whereas, the Tribe wishes to engage the Office of the Secretary [of the state of Montana] to provide a central filing system ("Central Filing System") in order to serve as the place (the "Central Filing

Office") for lenders to file financing statements to perfect security interests in personal property collateral that arise under the Tribal Act, and to provide certain administrative services relating thereto...." (Crow Tribe and Montana Secretary of State 2012)

In other words, this isn't full tribal control; Montana shares in the administration of this service. But this is still the exercise of practical self-determination, which the research shows is a fundamental underpinning for Indigenous community development success. It is self-determination because the arrangement ends full state authority over secured transactions. It is self-determination because the Native nation itself created the new legal regime. It is self-determination rather than colonization because the nation had the ability to give—and then gave—its consent to another government's authority. Eventually, the Apsáalooke Nation may opt to develop its own filing system, but until then, this is a good means of working towards that possible outcome.

A second complexity that Indigenous nations must address in the current environment for self-determination is the fact that some remaining opportunities to reclaim authority are more sensibly managed by multiple nations (or multiple governments) working together. Rationales for *not* "going it alone" include economies of scale, better management of conflicts of interest, and opportunities to leverage resources.

For example, a number of tribes in the northwestern United States banded together in 1979 to create the Northwest Indian Court System (NICS) (NICS 2012, HPAIED 2003). Many of the founding tribes are small in terms of population and, at least at NICS's inception, did not need—and could not afford—an array of full-time court personnel. By providing trial and appeals court judges, juvenile court judges, clerks, public defenders, lay advocates, code writers, and trainers whom tribes could employ on a part-time, full-time, short-term, or long-term basis, NICS offered a way for each nation to quickly formalize a full-service judicial system. In other words, NICS provided a means of institution sharing that made it possible for each tribe to reap the benefits of a full-service system. For NICS member nations, justice services are most effectively managed through organization on a larger, multi-tribe scale—yet each tribe is exercising practical sovereignty by no longer relying on non-Indian governments to provide court services and by freely making its own decision about how to secure those services.

In the mid-2000s, at meetings convened by the Union of Ontario Indians (2004) to address the development of its members' (forty-three First Nations in east-central Canada) emerging justice systems, delegates quickly identified conflict of interest as a reason to collaborate across First Nation governments. They raised questions about "how to develop creative solutions in addressing issues of conflict of interest where many First Nations are small and related by family" (7). But they soon concluded that "members would feel comfortable with an appeals and redress system outside of their own First Nation," "there is a need for a regional system," and "issues which cannot be addressed at a First Nation level may be addressed at an Anishinabek Nation level" (12; also see Morrison n.d., 19–21). In other words, these First Nations could administer true justice only by collaborating with each other.[7]

The Flandreau Santee Sioux Tribe collaborated not with another Native nation but with the city of Flandreau, South Dakota, to create a joint city–tribal police department. The checkerboarded reservation complicated law enforcement as officers and offenders frequently crossed onto and out of tribal land, and depending on the geography, different criminal justice rules prevailed. Worse, neither the city nor the tribe had adequate resources to effectively operate its own police department. By joining forces, the tribe and city were able to address the region's complex jurisdictional issues, pool their funds, and make the most of their joint staff, administrative, infrastructural, and financial resources.

In each of these examples, Native nations are exercising self-governance—they are making self-determined choices about how government functions will be managed on behalf of their citizens—although they are not doing (or are not planning to do) all of the work themselves. In fact, the examples highlight the various arrangements an Indigenous government might pursue to accomplish the tasks of government, arrangements that are a greater aspect of self-determination today than they were twenty years ago:

- A nation may opt to work in partnership with another government or governments (which may be Indigenous or not).

- It may opt to have an external government (Indigenous or non-Indigenous) carry out the function (a choice that might include leaving a function with an external government, compacting with an external government to take on a particular function, or shifting functional management from one external government to another).

- It may contract with a non-governmental organization to provide the service.

Can't a Tribe Have Capable Institutions While Still Allowing Elected Officials to Make Business Management Decisions?

Key advice concerning the structure of governing institutions that emerges from the nation-building approach is to separate business decision making from political decision making. In other words, running a business and representing a constituency are two different jobs, and tribes—and their businesses—fare better when the two are not mixed.

The evidence for this point comes from three primary sources. The first is an extensive and persuasive set of anecdotes that demonstrate the greater chances of business success when political priorities are not part of the management equation.[8] For example, they include the comparison—within a single Native nation—of a tribally owned electronics firm with an independent board of directors that was able to sustain profitability over many years with a post-and-pole business operating under the tribal council's direction, which ultimately faced crippling labour costs.

The second source of evidence was presented in its initial form in "Reloading the Dice" (Cornell and Kalt 1992, 32). Results of an informal poll of tribal leaders and program managers showed that tribally owned businesses were much more likely to succeed if they had an independent board of directors, as opposed to a tribal council acting as a de facto board. Today, the Native Nations Institute uses the following table, summarizing still more responses, to make the point:

Table 1. The Advantages of the "Separated Model"[9]

Enterprise Status	Council-Run Model	Separated Model
Profitable	31	48
Not Profitable	32	10
Ratio of Profitable to Not Profitable	1:1	5:1
% Profitable	49%	83%

Source: Executive Education curriculum, Native Nations Institute, University of Arizona, Tucson, 2013.

Econometric analysis offers a third source of proof. Both Jorgensen and Taylor (2000), which considers a broad range of both tribal and non-tribal Indian-owned businesses, and Hoberg et al. (2008), which looks more narrowly at First Nations–owned forestry enterprises, demonstrate that measures of political separation are strongly correlated with greater business profitability, even after controlling for other variables relevant to business success. Jorgensen and Taylor additionally demonstrate that businesses free from political influence are more likely to generate sustained employment.

Nonetheless, Native nations continue to struggle with the advice that businesses should be removed from political control. In part this is because of the stark way the advice has been summarized; "separation of business from politics" often has been understood as an arrangement that bars elected officials from having any role in enterprise management. But when leaders of First Nations and tribes and the principals of their businesses say, "That doesn't fit with how we need to do things. We actually do have elected officials on our board and it works really well," it pays to ask a follow-up question: "What is the practical influence those leaders have?" Many times, elected officials hold seats on the board, in a voting or ex officio capacity, without having determinative power over board decisions.

The chief executive officer of Ho-Chunk, Inc., the Winnebago Tribe of Nebraska's storied corporation, is one such dissenter. He posits that the strictest form of separation is unnecessary, but answers the follow-up question with the explanation that only two of the five seats on the company's board of directors are reserved for tribal council members. Two of five are too few to change corporate policy on their own but enough to aid in council–company communication. The two councillors bring the tribe's political directions for the company to the boardroom and return information about the company's activities to the council. In fact, this organizational arrangement is one of several lines of mandated communication between the corporate and political bodies established in Ho-Chunk, Inc.'s charter. Such mechanisms provide opportunities for politicians and business leaders to gather information, express concerns, communicate triumphs, and so on, increasing the probability that the corporation remains aligned with the strategic direction set by the nation's elected representatives (Ash Center 2001; HPAIED 2008, 124–25; Dreeszen 2012; Ho-Chunk Inc. 2013).

The leader of a British Columbia First Nation is another such dissenter. He has stressed to us that small community size is the reason his band has politicians—or at least politically connected individuals—on its corporate board. In small communities, there are relatively few adults, and even fewer with interests and skills appropriate to leadership (or politics or business or other community organizations), and relationships tend to be dense—everyone is connected to everyone else. Strict conflict-of-interest rules are difficult to apply in such settings, and a business's board may reflect these difficulties. Again, however, many small tribes and First Nations respond to this situation with "good corporate housekeeping" rules that establish (for example) limits on the number of politicians serving, reporting requirements to ensure transparency about relationships, and standards for recusing oneself from decision making.

Grant and Taylor (2007) explore these ideas in depth and offer a better summary phrase to describe the institutional ideal. Rather than a "separation" between business and politics, they refer to "managing the boundary" between business and politics. Their more nuanced version of the nation-building principle is that there is a greater probability of sustained enterprise success when there is an effectively managed boundary between business and politics.[10]

When other tribal leaders and the principals of their businesses say, "That doesn't fit with how we need to do things, we have elected officials on our board and it works well," they answer the follow-on question about the practical influence of tribal elected officials quite differently. They say, "Well, our council is our board, and that works for us." Sometimes they also point to their tribal enterprise's success—its remarkable profit levels, significant corporate growth, and capacity to generate substantial benefits for the nation. Have they proven the nation-building principle wrong?

The answer is no. The empirical evidence in support of separation is diverse, compelling, and accurate. Numerous tribal corporations are growing their profits, their nations' economies, and tribal government revenues because—or at least in part because—they are free to make market rather than political decisions. Some are clear that the shift away from political management has been the key to ending ongoing drains on corporate budgets and moving towards positive balance sheets.[11] Even the cases of managed boundaries rather than full separation reinforce the finding rather than disprove it, as the rules put in place to manage the boundary emphasize how important separate roles are.

So how can the case be made in those nations where a lack of full or managed separation is still the established arrangement? Certainly, some politicians may be unwilling to give up the opportunity to use the nation's businesses to dispense political favours; it remains unclear how to change their minds. But others may be wrestling with a more tractable problem: the lack of evidence *in their particular case* that changing the institutional structure would be good for the nation. For them, an exploration of the counterfactual may be helpful: what would happen if they were not in charge?

During a 2012 conversation on this topic with appointed and elected leadership of an Ojibwa nation that I helped facilitate, discussion was both considered and laced with humour. In response to the enterprise CEO's impassioned defence of the tribal council as the corporate board, a defence that included very specific citations of how well the business was doing, another tribal employee quipped, "But just think of how much *better* we'd be doing if the council was not involved!" There was laughter and an emerging sense that this just might be an issue the nation ought to address.

Tribal leaders might also usefully remember that the need for rules does not necessarily arise from their own behaviour but from the unpredictable behaviour of future elected leaders. Today's politicians may constitute a talented corporate board. But what of tomorrow's? Rules concerning separation may prevent future leaders from using the nation's enterprises for their own purposes and help protect the gains made from current enterprise success.[12] What legacy do today's leaders want to leave? Will they be remembered for their business acumen, or for their failure to establish a set of rules and community expectations about how the nation's assets should be managed?

Twenty years on, the advice to separate business from politics remains sound. Successful implementation requires a persuasive argument for change, a set of rules that fit the nation's needs, and a commitment on the part of a nation's political and corporate leaders to live the rules—to re-enact them—every day.

How Can a Native Nation Pursue Cultural Match in its Institutions and Practices?

Constitution writing is currently an area of intense activity among both First Nations and American Indian nations. In Canada, an increasing number of opportunities to escape all or part of the Indian Act are a primary driver. In the United States, Native nations are realizing that wholesale reform (writing a brand new constitution) often is preferable to making adjustments around the edges of so-called Indian Reorganization Act constitutions.

Given this concentrated activity, many Native nations have new opportunities to explore the meaning of cultural match for their government structures. The nation-building principle is that cultural match is a means of institutional legitimacy: citizens are more likely to adhere to political institutions (rules) that match their community's conceptions of how political authority ought to be distributed and exercised. As a result, government is more likely to produce results for citizens.

But what arrangements really constitute cultural match? Does honouring tribal culture mean that all "Western" governing mechanisms are suspect? Does cultural match mean returning to the political arrangements the nation had before the Indian Act (Canada) or Indian Reorganization Act (USA) took effect? Does it mean going back even further, to a pre-contact type of political organization?[13]

These questions have been the subject of intense debate in many Native communities, yet the answer to each one is only "maybe." There is no standard test of "Indigeneity" for governing institutions. There is no time period everyone can look to and say, "In general, cultural match is achieved by looking at what was going on then." The answers are unique, and only an individual nation can work out the contours of cultural match for itself.

Fortunately, several principles offer general guidance:

1. **Reflect on Everyday Life:** It can be hard to spot your own culture. Like your own accent (or lack of one!), you don't notice it until you are exposed to something different. To you, it's just the way things are. This reality can make conversations about the "cultural match" of constitutional principles difficult; a search begins for the odd or different. People may end up saying, "There's nothing special about our culture," or go to the other extreme and talk about "what the [non-Native] anthropologists said." Without uttering the words "government" or "culture," a more productive conversation might have community participants consider questions such as: When you were growing up—or when your parents or grandparents were younger—how did the community make decisions? How did it choose between conflicting ideas? How did it deal with disputes? Who was responsible for carrying out community decisions? How did people know what their roles were? These queries start to reveal cultural ideas about governance—which people otherwise may not have identified because they simply were the everyday way of doing things.

2. **Acknowledge That Culture Changes:** Richard Luarkie, governor of Laguna Pueblo, has noted that only recently have women been

selected as political leaders of the pueblo. All past history would identify their service as an illegitimate form of leadership. But Governor Luarkie instead has explained that women's new role is evidence of culture changing—on Laguna's terms, in Laguna's way—and that it is not the first time Laguna political culture has evolved. He points to the changes made in response to the Spanish invasion, to the Pueblo revolt, and to impositions by the American government. The Laguna have lived in a geography now known as western New Mexico for hundreds of generations, and their chosen ways of exercising self-rule have changed in response both to the specific challenges the pueblo has faced and to the changing sense among the population of what is proper and right (Luarkie 2012). Being too bound to the past in the quest for cultural match suggests that culture lives in display cases instead of in relationships among community members—a suggestion that surely is not true.[14]

3. **Ask the Right Question:** The most prominent landmark in my home city—St. Louis, Missouri—is the Gateway Arch. It marks the confluence of the Missouri and Mississippi rivers as a key access point to the American west for European colonizers. St. Louis was a fulcrum of North America's southern fur trade in the eighteenth century; it was the first major United States outpost of Belgian and French Jesuits seeking to bring their brand of religion and learning to the western populations; and it was the site from which Meriwether Lewis and William Clark embarked with their Corps of Discovery. It is a common "suppose" in our family to imagine what life in the American west would have been like in the absence of our city and the changes that the masses passing through it perpetrated for Indigenous peoples. What would the history of Native people have been if American expansion had stopped at this point rather than surged through the gate? Western Indigenous nations still would have had to deal with the Americans and other new migrants, but as neighbouring governments rather than occupiers. These nations still would have progressed apace into the nineteenth, twentieth, and twenty-first centuries, responding to new geopolitical alignments, new technologies, and the opportunities

of business and trade. For Native nations that today are considering cultural match in the (re)construction of their political institutions, this suppose exercise is useful. It gets to the right question: How would each Native nation's government have developed (what would it have looked like? how would it have been structured?) had it continued on the path it was on before colonial interruptions?

4. **Don't Issue a Blank Cheque:** Cultural match with "a blank cheque" would mean that any set of political institutions that matches a nation's cultural ideas of how authority should be distributed and exercised is acceptable for that nation. But this approach ignores the fact that the test for appropriate Indigenous political institutions is a twin test. Not only must nations ask, "Do the institutions have cultural legitimacy?" but they must also ask, "Are they effective?" In other words, cultural match is tempered by the need for institutions that work in the current environment. Are the institutions capable of meeting contemporary demands for intergovernmental relationships, economic development, community education, dispute resolution, and social service provision, among other concerns? If not, the cultural form must be modified and a new form engineered. Then the process of determining this new form is the key component of legitimacy: Is the process Indigenously chosen? Is the range of possible governing structures under the control of the Indigenous community? (Cornell 2007, 71–77).

5. **Allow for Structured Breathing Room:** One characteristic of the United States constitution may provide valuable guidance to Indigenous constitution drafters concerned about the creation of culturally legitimate institutions: its length. While the United States constitution describes an entire structure for government, it is nonetheless fairly brief, leaving much to be worked out through its use. In other words, the American framers left the door open for questions about the legitimate structure and conduct of government. Over time, these questions have played out as cases of legislative, executive, and state action and of constitutional interpretation by the United States Supreme Court; each action or case has served to clarify the constitution and organically hone cultural

match (especially through the application and development of common law, which is found in previous case law and in custom and tradition). Of course, this process of refinement through interpretation only works if the checks and balances in the constitution are robust enough to prevent unscrupulous individuals from controlling government in its entirety, in which case questions concerning the legitimate operation of government might never be aired. But if a balance is struck between relatively open weave[15] constitutional language and very clear separations of power,[16] a constitution can create structured breathing room for its own implementation: some aspects of government are left to be worked out, allowing more time for cultural considerations to enter in. Certainly, if the nation decides to do so, it can then institutionalize these ways of doing business in a constitutional amendment.[17]

While this section has concentrated on constitution writing and reform as a reason that the idea of cultural match in nation building remains a front-and-centre issue for American Indian nations and First Nations, other Indigenous government innovations also emphasize its currency. For example, some Indigenous nations apply the legitimacy test to governing institutions below the constitutional level—in their bureaucracies, law enforcement divisions, social service delivery programs, and so on—in an attempt to strengthen the rule of law (Begay et al. 2001; Brimley et al. 2007) or improve overall program functioning (Cornell et al. 2013; Jorgensen 2004).

How Can Native Nations Stay on a Strategic Path That Looks to the Seventh Generation?

Planning is a familiar activity in American Indian and First Nations communities. Sometimes it occurs because a non-Indian government requires it for funding purposes, sometimes it is a response to an economic opportunity or revenue windfall, and sometimes a tribe or First Nation uses planning as a way to gain control over its future. It may result from a mixture of these reasons.

Often, Native nation and First Nation plans address specific activities or target areas: housing, natural resource management, economic development, health care, or education. Some of these plans have had high value for Native nations. They have helped them sustain resources, rejuvenate eroding assets, and build new community assets. For example, because they planned effectively, the Menominee Nation and Confederated Salish and Kootenai Tribes have healthy forests that will produce revenue and other amenities over the long term (Berry 2009; Nesper and Pecor 1993; Trosper 2007). The Cherokee Nation has new, young cohorts of Cherokee-language speakers (HPAIED 2005). The Swinomish Indian Tribal Community has authority over all lands and waters within its checkerboarded reservation (HPAIED 2000; Zaferatos 2004). And the Tulalip Tribes have successfully addressed the interrelated problems of crime, substance abuse, and youth disaffection (HPAIED 2006).

A key factor in these plans' success is their true seventh-generation nature: they embrace broad principles of nationhood and sustainability. To insert the principle of nationhood into strategic planning is to recognize that "seventh generation" is a plural noun. It does not refer to a single individual's future or that individual's family's prospects; it refers to the *nation's* future and *all future citizens'* prospects. Seventh-generation planning doesn't simply ask what is desired for a particular resource in the future; it also asks how choices the nation faces today affect the survival of the tribe as a collective body. To insert the principle of sustainability into strategic planning is to recognize that only through deliberate behaviour today—behaviour that may come with certain short-term costs—will a people (a nation) reach the future they desire. Caring for the seventh generation may mean that some citizens are less well off today than they might have been if an alternative strategy had been pursued. Maybe, for example, they would have been monetarily richer if the tribe had developed a piece of land according to its highest dollar return, or cut all the timber this year that it could have sold, or invested less staff time in learning new techniques and more in generating current profits, and so on.

Yet these two elements—an understanding that decisions today can affect the survival of the nation, and that survival may mean leaving some value in the ground, in the bank, or otherwise with the tribe—tend to be missing from one of the most common types of plans Native communities make: revenue distribution plans.

By virtue of American Indian nations' and First Nations' success at flexing their self-government muscles, they increasingly are in the position of having significant amounts of cash available on a one-time or ongoing (but not unlimited) basis. This revenue may originate in legal settlements, royalty payments, or enterprise revenues. To their credit, many tribes do have some sort of plan for how to use the money. But perhaps to their discredit, many of these plans also include significant per capita payouts to Native citizens.

The reasons for these payouts are diverse. For example, because so many Native communities and individuals in the USA and Canada have low incomes, per capita distributions to citizens may be a way to help them make ends meet. In some cases, tribal and First Nation governments do not have a good record of using money well, and distributing it to citizens may seem like better stewardship. Economists (with a degree of libertarian zeal) might argue that individual citizens have a better sense of the highest and best use of these dollars than do governments. But some reasons for distribution are less laudable, and certainly less strategic in a seventh-generation sense. Pressure for per capita payments may arise simply because the resource under consideration is so fungible (money is easier to imagine distributing than is a stand of timber or coal from a mine); or because politicians see the promise of distributions (or higher distributions) as a quick way to win votes; or because the population is demanding their "rights as members" rather than thinking about their "responsibilities as citizens" (Cornell et al. 2007b).

But all of these reasons—whether good, bad, or neither—tend to underscore the absence of seventh-generation thought and the considerable urgency of community-wide strategic thinking and planning. Without it, nations will find it difficult to pull back from the process of dissipating the nation's estate (that is, their overall national assets).

The challenge is for Indigenous nations to find a way to back far enough away from the question of "What do we do with this money?" to be able to consider the bigger-picture questions of "Who are we?" and "Where do we want to go?" As shown in Table 2, they need to find a way to shift the conversation and community view of the resources from an individual/present focus to a collective/future focus.[18]

Table 2. A Shift in Thinking

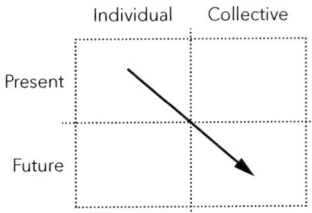

Source: Cornell et al. 2007b.

How to accomplish such thinking—and, ultimately, create a seventh-generation strategic plan for the nation's financial resources that leaders and citizens will follow—is a difficult question. Community-wide educational processes undertaken ahead of planning conversations can make a difference. Messaging from community and elected leaders can help as well. In both instances, the fact that this is the nation's money, not individual money, should be emphasized. Processes that allow citizens to reach these conclusions themselves (so that they are epiphanies rather than the result of scoldings) may be best of all.

The leaders of the Citizen Potawatomi Nation have thought about this problem a lot. Their nation's wealth built slowly, so they have had the advantage of implementing strategic planning via the nation's budget process instead of having to deal with a sudden new revenue windfall or income stream. In so doing, they have worked to commit new revenues to government development, programs, and services that have tangible results for citizens. Now, when citizens ask, "Where is my per capita revenue distribution?" the nation's leaders are able to say, "It's in the health care centre, the lacrosse fields, our scholarships, our justice system, our community housing, our home purchase down payment assistance..."

The Mashantucket Pequot Nation experienced a more painful transition to community/future thinking. When the global financial crisis hit in 2008–9, the nation's casino became over-leveraged. The situation was dire; it was clear to the Pequot that if they did not change their financial position quickly, they were at risk of losing even their sense of identity as a nation. In 2010, the tribe's leaders announced an end to the per capita payments that had propelled many tribal citizens to great individual wealth; payments were completely phased out by 2012. With change and a substantially revised revenue plan, the nation is today on a more sustainable financial path. (More information on this story can be found in Administrator, American Indian Report 2010; Hallenbeck 2012; and ICTMN Staff 2012.)

Yet neither of these cases really answers the question of how to educate citizens and political leaders or to help them make and stick to seventh-generation plans. The Citizen Potawatomi Nation example, while instructive, doesn't provide illustration of how to work through community education and make an adherence-inspiring community plan. And no nation really wants to experience the shock therapy delivered to Mashantucket Pequot. What this discussion most clearly points to is a critical need for new research. Because revenue distribution questions are a persistent part of life in Indigenous communities, what else can help them make the shift from short-term to long-term thinking, and from addressing individual issues to addressing broad community concerns?[19]

Concluding Remarks

So how do the nation-building findings really fare twenty years on? They're still applicable. They're still meaningful. They're still useful. In fact, many issues that Indigenous nations face today argue for ongoing application of the findings and for issue- and topic-specific extensions of the research.

The Harvard Project and Native Nations Institute have done some of that work, and this paper points to publications with relevant information and insights. We will continue in these efforts. But much work remains to be done, a conclusion that suggests a research agenda for others: rather than working to disprove the nation-building findings or dismissing them as irrelevant or too old, academics, policy analysts, and consultants interested in Indigenous political organization and community development should concentrate on generating data about how to use the findings and how to answer new questions their implementation raises.

Our goal and the goal of other academics, analysts, and consultants in the field should be to get as much nation-building information into the hands of Indigenous nation leaders as possible, helping them jump-start and sustain the benefits of a nation-building orientation.[20] We also do well to remember that data in support of nation building is a powerful persuasive tool in the non-Native world. Armed with research results, we can stand in partnership with tribes and First Nations in reminding external governments' policy-makers—many of whom continue to devise policies aimed at colonizing and assimilating Indigenous peoples—that Indigenous nation building is the best pathway towards mutually desired improvements in socio-economic conditions.

Of course, the most important future work lies not with researchers and policy analysts but with Indigenous leaders—and leadership is the component of nation building not yet discussed in this essay. Nation-building leadership has brought the nations wrestling with these complex, second-wave nation-building issues to where they are today. Their efforts have laid bare the need for a more nuanced approach to self-governance and self-determination, for a managed boundary between business and politics, for a reflective search for cultural match in institution building, and for new tools to bridge the divide between individual-benefit politics and strategic planning. That same public-spiritedness is required to address these concerns. It is the job of community and political leaders to bring new thinking about nation building into their communities, to apply it in appropriate ways to meet their nations' needs, to tell the story of how things can be different, and to stick with the changes that work.

Notes

1. Miriam Jorgensen is the research director of the Harvard Project on American Indian Economic Development and of its sister organization, the Native Nations Institute for Leadership, Management, and Policy at the University of Arizona. She has been an affiliate of the Harvard Project since 1989.

2. Some refer to the Harvard study as a single piece of work; it is not. The Harvard Project is a research, policy analysis, and outreach organization, which, along with its sister institution, the Native Nations Institute at the University of Arizona, continues to research nation building and create usable tools for Indigenous nations. The organizations have conducted multiple studies and research projects and have produced more than two hundred papers, reports, and advisory documents for Native nations and Native-serving organizations.

3. The point is also evident among the numerous tribes who have received "Honoring Nations" awards. See Honoring Contributions in the Governance of American Indian Nations, part of the Harvard Project on American Indian Economic Development, at http://www.hpaied.org/honoring-nations/about-honoring-nations, retrieved November 19, 2012.

4. The results were startling because of their descriptive summary: Native nations whose activities reflect nation-building principles also evidence more effective use of resources, more economic and community development, and a stronger defence of tribal sovereignty. They were provocative because they offered an evidentiary defence of tribal self-determination and sovereignty (previously, the arguments in support of self-determination were legal and moral, but this research showed that self-determination paid off for Indigenous welfare), and because of their possible prescriptive power (the principles point to necessary—although not sufficient—ingredients for the creation of a political-economic environment conducive to self-determined Indigenous community progress).

5. In the United States, many transfers took place under the guidelines laid out in Public Law 93-638 (1975) and its amendments. In Canada, many fiscal transfers took place through contribution agreements and multi-year funding agreements between Canada and First Nations.

6. I have borrowed the term "work toward" from Jeff Davis, Assistant United States Attorney, Western District of Michigan. Personal communication, September 10, 2012.

7. The Union of Ontario Indians' discussions also point to a related observation. Sometimes effective self-rule can occur only as Indigenous nations "reconstitute" themselves as larger communities that reflect more functional pre-colonial societies (Cornell 2013a).

8. As a colleague has quipped, "This cascade of anecdotes is so extensive that even an academic might be able to see that there's something of significance going on here." My own first site visit on behalf of the Harvard Project on American Indian Economic Development in autumn 1989 generated one such anecdote. On a tour of a Great Plains tribal community seeking assistance in valuing economic losses from Missouri River flooding, my guide (a tribal citizen and economic development expert) told me that in his tenure, the tribal government had started twenty-nine businesses, all under tribal council management, and only one remained open.

9. If the data from note 10 were added to Table 1, the "% profitable" entry for the council-run model would fall to 35 percent.

10. Improved communication is an important reason for a managed boundary, but not the only one. In small nations, where relatively few individuals are available to manage businesses and govern the nation, it might be impossible to construct an enterprise board that is free of political relationships (most citizens who might sit on the board would have a significant kinship relationship to at least one politician). In such cases, a managed boundary may be the only choice.

11. One such example is found at http://www.osageshareholders.org/_disc73/00000155.htm, retrieved February 16, 2013.

12. Even if those future councils end up installing themselves as boards of directors anyway, the fact that rules had to be changed may slow their actions down a little.

13. While these questions accept the validity of constitutionalism, some critics argue that constitutions themselves are non-Indigenous and suggest that "real cultural match" is to forgo a constitution altogether. But this argument misses a key point. All human societies that persist and produce value for their citizens have governing rules. These rules, even if they are unwritten, are constitutions. Given this understanding, constitutions are not non-Indigenous creations, they are *human* creations. See Cornell 2013b and Cornell, Curtis, and Jorgensen 2004.

14. This guidance may be especially helpful for nations that experienced significant cultural losses through colonization—through forced removal from Indigenous lands, forced placement in boarding schools, and necessary accommodations to colonizers' religions. *All* commun-

ities' cultures evolve. It may not be necessary to be fully conversant in historical ways for citizens to understand what the community's Indigenous governance culture is *today*.

15. "A weave in which warp threads never come together, leaving interstices in the fabric." Free Online Dictionary, http://www.thefreedictionary.com/open+weave, retrieved February 16, 2013.

16. This also can be referred to as "allocations of responsibility." Thus, "checks and balances," "separations of power," and "allocations of responsibility" are all versions of the same idea: no one part of government should have so much responsibility and control that the office bearer in that position can usurp the functions of government for his or her own purposes. (My thanks to Don Wharton of the Native American Rights Fund for suggesting "allocations of responsibility" as an alternative term; personal communication August 2010.)

17. This point has both a present and a future dimension. For the present, framers can rely on constitutional cases to help solidify cultural match, putting less pressure on themselves to work out all the nuances for their generation. Looking to the future, the process helps accommodate cultural change as well; it can be addressed through the application of common law, which evolves with culture, to each newly raised constitutional test. In sum, constitutional interpretation is both a means of and an opportunity for applying contemporary custom and tradition.

18. A version of this table first appeared in Cornell et al. 2007b.

19. While this section has focused on the potential of per capita financial payments to foster "get yours now" political pressures, other resource distributions can do the same thing. For example, the pressure to distribute land in some First Nations communities has the same flavour of member entitlement. Here too, the individual/present orientation has the potential to put the very future of the nation at risk.

20. There is a convergence between this point and the point made in the final paragraph. The best way to get nation-building information into the hands of Indigenous leaders is through education and professional development. Such training will help tribal and First Nation leaders discern and implement the most appropriate strategies for governance—and nation—strengthening. Education and professional development programs in Indigenous nation building have been part and parcel

of the Harvard Project and Native Nation Institute's work since the mid-1990s, and a number of related programs are now on offer or under development across the United States and Canada.

References

Administrator, American Indian Report. 2010. "Mashantucket Pequot Eliminates Per Cap Payments to Members." *American Indian Report.* July 10. Accessed June 11, 2014. http://www.americanindianreport.com/wordpress/2010/07/mashantucket-pequot-eliminates-per-cap-payments-to-members/.

Ash Center for Democratic Governance and Innovation. 2001. "Ho-Chunk, Inc." Harvard Kennedy School, Cambridge. Accessed June 11, 2014. http://www.innovations.harvard.edu/awards.html?id=3675.

Begay, Manley, Stephen Cornell, Miriam Jorgensen, and Nathan Pryor. 2007. "Rebuilding Native Nations: What Do Leaders Do." In *Rebuilding Native Nations: Strategies for Governance and Development,* edited by Miriam Jorgensen, 275–95. Tucson: University of Arizona Press.

Begay, Manley, Miriam Jorgensen, Susan Michaelson, and Stewart Wakeling. 2001. *Policing on American Indian Reservations: A Report to the National Institute of Justice.* Washington, DC: National Institute of Justice, United States Department of Justice.

Berry, Alison. 2009. "Two Forests Under the Big Sky: Tribal v. Federal Management," PERC Policy Series No. 45. Bozeman, MT: PERC.

Brimley, Stephen, Stephen Cornell, Joseph Thomas Flies-Away, Miriam Jorgensen, and Rachel Starks. 2007. "Resurgent Justice: Rebuilding the Mohawk Justice System." Tucson: Native Nations Institute, Udall Center for Studies in Public Policy, University of Arizona.

Caves, Richard E., and Matthew B. Krepps. 1994. "Bureaucrats and Indians: Principal–Agent Relations and Efficient Management of Tribal Forest Resources." *Journal of Economic Behavior and Organization* 24 (July): 133–51.

Champagne, Duane, and Carole Goldberg. 2012. *Captured Justice: Native Nations and Public Law 280.* Durham: Carolina Academic Press.

Cornell, Stephen. 2007. "Remaking the Tools of Governance: Colonial Legacies, Indigenous Solutions." In *Rebuilding Native Nations: Strategies for Governance and Development,* edited by Miriam Jorgensen, 57–77. Tucson: University of Arizona Press.

——. 2013a. "Reconstituting Native Nations: Colonial Boundaries and Institutional Innovation in Canada, Australia, and the United States." In *Reclaiming Indigenous Planning*, edited by Ted Jojola, David Natcher, and Ryan Walker. Montreal: McGill-Queen's University Press.

——. 2013b. "'Wolves Have a Constitution': Continuities in Indigenous Self-Government." Unpublished paper. Tucson: Native Nations Institute, Udall Center for Studies in Public Policy, University of Arizona.

Cornell, Stephen, and Joseph P. Kalt. 1992. "Reloading the Dice: Improving the Chances for Economic Development on American Indian Reservations." In *What Can Tribes Do? Strategies and Institutions in American Indian Economic Development*, edited by Stephen Cornell and Joseph P. Kalt, 1–59. Los Angeles: American Indian Studies Center, University of California, Los Angeles.

——. 1993. "Culture as Explanation in Racial and Ethnic Inequality: American Indians, Reservation Poverty, and Collective Action." Report 93-2, Project Report Series. Cambridge, Massachusetts: Harvard Project on American Indian Economic Development, John F. Kennedy School of Government, Harvard University.

——. 1995. "Where Does Economic Development Really Come From? Constitutional Rule Among the Contemporary Sioux and Apache." *Economic Inquiry* 33 (July): 402–26.

——. 1997. "Successful Economic Development and Heterogeneity of Governmental Form on American Indian Reservations." In *Getting Good Government: Capacity Building in the Public Sectors of Developing Countries*, edited by Merilee S. Grindle, 257–96. Cambridge, Massachusetts: Harvard Institute for International Development.

——. 1998. "Sovereignty and Nation-Building: The Development Challenge in Indian Country Today." *American Indian Culture and Research Journal* 22 (3): 187–214.

——. 2000. "Where's the Glue: Institutional and Cultural Foundations of American Indian Economic Development." *Journal of Socio-Economics* 29: 443–70.

——. 2007. "Two Approaches to the Development of Native Nations: One Works, the Other Doesn't." In *Rebuilding Native Nations: Strategies for Governance and Development*, edited by Miriam Jorgensen, 3–33. Tucson: University of Arizona Press.

Cornell, Stephen, Catherine Curtis, and Miriam Jorgensen. 2004. "The Concept of Governance and Its Implications for First Nations." *Joint Occasional Papers on Native Affairs*, No. 2004-02. Tucson and Cambridge, MA: Native Nations Institute for Leadership, Management, and Policy, and Harvard Project on American Indian Economic Development.

Cornell, Stephen, Miriam Jorgensen, Joseph P. Kalt, and Katherine Spilde Contreras. 2007a. "Seizing the Future: Why Some Native Nations Do and Others Don't." In *Rebuilding Native Nations: Strategies for Governance and Development*, edited by Miriam Jorgensen, 296–320. Tucson: University of Arizona Press.

Cornell, Stephen, Miriam Jorgensen, Stephanie Carroll Rainie, and Rachel Starks. 2013. "Self-Determination and Native American Health Care: The Shift to Tribal Control." Unpublished paper. Tucson: Native Nations Institute, Udall Center for Studies in Public Policy, University of Arizona.

Cornell, Stephen, Miriam Jorgensen, Stephanie Carroll Rainie, Ian Record, Ryan Seelau, and Rachel Starks. 2007b. "Per Capita Distributions of American Indian Tribal Revenues: A Preliminary Discussion of Policy Considerations." Tucson: Native Nations Institute, University of Arizona.

Crow Tribe of Indians and Montana Secretary of State. 2012. "Compact between Crow Tribe of Indians/Apsaalooke Nation and Office of the Montana Secretary of State for a Joint Sovereign Filing System." Crow Agency and Helena, Montana.

Dixon, Mim, Cynthia Mala Smith, David Mather, Yvette Roubideaux, and Brett Lee Shelton. 1998. *Tribal Perspectives on Indian Self-Determination and Self-Governance in Health Care Management*. Denver: National Indian Health Board.

Dreeszen, Dave. 2012. "Ho-Chunk, Inc. has grown into global enterprise." *Sioux City Journal*. May 31. Accessed June 11, 2014. http://siouxcityjournal.com/news/local/a1/ho-chunk-inc-has-grown-into-global-enterprise/article_cdb7f26f-3442-5839-9ae8-4698b7856422.html?comment_form=true.

Grant, Kenneth, and Jonathan B. Taylor. 2007. "Managing the Boundary between Business and Politics: Strategies for Improving the Chances for Success in Tribally Owned Enterprises." In *Rebuilding Native Nations: Strategies for Governance and Development*, edited by Miriam Jorgensen, 175–96. Tucson: University of Arizona Press.

Hallenbeck, Brian. 2012. "Mashantuckets end payment to tribal members." The Day: Connecticut. March 2. Accessed June 11, 2014. http://www.theday.com/article/20120302/NWS01/303029924/1018.

Hoberg, George, Harry Nelson, William Nikolakis, Peggy Smith, and Ronald L. 2008. "Institutional Determinants of Profitable Commercial Forestry Enterprises among First Nations in Canada." *Canadian Journal of Forest Research* 38: 226–38.

Ho-Chunk Inc. 2013. "Corporate Profile: Board of Directors." Accessed May 31. http://www.hochunkinc.com/corporateprofile/boardofdirectors.html.

HPAIED (Harvard Project on American Indian Economic Development). 2000. "Honoring Nations: 2000 Honoree." Swinomish Indian Tribal Community, LaConner, Washington. Accessed January 27, 2013. http://hpaied.org/images/resources/publibrary/Swinomish%20Cooperative%20Land%20Use%20Program.pdf.

——. 2003. "Honoring Nations: 2003 Honoree." Northwest Intertribal Court System, Mountlake Terrace, Washington. Accessed May 19, 2013. http://hpaied.org/images/resources/publibrary/Northwest%20Intertribal%20Court%20System.pdf.

——. 2005. "Honoring Nations: 2005 Honoree." The Cherokee Nation, Tahlequah, Oklahoma. Accessed January 27, 2013. http://hpaied.org/images/resources/publibrary/Cherokee%20Language%20Revitalization%20Project.pdf.

——. 2006. "Honoring Nations: 2006 Honoree." Tulalip Tribes, Tulalip, Washington. Accessed January 27, 2013. http://hpaied.org/images/resources/publibrary/Tulalip%20Alternative%20Sentencing%20Program.pdf.

——. 2008. *The State of the Native Nations: Conditions under U.S. Policies of Self-Determination.* New York: Oxford University Press.

ICTMN Staff. 2012. "Foxwoods Reaches Accord on Debt Restructuring." *Indian Country Today Media Network.* August 3. Accessed June 11, 2014. http://indiancountrytodaymedianetwork.com/2012/08/03/foxwoods-reaches-accord-debt-restructuring-127184.

Jorgensen, Miriam. 2000. "Bringing the Background Forward: Evidence from Indian Country on the Social and Cultural Determinants of Economic Development." PhD diss., Harvard University.

———. 2004. "History's Lesson for HUD and Tribes." *Joint Occasional Papers on Native Affairs,* No. 2004-01. Tucson and Cambridge: Native Nations Institute for Leadership, Management, and Policy, University of Arizona, and Harvard Project on American Indian Economic Development, Harvard University.

Jorgensen, Miriam, and Jonathan Taylor. 2000. "What Determines Indian Economic Success? Evidence from Tribal and Individual Indian Enterprises." *Red Ink* (Spring): 45–51.

Krepps, Matthew B. 1992. "Can Tribes Manage Their Own Resources? A Study of American Indian Forestry and the 638 Program." In *What Can Tribes Do? Strategies and Institutions in American Indian Economic Development,* edited by Stephen Cornell and Joseph P. Kalt, 179–203. Los Angeles: American Indian Studies Center, University of California, Los Angeles.

Luarkie, Richard. 2012. "Culture and Nation Building." Presentation at Bush Foundation Native Nation Rebuilders Program, April 10. Spearfish, South Dakota.

Morrison, Caitlin Wakara. n.d. *The 10-Year Talk: A Summary of the Restoration of Jurisdiction Community Consultation, 1998–2008.* North Bay, ON: Union of Ontario Indians.

Native Nations Institute. 2013. "Executive Education curriculum." Tucson: University of Arizona.

Nesper, Larry, and Marshall Pecore. 1993. "'The Trees Will Last Forever': The Integrity of Their Forests Signifies the Health of the Menominee People." *Cultural Survival* 17 (1): 28–31.

NICS (Northwest Intertribal Court System). 2012. "About NICS." Accessed November 9. http://www.nics.ws/.

Trosper, Ronald L. 1995. "Traditional American Indian Economic Policy." *American Indian Cultural and Research Journal* 19 (1): 65–95.

———. 2007. "Indigenous Influence on Forest Management on the Menominee Indian Reservation." *Forest Ecology and Management* 249 (2007): 134–39.

Union of Ontario Indians. 2004. "Appeals and Redress Workshops and Conference: Final Report 2004." Restoration of Jurisdiction Project. North Bay, ON: Union of Ontario Indians.

Zaferatos, Nicholas Christos. 2004. "Developing an Effective Approach to Strategic Planning for Native American Indian Reservations." *Space and Polity* 8 (1): 87–104.

Chapter 7

Aboriginal Approaches to Business Leadership and Entrepreneurship in Australia

Dennis Foley

Abstract

This chapter describes Aboriginal leadership and entrepreneurship pre- and post-colonial in case studies centred within the state of Victoria, Australia. It includes a case study of an eight-thousand-year-old Aboriginal enterprise that included trade networks extending across nearly one-third of the continent. It also describes contemporary case studies that illustrate the complexity of Aboriginal enterprise, leadership, and sustainable economic development in the Gippsland region of eastern Victoria.

A Long History of Aboriginal Enterprise in Victoria

I take time to acknowledge and thank the elders past and present for their knowledge that they have shared, with a special acknowledgement to Damien Bell and his family for their care and guidance in this research.

Aboriginal entrepreneurship and enterprise in the state of Victoria, Australia, are not new. Participation in enterprise and entrepreneurial activity for the Gunditjmara people of western Victoria dates back to over eight thousand years. There is evidence in Victoria of one of the world's oldest-known commercial hubs of farming, harvesting, and "manufacturing" in large-scale production of a value-added product. The product was distributed in standardized packaging, incorporating a supply chain and product marketing over thousands of kilometres to a consumer base estimated to number as many as ten thousand people (Builth 1996, 2000, 2002, 2004, 2006, 2009).

The Gunditjmara people's aquaculture infrastructure of dams, channels, and holding ponds, combined with their smoked eel industry, is arguably one of the oldest surviving recorded "business" undertakings known to the modern era. By its sheer size and complexity of resource management and human labour interaction in the production and distribution of product, it was a marvel of technology, leadership, ordered enterprise, and efficiency in land-use management.

Economic development and activity by Australian Aboriginal people have always been subject to opportunity recognition of potential products, their qualities, supply and demand, plus effective marketing and transportation of the product. Above all, economic development necessitated access to sustainable resources to support those involved in the chain of production and distribution. This included permanent water supplies and basic commodities, involving a ready supply of complex foods, shelter, timber, and human resources.

When these conditions have been available and sustainable, Aboriginal people have changed their patterns of social behaviour to suit the demand for the product. As an example, one coastal group refrained from spending countless hours making weapons when the surplus goods and services they already produced efficiently could be used to purchase required weapons cheaply from within their inland trade networks. This led to the obsolescence of boomerang production in some areas of Australia (Trudgen 2000). Likewise, highly valued stone axes were not made by all Aboriginal groups; rather, they were in fact crafted by artisans, and raw material and finished products were traded over vast distances.

This involved the quarrying and transport of raw material in different stages of production by distinctly different language groups. From arid desert, across temperate terrain, over hundreds of kilometres, the raw product in various stages of milling was traded until it reached the artisans in a coastal environment, who would shape the product into the finished artifact. The value added was highly prized, and the final product in turn was traded back to the original site at a considerably inflated price (Tibbert 2005).

The combination of available natural resources and opportunity recognition by Aboriginal leaders helped to determine whether a society continued to be predominantly hunter-gathering or became more entrepreneurial. The Gunditjmara are an example of the latter, which enabled them to make dramatic modifications to their natural environment and later led to a semi-sedentary existence (Builth 1996, 2000, 2002, 2004, 2006, 2009).

Other examples of Victorian Aboriginal enterprise and entrepreneurship are found during the colonial period. In March 1862, two great Aboriginal leaders, Simon Wonga and William Barak, led forty Wurundjeri, Taungurong (Goulburn River), and Boonwurrung people over the Black Spur and squatted on a traditional camping site at Badger Creek, near what is now called Healesville, requesting ownership of the site. They were concerned at the loss of their land and were anxious to have this land officially approved by the state so they could move down and establish themselves. A small area of land was finally gazetted on June 30, 1863, and called Coranderrk, at their request. They started with a population of around forty people; by 1865, this had grown to 105, making it Victoria's largest Aboriginal reserve at the time. Within four years the mission's residents had cleared much of the property to develop a competitive farming community.

Coranderrk's first manager, John Green, worked closely with the Aboriginal leaders to build housing and plant crops of hops, wheat, and vegetables. By the mid-1870s, Coranderrk had become a large village with a schoolhouse, bakery, and butcher. The growing community's hard work and dedication had made Coranderrk a highly productive farm and a valuable area of land. A small timber mill was also established on the site, which was used in the expansion of their buildings. In many ways they were self-sufficient and entrepreneurial, selling both dressed timber and fencing lumber to surrounding farmers, in addition to working as shearers or labourers on nearby properties to gain extra income to purchase equipment that they needed in their own farm operations. Coranderrk Station ran very successfully for many years as an Aboriginal enterprise selling wheat, hops, and crafts to the growing market of Melbourne. The produce from the farm won first prize at the Melbourne International Exhibition in 1872 (Broome 2005, 2006; Christiansen and Ellender 2001).

However, what was a successful Aboriginal enterprise was eventually destroyed by bureaucracy, for the success of the mission and the entrepreneurial actions of its hard-working inhabitants had not escaped the notice of members of the Aboriginal Protection Board, who argued that it was in the community's own interests for it to be moved. A combination of poor management by the Aboriginal Protection Board, alleged corruption, and non-Indigenous farming lobbies who wanted the land led to Coranderrk's closure in 1924 (Broome 2005, 2006).

The Gunditjmara and Coranderrk are only two of many examples of Australian Aboriginal enterprise. The entrepreneurial spirit of Victorian Aboriginal people can also be found in Shepparton-Mooroopna and surrounding towns along the Murray Valley, and indeed all over Victoria if you strip away the colonial layers of myths and mistruths and the non-Aboriginal recording of history.

Aboriginal Enterprise

Not all Aboriginal people led a purely foraging, nomadic life. Heather Builth's (1996, 2000, 2002, 2004, 2006, 2009) seminal work has contributed towards the debunking of old stereotypes and prejudices about Aboriginal Australians as foragers or hunter-gatherers before European colonization (Broome 1994, 9–21; Lloyd 2010). Early anthropologists' ideas led to some very negative stereotypes that still haunt Aboriginal Australia today (Morton 1998). Other anthropologists, including Gillian Cowlishaw (1982, 1988, 2003a, 2003b) and Andrew Lattas and Barry Morris (2010), argue that the discipline should review itself and be accountable. Jon Altman and Melinda Hinkson's (2010) edited text *Culture Crisis: Anthropology and Politics in Aboriginal Australia* intensified the criticism directed at a discipline where the Indigenous voice is not given full recognition. Non-Indigenous anthropologists need to record and interpret more of the Indigenous discourse about ownership and not publish external perspectives just from the Western perspective (Keen 2010, 57).

Entrepreneurship is an interdisciplinary area of study, drawing on anthropology, archaeology, history, business, and several other disciplines. Entrepreneurship scholars need to be aware of, and grounded in, these wider debates and issues. In the past there has been a dominance of non-Indigenous scholars in the research area of Australian Indigenous entrepreneurship, coloured by Eurocentric views and assumptions (Foley 2007, 2008a). In order to include Indigenous voices and viewpoints in the study of entrepreneurship and management, we need to establish a balanced understanding of the cross-cultural dimensions of the relevant issues and multiple perspectives within our research (Barney and Mackinlay 2010).

Gippsland Aboriginal Enterprise

I will now discuss some contemporary Gippsland Aboriginal enterprises. It is the demographics of Gippsland that determine the scope of the Aboriginal enterprises within that area. Gippsland is a large rural region in Victoria beginning immediately east of the suburbs of Melbourne, stretching to the New South Wales border, lying between the Great Dividing Range to the north and Bass Strait to the south. The region is best known for its primary production in mining, power generation, and farming, as well as its tourist destinations. The Gippsland region covers a land area of 41,524 square kilometres. It is the traditional country of the Gunai/Kurnai and parts of the Boonwurrung Aboriginal nations. The region comprises six local government areas that for the most part are very supportive of Aboriginal economic development.

The Australian Bureau of Statistics' 2006 census reported a population of 239,647 for Gippsland, with an Aboriginal population of 3,064 persons, consisting of 1,508 males and 1,556 females (ABS 2006). The Aboriginal population makes up just 1.3 percent of the total population of the Gippsland region, which is higher than the proportion for all of Victoria, which sits at 0.6 percent (Ayton 2008). Even so, Aboriginal people are underrepresented in the region in comparison with the national total population ratio of 2.5 percent (ABS 2007), and this has an impact on the number of Aboriginal businesses in

Gippsland. With such a small population, the development of Aboriginal enterprise is statistically limited.

The Gippsland Aboriginal business community follows a trend that sees a high prevalence of Aboriginal businesses in the hospitality and tourism industries that have questionable long-term sustainability prospects. Research indicates that the economic returns from tourism in comparison with Aboriginal investment can be comparatively small; the Aboriginal traditional owner can even be treated commercially unfairly by other business operators (Foley 2008b; Haynes 2010; Ryan 1997). The small returns from Indigenous tourism lead to many Aboriginal tourism ventures ceasing to operate once the government seed funding expires (Birdsall-Jones, Jones, and Wood 2007; Russell-Mundine 2007). Tourism as a motor for Aboriginal small business creation has been promoted by a mix of previous and current state and federal governments who speak of sustainability. The reality in many cases has been a lack of knowledge of the industry, the tourism product, the consumer, or the needs of the Aboriginal service provider, resulting in failure of the Aboriginal tourism product (Russell-Mundine 2007; Ruhane and Whitford 2010).

It is not uncommon in some geographic areas to see Aboriginal copycat businesses—businesses very similar (or identical) in nature and service to another Aboriginal enterprise contesting or vying for a small tourist marketplace. Traditionally, one business starts up and another person thinks the first person is so successful that they can do the same thing without undertaking a market evaluation, and then within a short period there are two identical businesses competing for a market that may not be able to support both of them. This has happened in the recent past in Gippsland. Previous research on copycat businesses that looked at Pacific Islander entrepreneurs has been expanded upon with a more recent Australian study that indicates too many Aboriginal small business start-ups should never have progressed past the initial planning stage (Cheshire 2001; Foley 2005, 2011).

Indigenous Business Australia has identified this as one of the many problems with the former Aboriginal and Torres Strait Islander Commission (ATSIC) loan portfolio. This is one reason why commercial business funding now requires a substantial business plan to ensure Aboriginal entrepreneurs are looking at sustainable businesses within the hospitality and tourism-related industry. Having said all this, many a successful business person commences an entrepreneurial career by selling art, making boomerangs, or conducting local tours. The experience they gain is invaluable in their professional and social capital development for when they move on to another, more sustainable business. Thus, tourism-based, cultural/hospitality-based, or art-based businesses are the nursery in which many Aboriginal people gain the social capital necessary to be successful business persons (Bennett and Gordon 2007; Foley 2010).

The key to this development of business expertise is Aboriginal entrepreneurs' interaction with the dominant society's business environment (Foley and O'Connor 2013). The Aboriginal entrepreneur learns business processes through their networking within the dominant culture in these nursery-type businesses. Effectively, these industries assist in the development of Aboriginal social capital, as entrepreneurs learn how to network and do business with white folk (Bennett and Gordon 2007; Foley 2008c, 2010).

Currently, Gippsland has several Aboriginal cultural tour–type companies, with short guided tours and cultural demonstration training, including one Aboriginal ecotour enterprise, two established Aboriginal retail art centres, and two established artifact makers. Predominantly, they service the Australian domestic tourist market. There are also two dance troupes—one established and one fledgling—servicing the needs of the local community existing within the local cash economy. This is where these small businesses are interesting, because they are off the major tourist routes. They do get access to the occasional backpacker or motorhome convoy, and a growing number of international travellers who are doing self-guided Australian experiences. Mostly, though, their clientele is the domestic market. School education programs form a sizable component of their tours and teaching. These small Aboriginal businesses principally sell their cultural stories and Aboriginal history to a broader Australian client base who want to learn about the local Aboriginal culture. Some have allowed their businesses to exploit a universal stereotype of the Australian Aboriginal playing the didgeridoo, which is alien to Gippsland Aboriginal traditional knowledge.

The tours are relaxed and flexible, providing an interactive experience of the local history and culture. A Bairnsdale company offers several interesting guided tours in and around the national and state parks along walking tracks, sharing land-use and ecological management knowledge together with creation stories on the tracks that their ancestors used. This is an example of insider-outsider theory in application, where the operators blur the lines of demarcation between the Aboriginal and non-Aboriginal (Merton 1996). When a tourist is exposed to Aboriginal culture and history within an intimate setting such as this, they have crossed boundaries, establishing an understanding within a new cultural interface (Nakata 2007). These operators use epistemologies informed by identity and culture that enable the participant to understand Aboriginal cultures. Those who listen deeply leave these tours with a new understanding and comprehension of Aboriginal Australia. Common experiences forge common understanding and address issues of the Aboriginal voice and narrative (Martin 2008).

There are four levels of Australian Aboriginal businesses:

1. **The Nursery Industries**: Low-cost hospitality, tourism, art, and artifact production—businesses that require little knowledge or low set-up costs, including takeout food and/or greengrocers.

2. **Complex Retail and/or Service Industry**: Trade-based service providers, complex retail stores, and businesses in the hospitality industry that require substantial investment and industry knowledge.

3. **Professional Industry**: Businesses requiring high levels of education and professional expertise, as well as human/social and financial capital.

4. **Multinational and National Industry**: Calls for high levels of business acumen and established business experience over many years, with proven track records in governance/management and product diversification.

Gippsland is well represented in the first category. There are no known examples of the third and fourth levels in this region. However, there are two well-known businesses that fall into category two. One is a relatively large arts corporation that has been involved for fourteen years in the development of Aboriginal art beyond the Nursery stage; it has a well-established retail outlet promoting local artists and supplying several well-known public art galleries and private collectors. The other business is unlike what we normally think of as an Aboriginal enterprise, breaking into new retail/service areas. It is in fact a conglomeration of several small businesses. These include a concrete fabrication business, supplying culverts, plumbing and builders' concrete structural needs, and wholesale retail gardening products. There is also a propagation nursery and an Indigenous revegetation service supplying public authorities, environmental groups, land care groups, farmers, and commercial and domestic clients. A side industry is a fencing contracting arm, supplying and installing a wide range of commercial and domestic fencing. This company employs and trains Indigenous staff whenever possible.

There are several other trades-based Aboriginal enterprises in Gippsland, including several builders, plumbers, electricians, tilers, and mechanics, for example. Most of these tradesmen, however, do not identify within the workplace as Aboriginal enterprises. Some fear being stereotyped as providing inferior work, as follows: "Your Aboriginality can be used as an excuse to find something wrong in your workmanship and an excuse not to pay you the full contract" (interview with tradesman, June 2008[1]). One of the greatest impediments facing Aboriginal business in Australia today is the negative racial attitudes towards Aboriginal people, which have a direct correlation to effective leadership within Australian Aboriginal society (Foley, 2005, 2007, 2008a, 2011).

Future for Indigenous Business

This chapter has showcased eight thousand years of enterprise and entrepreneurial activity in the southeastern regions of the Australian continent. National developments in the last few years include the creation of the Indigenous Business Council of Australia, the estab-

lishment of numerous Aboriginal business chambers of commerce—
Mandurah Hunter Aboriginal Business Chamber being the longest
established—and the recent creation of the Australian Minority
Supplier Council, now known as Supply Nation.

Aboriginal Australians operating in small to medium enterprises
generally face the same barriers as Indigenous people in employment:
poor numeracy and literacy, less opportunity to complete tertiary
education, poorer health, larger families, more dependants, fewer
assets, inhibited access to finance/capital, and the cultural pressure
to share resources (Foley 2005, 2007, 2008a). Many Indigenous
business owners, like those previously outlined in the Gippsland
study, have also experienced discrimination. Mainstream business
support hubs, such as Business Enterprise Centres and chambers of
commerce, are not skilled or equipped to support Indigenous people
facing these barriers. This has resulted in Aboriginal enterprises not
receiving adequate support to access government programs that exist
to support them. There was a need for something new—independent
of government but working in partnership with government—to
support a more user-friendly environment for Aboriginal business
operators. Mandurah HIBC, a not-for-profit Aboriginal-controlled
organization, was established to fill this need. Mandurah HIBC's aim
was to eventually become a one-stop shop for Indigenous business
and industry engagement that would support the establishment and
growth of Indigenous business and employment.

An exciting development in the maturing of Indigenous economic
activity in Australia has been the founding of the Indigenous Business
Council of Australia (IBCA), which was developed in partnership with
Aboriginal and Torres Strait Islander business leaders and Indigenous
business associations as the key national representational body for independent Indigenous business. IBCA focuses on Indigenous business
issues. The establishment of the Council mirrors the achievements
of the inspirational community leaders of the 1970s and 1980s, which
resulted in the establishment of Indigenous-controlled legal, medical,
and housing organizations in Australia.

During 2007 and 2008, a number of leading peak organizations were
examined in an effort to identify a model for a new national Indigenous

business organization. By mid-2008, the draft national Indigenous business model had gained considerable support from Indigenous business leaders, owners, and organizations. In 2009, a meeting was conducted in Adelaide that brought together a number of Indigenous business chambers, associations, and representatives from across the nation. The Indigenous Business Council of Australia was formed to act as a federal representative body and was formally registered under the Corporations Act 2001 as a public company limited by guarantee in 2011, with Neil Willmett elected as the Council's inaugural president.

Five years earlier, in 2006, the first Indigenous-controlled business chamber in Australia was established. This grassroots initiative was the Mandurah Hunter Indigenous Business Chamber (Mandurah HIBC), formed to provide Aboriginal people and organizations of the Hunter Region with a forum through which they could be supported, and in turn support each other in business. Prior to the establishment of Mandurah HIBC, Indigenous people operating businesses across Australia were generally not participating as members of business chambers and other business networks. This resulted in lost opportunities to build strategic alliances and networks in business. More importantly, they were not networking with each other, resulting in cultural isolation and a general feeling of being unsupported.

Since then, the South East Queensland Indigenous Chamber of Commerce was established in late 2006, followed by other Indigenous business networks such as the Pilbara Aboriginal Contractors Association (PACA) in 2008 and the Northern Territory Indigenous Business Network in 2009, Kinnaway in Victoria (a spinoff of the state government–funded Koori Business Network), and more recently the Central and Western Queensland Indigenous Chamber of Commerce (CAWQICC) and the Cairns-based Indigenous Business Network North Queensland (IBNNQ).

In 2009, the Australian Indigenous Minority Supplier Council (AIMSC) was established, similar to the US Small Business Association model for minorities. AMSIC recently changed its name to Supply Nation. It was established to assist a growing, vibrant, and sustainable Indigenous enterprise sector by integrating Indigenous small- to medium-sized enterprises into the supply chains of Australian companies and government agencies. It advocated on behalf of the Indigenous business community to foster business-to-business transactions and commercial partnerships between corporate Australia, government agencies, and Indigenous business. It facilitated the exchange of information and the conducting of research into the integration of Indigenous business into the Australian economy.

Currently, the Supply Nation website indicates that it has 190 members, including representatives of corporate Australia, not-for-profit companies, and Australian government agencies, all of which are committed to doing business with Supply Nation–certified suppliers. There are 169 Indigenous businesses certified by Supply Nation as ready to "do business." Since 2009, Supply Nation has claimed to achieve $48 million worth of transactions between Supply Nation members and Supply Nation–certified suppliers, with $31 million worth of contracts awarded to Supply Nation–certified suppliers.

Australian Aboriginal enterprise has made quantum leaps since I first began my research twenty years ago. However, IBCA and the major Aboriginal chambers of commerce lack any real government support. Supply Nation receives favourable financial assistance at the expense of the state chambers and the federal representative body, which provide a necessary support mechanism in the economic development of Aboriginal Australia. If not for the work of the Indigenous chambers, there would be few Aboriginal businesses for Supply Nation, so each organization needs the other. Unfortunately, the federal government funds only one. A lacuna exists in government officials' understanding of Aboriginal economic development, as they prioritize funding for short-term Aboriginal employment strategies and Supply Nation at the expense of long-term, economically sustainable business models that result in real growth in the Aboriginal economic sector. What is evident, even so, is the fortitude of Aboriginal entrepreneurs who struggle with nominal capital, financing, and literacy, and yet are still able to achieve business success.

Conclusion

The role model of an entrepreneur generally reflects the cultural assumptions of the dominant settler society. Aboriginal Australians are not reflected in that model. In fact, in the study of entrepreneur-ship in Australia, the Aboriginal as entrepreneur is not there. Yet, as we see, there is a long history of Aboriginal entrepreneurs. Through colonization much was lost. Aboriginal Australia, in general, operates within a mainstream business framework, often at the expense of its own cultural capital. The arrival of British colonists stifled Aboriginal enterprise. Aboriginal people suffer low levels of cultural and financial capital due to almost two centuries of subjugation, which have limited family and cultural opportunity to maintain enterprise skills and accumulate financial wealth.

Gippsland Aboriginal enterprises are, however, forging new stan-dards of interaction in many instances. Some of the tour companies highlighted in this chapter are interacting with non-Indigenous Aus-tralia in a very positive manner based on Aboriginal customs. Those operating in the building industry as tradesmen or suppliers are also positive role models. Aboriginal tourism operators, small business persons, and entrepreneurs are obtaining valuable skills and regaining former culturally held attributes so long denied.

Invariably, entrepreneurs are measured in the modern marketplace on their performance, not by the colour of their skin or the ethnicity of their parents. It is the acquisition of a level playing field for the Australian Aboriginal entrepreneur that is the societal challenge in Australia today. Aboriginal chambers of commerce are facing this challenge to ensure support for the continued growth of Aboriginal enterprise and leadership in a commercial world.

Notes

1. Interview conducted in confidentiality, therefore name of interviewee withheld by mutual agreement.

References

ABS (Australian Bureau of Statistics). 2006. "Community Profile Series: Gippsland (Statistical Region): 2006 Census of Population and Hous-ing." Accessed August 22, 2011, http://www.censusdata.abs.gov.au/ABSNavigation/prenav/LocationSearch?locationLastSearchTerm=gippsland&locationSearchTerm=gippsland&newarea=2976&collection=

Census&period=2006&areacode=&geography=&method=&product-label=&producttype=Community+Profiles&topic=&navmapdisplayed=true&javascript=true&breadcrumb=PL&topholder=0&leftholder=0&currentaction=104&action=104&textversion=false&subaction=2.

————. 2007. "4705.0 - Population Distribution, Aboriginal and Torres Strait Islander Australians, 2006." Accessed August 22, 2011, http://www.abs.gov.au/ausstats/abs@.nsf/mf/4705.0.

Altman, Jon, and Melinda Hinkson, eds. 2010. *Culture Crisis: Anthropology and Politics in Aboriginal Australia.* Sydney: UNSW Press.

ATSIC (Aboriginal and Torres Strait Islander Commission) and the Office of National Tourism. 1997. "Tourism Industry Strategy." Accessed October 24, 2005, http://pandora.nla.gov.au/pan/41037/20050516/www.atsic.gov.au/programs/industry_Strategies/tourism_industry_strategy/default.html.

Ayton, Linda. 2008. "Aboriginal Statistical Profiles: Statistics collected by local government area on the Aboriginal population of Gippsland." Department of Human Services Gippsland Region. Accessed on August 22, 2011, http://www.dhs.vic.gov.au/__data/assets/pdf_file/0006/383910/GS103.pdf.

Barney, Katelyn, and Elizabeth Mackinlay. 2010. "Transformative learning in first year Indigenous Australian studies: Posing problems, asking questions and achieving change. A Practice Report." *International Journal of the First Year in Higher Education* 1 (1): 91–99.

Bennett, Judy, and Wilfred Gordon. 2007. "Social Capital and the Indigenous Tourism Entrepreneur." In *Striving for Sustainability: Case studies in Indigenous tourism,* edited by Jeremy Buultjens and Don Fuller, 333–70. Lismore, New South Wales: Southern Cross University Press.

Bird Rose, Deborah. 2001. "The silence and power of women." In *Words and Silences: Aboriginal women, politics and land,* edited by Peggy Brock, 92–116. Sydney: Allen & Unwin.

Birdsall-Jones, Christine, Roy Jones, and David Wood. 2007. "Great expectations: Indigenous land-based tourism in regional Western Australia." In *Striving for Sustainability: Case studies in Indigenous tourism,* edited by Jeremy Buultjens and Don Fuller, 187–209. Lismore, New South Wales: Southern Cross University Press.

Broome, Richard. 1994. *Aboriginal Australians: A history since 1788.* 2nd ed.

Sydney: Allen and Unwin.

——. 2005. *Aboriginal Victorians: A History Since 1800*. Sydney: Allen and Unwin.

——. 2006. "'There Were Vegetables Every Year Mr. Green was Here': Right Behaviour and the Struggle for Autonomy at Coranderrk Aboriginal Reserve." *History Australia* 3 (2): 1–17.

Builth, Heather. 1996. "Lake Condah Revisited: Archaeological Constructions of a Cultural Landscape: Reconstructing the cultural records of an Indigenous community by the use of archaeology, anthropology, archival research, oral history, geomorphology and palaeo-landscape studies." Unpublished honours thesis, Flinders University, Adelaide.

——. 2000. "The Connection Between the Gunditjmara Aboriginal People and their Environment: The case for complex hunter-gathers in Australia." In *Environment-Behaviour Research on the Pacific Rim: Proceedings of the 13th People and the Physical Environment Research Conference*, edited by Jacqui Hunt, Gary Moore, and Louise Trevillion, 197–221. Faculty of Architecture, University of Sydney, Sydney.

——. 2002. "The Archaeology and Socioeconomy of the Gunditjmara: A Landscape Analysis from Southwest Victoria, Australia." Unpublished PhD diss., Flinders University, Adelaide.

——. 2004. "The Mt. Eccles Lava Flow and Gunditjmara: A Landform for all Seasons." In *Environmental History of the Newer Volcanic Province of Victoria: Proceedings of the Royal Society of Victoria* 116 (1), edited by A. Peter Kershaw.

——. 2006. "Gunditjama Environmental Management: The development of a fisher-gather-hunter society in temperate Australia." In *Beyond Affluent Foragers: Rethinking hunter-gatherer complexity*, edited by Colin Grier, Jangsuk Kim, and Junzo Uchiyama, 4–23. Oxford: Oxbow Books.

——. 2009. "Intangible Heritage of Indigenous Australians: a Victorian example." *Historic Environment* 22 (3): 24–31.

Cheshire, C. L. 2001. "Business and Family in Micronesia." *Micronesian Seminar*. Manoa, Hawai'i: Pacific Business Center Program, University of Hawaii.

Christiansen, Peter, and Isabel Ellender. 2001. *People of the Merri Merri: The Wurundjeri in Colonial Days*. Merri Creek, Victoria: Merri Creek Management Committee.

Cowlishaw, Gillian. 1982. "Socialisation and subordination among Australian Aborigines." *Man* 17 (3): 492–507.

———. 1988. *Black, White or Brindle: Race in Rural Australia*. Cambridge: Cambridge University Press.

———. 2003a. "Euphemism, Banality, Propaganda: Anthropology, Public Debate and Indigenous Communities." *Australian Aboriginal Studies* 2003 (1): 2–18.

———. 2003b. "Disappointing Indigenous People: Violence and the Refusal of Help." *Public Culture* 15 (1): 103–25.

DETYA (Department of Education, Training, and Youth Affairs). 2000. *Higher Education Students Time Series Tables, 2000: Selected Higher Education Statistics*. Canberra: Commonwealth of Australia.

Flood, Josephine. 2006. *The Original Australians: Story of the Aboriginal People*. Sydney: Allen & Unwin.

Foley, Dennis. 2005. "Understanding Indigenous Entrepreneurs: A Case Study Analysis." Unpublished PhD thesis, School of Business, University of Queensland, Australia. Accessed 1 September, 2011, http://espace.library.uq.edu.au/view/UQ:179923.

———. 2007. "Do we understand Indigenous entrepreneurship?" *20th SEAANZ Conference Proceedings*. Manukau City, New Zealand, September 24.

———. 2008a. "Indigenous (Australian) entrepreneurship?" *International Journal of Business and Globalisation* 2 (4): 419–36.

———. 2008b. "What Determines the bottom Line for Māori Tourism SMEs? Small Enterprise Research." *Small Enterprise Research: The Journal of SEAANZ* 16 (1): 86–97.

———. 2008c. "Does culture and social capital impact on the networking attributes of Indigenous entrepreneurs?" *Journal of Enterprising Communities: People and Places in the Global Economy* 2 (3): 204–24.

———. 2010. "The function of Social (and Human) Capital as antecedents on Indigenous entrepreneurs networking." *New Zealand Journal of Employment Relations* 35 (1): 65–88.

———. 2011. "Aboriginal Enterprise and Entrepreneurship in the Gippsland: a tool in the Reconciliation kit." In *Reconciliation in Regional Australia: Case Studies from Gippsland*, edited by Andrew Gunstone, 108–26. North Melbourne: Australian Scholarly Publishing.

Foley, Dennis, and Allan John O'Connor. 2013. "Social Capital and the

Networking Practices of Indigenous Entrepreneurs." *Journal of Small Business Management* 51 (2): 276–96.

Haynes, Chris. 2010. "Realities, simulacra and the appropriation of Aboriginality in Kakadu's tourism." In *Indigenous Participation in Australian Economies: Historical and Anthropological Perspectives*, edited by Ian Keen, 165–85. Canberra: ANU E Press.

Keen, Ian. 2010. "The interpretation of Aboriginal 'property' on the Australian colonial frontier." In *Indigenous Participation in Australian Economies: Historical and Anthropological Perspectives*, edited by Ian Keen. Canberra: ANU E Press.

Lattas, Andrew, and Barry Morris. 2010. "The politics of suffering and the politics of anthropology." In *Culture Crisis: Anthropology and Politics in Aboriginal Australia*, edited by Jon Altman and Melinda Hinkson, 61–88. Sydney: UNSW Press.

Lloyd, Christopher. 2010. "The emergence of Australian settler capitalism in the nineteenth century and the disintegration/integration of Aboriginal societies: hybridisation and local evolution within the world market." In *Indigenous Participation in Australian Economies: Historical and Anthropological Perspectives*, edited by Ian Keen, 23–40. Canberra: ANU E press.

Martin, Karen L. 2008. *Please Knock Before You Enter: Aboriginal regulation of Outsiders and the implications for Research.* Teneriffe: Post Pressed.

Merton, Robert K. 1996. *On Social Structure and Science.* Chicago: University of Chicago Press.

Morton, John. 1998. "Essentially Black, Essentially Australian, Essentially Opposed: Australian Anthropology and its Uses of Aboriginal Identity." In *Pacific Answers to Western Hegemony: Cultural Practices of Identity Construction*, edited by Jürg Wassmann, 355–85. New York & Oxford: Berg.

Nakata, Martin. 2007. *Disciplining the Savages: Savaging the Disciplines.* Canberra: Aboriginal Studies Press.

Ruhane, Lisa M., and Michelle M. Whitford. 2010. "Australian Indigenous tourism policy: practical and sustainable policies?" *Journal of Sustainable Tourism* 18 (4): 475–96.

Russell-Mundine, Gabrielle. 2007. "Key Factors for the successful development of Australian Indigenous entrepreneurship." *Tourism* 55 (4): 417–29.

Ryan, Chris. 1997. "Maori and Tourism: A Relationship of History, Constitutions and Rites." *Journal of Sustainable Tourism* 5 (4): 257–78.

Tibbert, Kevin. 2005. "Community specialisation, standardisation and exchange in a hunter-gatherer society: a case study from Kalkadoon country, Northwest Queensland, Australia." Unpublished PhD thesis, James Cook University, Australia. Accessed November 16, 2010, http://eprints.jcu.edu.au/1255.

Trudgen, Richard. 2000. *Why warriors lie down and die: towards an understanding of why the Aboriginal people of Arnhem Land face the greatest crisis in health and education—Djambatj Mala.* Northern Territory, Australia: Why Warriors.

Chapter 8

Leadership Success in Overcoming the Environmental Constraints to Indigenous Entrepreneurial Activity in Canada

Bob Kayseas

Introduction

Historically, Canadian Indigenous[1] populations lived independently. Long before the encroachment of European settlers, they lived off the land. While existence in the Canadian climate was, at times, very harsh, and hunting and gathering to the cycles of nature not always rewarding, there was an independence to the lifestyle, and systems of beliefs and values that formed the foundation of societies that existed for thousands and thousands of years. The way of life of First Nations was deeply rooted in an acknowledgement of, respect for, caring about, and belief in the Creator (Clarkson, Morrissette, and Régallet 1992). There were clearly defined roles within the community. Leadership was an earned right, and the values of sharing and respect, for self, family, community, and the cultural group, were strong and very positive guides for individual and collective behaviour.

These traditional First Nations communities withstood thousands of years of the natural environment but could not overcome five hundred–plus years of colonial violation. The cultural and traditional beliefs and values of contemporary Indigenous communities were not unscathed by the challenges that came with European contact.

While Indigenous populations evolved and adapted to the significant changes in their life situations that accompanied the coming of the Europeans, there is much evidence that this evolution and adaptation have resulted in contemporary Indigenous communities with considerable challenges, social pathologies, and very low economic activity relative to mainstream Canada (Anderson 2005, 1–2; Calliou and Voyageur 2007, 135).

However, a window of opportunity exists to improve their socio-economic status. Indigenous Canadians are probably in the best position ever to "integrate economically with the mainstream, to partner with industry, and create wealth and opportunities for all" (Helin 2006, 30). The 2007 report of the Standing Senate Committee on Aboriginal Peoples stated, "In dozens of communities across Canada, Aboriginal involvement in economic development has done more to change the lives of Aboriginal people in the last decade than any number of government programs" (Sibbeston and St. Germain 2007, vii). There is a "potential to revivify and expand Aboriginal economies, open for them modern business opportunities and harness the use of traditional Aboriginal resources for modern economic development" (Dorey and Magnet 2007). Some Indigenous communities have successfully engaged in economic development at an "unprecedented level of success," by reducing reliance on social assistance from 85 percent of adults within the community to 25 percent and financing their government with own-source revenues in the $50-million range, with only $6 million in government transfer payments (Whitecap Dakota First Nation, n.d.). However, "for a significant segment of the Aboriginal population, some of whom continue to struggle to acquire even the most basic service, for their communities, such as adequate housing and health care, the promise held by economic development may still be far away" (Sibbeston and St. Germain 2007, vii).

One of the key elements of the economic development Canadian Indigenous communities are engaged in involves new venture creation at the band level. Indigenous communities are developing community-owned enterprises and are experiencing success all across the country. For example, the Osoyoos First Nation in the southern Okanagan of British Columbia, population 450, owns ten businesses and generates approximately $40 million in annual revenues from its enterprises (AANDC 2011). The Membertou First Nation, in Nova Scotia, is developing collective and individual self-reliance through the creation of community-owned businesses that generate jobs and own-source revenues that are used by the First Nations government. The Whitecap Dakota First Nation (n.d.) has reduced unemployment from 67 percent to 4 percent and reliance on social assistance by 100 percent—down to eight clients in 2010. Whitecap Dakota accomplished this impressive success through the creation of a range of community-owned business ventures that are supported by "responsible governance" and an "environment conducive for business." There are more examples of First Nations governments successfully engaging in entrepreneurial ventures. But what of those communities that "continue to struggle to acquire even the most basic services" (Sibbeston and St. Germain 2007, vii)? The success stories are inspiring. However, of the more than six hundred Indigenous bands across Canada, there are only a small handful that have gained success in business at a scale that can adequately address the challenges that exist within most Indigenous communities.

What lessons are to be learned from these First Nations success stories? What are the specific elements conducive to First Nations business success? Could the existence of entrepreneurial ventures in some communities be simply a timing issue—right time, right place, and right people? *Why* do some Indigenous communities exploit these new opportunities and others do not? *How* do communities exploit these opportunities? *What* have Indigenous communities done to create the environment in which entrepreneurial ventures can thrive? These questions encapsulate the essence of the research problem at the heart of this article.

This paper is derived from an empirical research project that I undertook over a three-year period that culminated in the completion of the requirements for a doctorate degree. The core question that I sought to answer was, "What makes for successful as distinct from unsuccessful entrepreneurship in the Canadian Indigenous on-reserve context?" To develop an adequate response to this question, I needed to understand how Indigenous context at the community level influences the entrepreneurial process.[2] The rationale for undertaking this research, in its simplest form, was to ask: If Indigenous communities are in fact using entrepreneurship as a primary economic development strategy, then must the research that attempts to inform the broader economic development agendas of Indigenous communities also speak specifically about how to do entrepreneurship within the contextual environments that exist in said communities?

The research project involved a qualitative study that used the case study method (Yin 1994) and the grounded theory methodology (Corbin and Strauss 1998). I visited six Indigenous communities over a three-year period beginning in 2008. Semi-structured interviews were used along with comprehensive analysis of documentary evidence. This paper will not provide a detailed explanation of the methodology, nor will it include a comprehensive review of the various literatures that informed the research. Instead, this paper will briefly highlight key aspects of the Canadian Indigenous on-reserve community, the rationale for recognizing the importance of context, and the entrepreneurial environment. Reference will be made to three case studies of "successful" Indigenous entrepreneurship to illustrate how communities can progress economically despite all the challenges that exist within the band context. These three communities form the sample for this research. It is assumed that, since it is the First Nation government that is largely responsible for creating facilitative factors and strategies to address inhibiting factors, a study such as this should focus on entrepreneurship at the band and community level. Therefore, entrepreneurship in this study is examined within the context of community-owned enterprises. Lastly, I conclude with a discussion of how the successful entrepreneurial communities offer proof that development of new enterprises can be successfully accomplished when communities understand the factors that facilitate or constrain new venture creation within their region.

Background to Contemporary Canadian Indigenous Economies

Years ago our people were self-reliant. We made our living by trapping and from whatever nature was able to provide for us. Our life was hard. It was not an easy life.... But we lived like men. Then the government came and offered welfare to our people.... When they offered us welfare, it was as if they had cut our throats. Only a man who was crazy would go out to work or trap and face the hardships of making a living when all he had to do was sit at home and receive the food, and all he needed to live. It seemed as if the government had laid a trap for us, for they knew that once we accepted welfare they would have us where they wanted.... I think this is where the government made its mistake.... We do not want welfare assistance from the government. I would rather see the government put its money where it would help us most.... Instead of sending us welfare, why does the government not send us the money to develop the resources that we have here so that people can make their living from these reserves? (Cardinal 1969, 63)

In his highly regarded book *The Unjust Society*, Harold Cardinal (1969) succinctly captures the essence of Canadian government policy regarding Indians. The book is a manifestation of the culture of dependence (Boldt 1993, 261). It provides insight into the mind of an Indigenous leader who feels powerless and dependent. He poses the question "why does the government not send us the money to develop the resources" with great conviction and sincerity, but to him the answer to solving the dependency on government transfers does not lie within his community or himself; to him, the remedy must come from the place that led to their dependence in the first place. On the other hand, Calvin Helin, a First Nations lawyer from British Columbia, offered an alternative view on how to address dependency on-reserve by arguing that Indigenous success can only be achieved through self-reliance. The dependency of many First Nations has resulted in a situation where people have been socialized into thinking that tragically high suicide rates, gross unemployment figures, and persistent abuse are normal (Helin 2006, 25). Social pathologies within Indigenous communities are not the causes of the underdevelopment of these communities. Rather, the underdevelopment is the cause of the poverty, ill health, and dependent culture (Frideres 1984, 52). The policy of the Canadian government after the signing of the treaties in the late 1800s was to segregate Indians geographically (through the reserve system), socially (by prejudice and discrimination), politically (through the introduction of a colonial system of governance and administration), and legally (through the Constitution and the Indian Act) (Boldt 1993, 171). The effect of this forced isolation—and the cutting off of the Indians' ability to live a traditional form of subsistence—was an involuntary move from a state of economic self-sufficiency to one of dependence (Boldt 1993, 172).

The following discussion offers a brief account of how underdevelopment affects entrepreneurship in Canadian Indigenous communities.

The Effects of Government Legislation and Policy on Contemporary Indigenous Entrepreneurship

The imposition of laws and policies disrupted Indigenous livelihoods, community values, and governance. For example, a headline— "Government Takes Over Pine Creek Management"—illustrates this:

Indian and Northern Affairs Canada (INAC) took over Pine Creek First Nation this week, turning control of the band government and finances over to a third-party manager. But it's not for the usual reasons, reserve residents say. They say that cutthroat politics, not bad debt, threw the western Manitoba Ojibway First Nation 437 kilometres northwest of Winnipeg into financial chaos this summer. Typically, bands are broke when Ottawa steps in and takes control. But in July, Indian Affairs decided to sideline the Pine Creek chief and four councillors over what Ottawa saw as a total breakdown in band government. "The situation at Pine Creek First Nation has severely deteriorated to the point that the First Nation is unable to function," stated a letter dated July 17 from regional Indian Affairs officials.... It cites numerous allegations of political interference in band management. Personality conflicts ruined the First Nations relationships with the only bank willing to lend it money, Ottawa says—consequently, loans were called in on the band's houses. The federal government alleges that safety standards fell apart and the health of the 1,191 people living on the reserve was threatened when staff stopped cleaning the tanks on the water trucks which deliver the only potable water on the reserve.... "Administration of programs and services are largely dysfunctional. There is direct involvement of councillors in administration. Staff are intimidated, mixed directions are sent to staff and political agendas take priority over services. There is no clear separation between administration and politics," the federal government's letter stated. (Paul 2008, C10)

This newspaper report from October 2008 underscores the complexities that exist and points to the degree of responsibility the band government possesses over the lives of its Indigenous constituents. Canada's Indigenous people who live within these reserves exist within a specific social, political, economic, and legislative environment (Anderson et al. 2004; Boldt 1993; Frideres and Gadacz 2001; Helin 2006; Newhouse 2000; RCAP 1996). First Nations may differ in the proportion of undesirable factors that interplay to define their world, but many of the factors contributing to a poor quality of life are common across many bands. The lands they live on are legally defined as "reserves" (Imai 1998). The federal government of Canada only recognizes one group of Aboriginal people, legally classified as Indians, as having the legal right to enjoy the benefits of reserve land and "Indian" status (Imai 1998, 24).

The legislation that the Government of Canada relies on to facilitate governance on Canadian reserves is the Indian Act. The Act provides the political and administrative constraints and boundaries within which three sets of officials—federal, provincial, and First Nations— must work. It was never created with self-determining governance in mind. Rather, its original purpose was to provide a legal framework within which the federal government could control Indigenous populations and to "enable social engineering." Fundamentally, it was a tool of assimilation (Abele 2007, 4; Coates 2008, 2).

Within First Nations society the Indian Act is omnipresent. While its effects are probably impossible to fully document, it is safe to say that its impact on First Nations economic development has reached mythical proportions. Some find its existence so overwhelming that economic development is not even attempted, while others recognize it as out of date and out of touch with modern realities and look for ways to work around its anachronistic requirements. Suffice it to say, any discussion of First Nations economic development will start with and constantly return to understanding and trying to work with this invasive legislation. (Shanks 2005)

The quote encapsulates the essence of the Indian Act and the constraints it poses to the development of entrepreneurial ventures and economic development projects within Indigenous communities. The manner in which it impacts livelihood and economic development is significant. The Indian Act clearly asserts control and ownership over reserve lands within the hands of the Crown, represented by Aboriginal Affairs and Northern Development Canada. This "invasive legislation" asserts federal government authority over all of the following areas in respect to reserve lands: improvements, compensation for loss of use, rights of temporary possession, transfer or cancellation of location tickets (a form of allocation to band members), remedy to trespass, approval of commercial transactions concerning reserve produce (in three provinces only: Alberta, Saskatchewan, and Manitoba), infrastructure maintenance, and the taking of reserve lands by authorities (such as provincial and municipal governments) (Abele 2007, 13). Therefore, while the Act confers authority on the band to develop bylaws in a wide range of areas (while maintaining the authority for final approval with the minister), it also limits the ability to act in many ways simply because of the restrictions on how land can be used.

The Royal Commission on Aboriginal Peoples characterized the impact of the policies outlined in the Indian Act as having the effect of removing Indian lands and property from the Canadian economic realm and setting them aside in enclaves (RCAP 1996). For example, while entrepreneurs in every municipality, town, city, and province of Canada can search for and discover business licensing requirements, business taxation regimes, zoning bylaws, and other land use policies, this is not so on reserve land. The manner in which an entrepreneur operates or begins to operate within the band is almost entirely defined by the band council as the governing body of that reserve. In the absence of any band-created bylaws or community-developed legislation, the entrepreneur is often left to navigate a process that is ad hoc and informal, thus increasing risks to investment.

Indigenous communities are effectively islands unto themselves (RCAP 1996). While the rest of Canada enjoys the benefits of a well-defined legal and property rights system, access to financial institutions, and zoning and bylaw regimes that are clearly defined, the majority of Indigenous persons who live on reserves exist in very different financial, regulatory, and legal realities. Individual entrepreneurs within Indigenous communities are not organized in a chamber of commerce or a board of trade (RCAP 1996). In the majority of Indigenous communities there is not likely to be an industrial park or commercial centre where local entrepreneurs are located. There are likely to be no clear "rules of the game" governing interactions between the private sector and band governments. Most bands are small. Possessed of very small populations, reserve economies can only support those businesses that can operate on a small scale, such as a corner store, a gas bar, a hairdresser, or an auto mechanic's shop (RCAP 1996).

A study prepared for Industry Canada utilized two sets of data to deepen the understanding of privately owned Aboriginal businesses and their prospects for growth. The authors found that Aboriginal people are less likely to own firms than other Canadians (Caldwell and Hunt 1998). The authors use information taken from the 1991 Aboriginal Business Survey conducted by Statistics Canada. That study reported that Aboriginal entrepreneurs fifteen years of age and older who owned a business accounted for 4.8 percent of the Aboriginal population, while the comparable figure was 6.6 percent for non-Aboriginal entrepreneurs in Canada's overall population. Those figures changed somewhat in the years between 1991 and 2004, when there were 27,195 self-employed Aboriginals, of whom approximately 14 percent were on-reserve entrepreneurs (3,920), and of the remaining 86 percent, half were Métis, more than one-third were female, and 61 percent resided in urban areas (Statistics Canada 2004). The number of Aboriginal on-reserve entrepreneurs only amounted to 1.3 percent of the overall on-reserve population of 286,159 in 2001. Furthermore, on-reserve entrepreneurs were more likely to "be home-based, seasonal or part-time, unincorporated, located in rural settings, more reliant on local community markets, and much more likely to exclusively have Aboriginal clients" (Statistics Canada 2004).

Another study examined Aboriginal entrepreneurship on four reserves in northern Ontario. Based on interviews with twenty-two entrepreneurs, the study found that 88.9 percent of the businesses were unincorporated, small, and had very few employees (Cachon 2000). The problems associated with business ownership identified by Cachon's respondents included: isolation from information channels, availability and conditions of entrepreneurship programs, almost no networking opportunities, small markets, higher costs and thus higher prices, and limited access to land.

Given the above discussion, one can infer why entrepreneurs within Canadian Indigenous reserves are so few. The inability to leverage any assets associated with reserve land has been an inhibiting factor that is very difficult to surmount. Section 89 of the Indian Act prohibits reserve land from being mortgaged or pledged in any manner; thus entrepreneurs cannot leverage their on-reserve assets for start-up financing (Caldwell and Hunt 1998). Other inhibiting factors include: lack of required management and business skills, limited sector-specific knowledge and information, the rural location of many reserves, and other legal and structural obstacles (Parkinson, n.d.). In addition, after years of suppression under the passive welfare system, entrepreneurs represent a new phenomenon in many Indigenous communities. They often have no role models or older-generation entrepreneurs to facilitate the growth of the entrepreneurial spirit. These issues concerning entrepreneurs within the Canadian reserve system do not only impact the individual pursuits of Indigenous people seeking to better their circumstances through new venture creation; these issues are also relevant in respect to community-owned enterprises.

Lastly, Indigenous communities stand in stark contrast to the Canadian mainstream relative to a number of factors that have been used to measure the "well-being" of a population (Armstrong 2001). The following statistical description is focused on the segment of the Canadian Indigenous population that live on reserve, and the data mainly comes from Canada's statistical agency reporting data from the

2006 census. The inclusion of these details in this paper is to provide evidence of the vast difference between Indigenous circumstances in Canada and those in which the general population live.

In 2006, the employment rate for the Indigenous on-reserve population was 39 percent, while the overall Aboriginal population's employment rate was 53.7 percent and Canada's was 62.4 percent (Statistics Canada 2008a). There was also a significant gap in median earnings. The on-reserve population had median earnings almost $10,000 less than the overall Aboriginal population, and more than $13,000 less than the general population. One form of income is social assistance. The difference in welfare dependency rates between on-reserve populations and other Canadians is alarming.

The incidence of social assistance for on-reserve populations has been considerably higher than for non-Aboriginal and other Aboriginal groups for some time. For example, data taken from the Royal Commission of Aboriginal Peoples showed that the on-reserve population had a 41.5 percent reliance on welfare, as opposed to 23.5 percent for Métis, 22.1 percent for off-reserve First Nations, and 8.1 percent for the general population (Helin 2006, 112). This translates into an on-reserve population reliant on welfare at a rate five times higher than the general population.

The 2006 census reported an estimated 555,400 adults aged twenty-five to sixty-four who identified as Aboriginal. One in three Aboriginal persons (34 percent) had not completed high school, and 21 percent had a high school diploma as their highest educational qualification (Statistics Canada 2008b). The First Nations population reported similar educational attainments: 38 percent had not completed high school and 20 percent had a high school diploma as their highest educational qualification. However, the on-reserve population reported significantly lower educational attainments than the off-reserve status Indians. The 2006 census reported that 50 percent of on-reserve populations between the ages of twenty-five and sixty-four had not completed high school. Another important statistic regarding educational attainment was completion of post-secondary studies. In 2006, 20 percent of off-reserve Indigenous people had a college diploma, compared with 14 percent of the on-reserve population.

Furthermore, an estimated 9 percent of the off-reserve population reported they had a university degree, while only 4 percent of their on-reserve counterparts reported having a degree (Statistics Canada 2008b, 19). These low levels of education have an impact on economic development opportunities and quality of life.

Housing is another critical component of overall family well-being (Bratt 2002, 14). The 2006 census reported that First Nations people were more than five times more likely to live in a crowded home, with crowding defined as more than one person per room (Statistics Canada 2008b, 45). Only 3 percent of the general population reported living in crowded conditions, while 15 percent of all First Nations reported living with more than one person per room. Moreover, overcrowding was especially prevalent on-reserve. Slightly more than one-quarter (26 percent) of the on-reserve populations lived in crowded conditions. There was also a considerably higher percentage of people who reported living in homes in need of major repairs in the on-reserve population. In fact, 44 percent of the on-reserve population lived in homes that needed major repairs, compared with just 7 percent of the general population and 28 percent of the overall Aboriginal population (Statistics Canada 2008b, 46).

The above census data, when combined with previous information, allows for a glimpse and an understanding of the contemporary Indigenous reserve community. The picture that emerges is one that seems out of place in a G8 nation, one of the world's wealthiest. Indigenous on-reserve populations live in a context of paternalistic government intervention and repressive systems of governance, and are "led" by leaders from within their own community who often may not have the requisite level of schooling, training, or aptitude for any of the tasks their position involves. Would-be entrepreneurs often cannot access information needed to start a business, almost no business licensing regimes exist, and they cannot leverage their property for start-up capital as most other mainstream entrepreneurs can, as a result of legislation that only applies to reserve lands. Ownership of reserve lands is placed in the hands of the Crown—which is where the final authority for the majority of development initiatives lies—instead of with the Indigenous populations and their governments.

Indigenous on-reserve communities experience socio-economic, political, and legal circumstances very different from the general population of Canada as well as other Aboriginal groups. Their leaders are tasked with the challenge of developing strategies to address their circumstances and creating opportunities for positive change and economic growth.

The success of a number of Indigenous communities has drawn the attention of government officials, society at large, and other Indigenous communities that have not yet achieved economic development success. Additionally, researchers have taken on the issue of underdevelopment of Indigenous communities by pursuing understanding of the factors associated with this phenomenon (Anderson and Bone 1995; Anderson 1997, 1999; Anderson et al. 2004, 2005; Anderson and Loizides 2006; Cachon 2000; Chataway 2002; Chiste 1996; Cornell and Kalt 1992, 2000; Cornell, Curtis, and Jorgensen 2004; Cornell 2006a, 2006b; Dana 1995; Harvard Project 2008; Hindle and Lansdowne 2005; Hindle and Moroz 2007; Loizides and Wuttunee 2005; McBride 2001; Newhouse 2000, 2002; RCAP 1996; Wien 2006). However, one of the challenges with the existing literature is the lack of focus directly on entrepreneurship within Indigenous communities and by Indigenous people. Entrepreneurship is recognized as a key ingredient, but it is often not examined in depth. This paper attempts to add knowledge specifically on this critical topic for Indigenous communities.

The next section briefly highlights the importance of the entrepreneurial environment.

The Entrepreneurial Environment and Context

It is widely recognized that "environmental forces" ranging from purely cultural and social currents to governmental regulations, bureaucracy, and institutional arrangements can either facilitate or inhibit the "driving force behind entrepreneurs" (El-Namaki 1988; Van de Ven 1993). The "entrepreneurial environment" is the combination of factors that play a role in entrepreneurship developing in a country or region. Van de Ven (1993), in a study outlining the "issues and processes" involved in the creation of an infrastructure that facilitates or constrains entrepreneurship, argued that there are deficiencies when a study only focuses on the characteristics or behaviours of an individual entrepreneur and treats the "social, economic, and political infrastructure for entrepreneurship as externalities."

In a recent book, Pierre-André Julien (2007) asked the question, "Why do some small regions grow while others—even those located close by—either fall into decline or find it difficult to keep up to the general economic trend?" (1). Julien posited a complex theory of local entrepreneurship that depends on a number of factors, two of which are:

1. The model of local entrepreneurship incorporates a broadly based perspective that takes into account the entrepreneur's origins, culture, life experiences, education, and training, as well as stake-holders such as family members, associates, employees, business partners, "or anyone else in the entrepreneur's milieu, who serve as a model or are able to provide useful information" (9).

2. It incorporates the geographic space the entrepreneur lives in, specifically focusing on the ability of that region to support entrepreneurial activity with resources including social, financial, and human capital, infrastructure, consumers, and institutions (10). Thus, it incorporates the locale, social capital, networking, and entrepreneurial culture within a given region.

Frederik Cornelis Stam (2003, 1) offered credible support for Julien's thesis when he asserted, "It is now recognized that economic competiveness depends to a large extent on non-economic factors... and the creation of structural competitiveness relies on a strong inter-dependence between economic and non-economic factors."

Ucbasaran, Westhead, and Wright (2001, 61–63) examined the focus of recent entrepreneurship research that pays particular attention to contextual and process issues. They made three important points that are worth including here:

1. The ability to make a connection between specific knowledge and a commercial opportunity requires a set of skills, aptitudes, insights, and circumstances that are neither uniformly nor widely distributed.

2. The extent to which individuals recognize opportunities and search for relevant information can depend on the makeup of the various dimensions of an individual's human capital.

3. Resources and assets, both tangible and intangible, and including human, social, physical, financial, and organizational capital, are accumulated throughout entrepreneurial careers.

These same issues contribute to the discussion concerning the entrepreneurial process within Indigenous communities. The literature describing the current circumstances of the people within Indigenous communities notes the limited number of entrepreneurs (Bherer, Gagnon, and Roberge 1990; Cachon 2000; Caldwell and Hunt 1998; Statistics Canada 2001). Other studies point to the low rates of human capital (Boldt 1993; Helin 2006; RCAP 1996). Both of these factors contribute to communities whose people do not have the skills, aptitudes, and insights needed to identify commercial opportunities. Moreover, the human, social, physical, financial, and organizational capital required to move effectively from conception of a commercial idea to the development of a business strategy is also in short supply.

Randall Holcombe (2003, 40) argued that a nurturing environment is more important over the long run than one that is created with explicit policy because of the nature of the entrepreneurial act. Holcombe stresses several important points:

1. Entrepreneurship is a key ingredient of a prosperous society. The existence of entrepreneurship requires a vibrant private sector as well as government policies that support the entrepreneurial act.

2. Governments must create stable economic environments, with efficient market institutions, protection of property rights, and minimal disincentives such as taxation, regulation, and redistribution.

3. Policy that "nurtures" entrepreneurship is more important than policy that encourages investment. The reason for this is that an environment conducive to entrepreneurship creates private incentives to invest.

Thus, entrepreneurship is essentially a local process bounded by the resources and cultural understandings of local environments (Romanelli and Schoonhoven 2004, 10). Entrepreneurship is embedded in the local context; it involves analyses of firms and industries as well as cities, regions, and countries (Audretsch, Keilbach, and Lehmann 2006). In fact, it is a behavioural process that involves the interaction of three critical elements: the individual, the venture, and the environment (Hoy 1995, 146). Contextual factors, including culture, availability of and access to natural resources, presence of economic barriers to employment, social capital, and access to financial resources, and individual factors, such as life situation, aspirations, skills, and alternatives, all shape the activity that may or may not occur (Devaughn et al. 2001, 11).

The studies reviewed above all note that the environments that entrepreneurs exist within can impact their eventual entry into business ventures and possibly the outcomes of that activity. In other words, the existence of highly supportive entrepreneurial environments can actually "create" entrepreneurs (Gartner 1985). Since the environmental context plays a very significant enabling/constraining role in new venture formations, many of the challenges that exist within Indigenous communities certainly must have an impact. One important aspect of the entrepreneurial environment is the notion that governments have a significant role in the formation of various factors associated with enabling/constraining contexts. Within the Canadian Indigenous community, the primary legal, political, and economic environment is articulated in the Indian Act, which contributes significantly to the lack of or existence of an entrepreneurial environment. Furthermore, the low levels of human capital available within a given community constrain that community from engaging successfully in the various aspects of the entrepreneurial process. In the absence of someone within the community who has the ability to perceive an entrepreneurial opportunity, other economic activities became more prevalent—such as a reliance on government funding. The prevailing situation in many Canadian Indigenous bands reflects lower levels of education, lower employment rates, and considerably lower levels of entrepreneurial activity. All of these factors contribute to low rates of new venture creation and act as constraints.

Other factors constraining entrepreneurial activity in Indigenous communities include remote location and lack of infrastructure. In 2001, almost 400 of the 615 Canadian bands—65 percent—were located in areas classified as either rural (between 50 and 350 kilometres from the nearest service centre); remote (over 350 kilometres from the nearest service centre); or "special" (no year-round road access to a service center) (McHardy and O'Sullivan 2004, 17). Many northern communities are situated in locations with physical barriers such as rivers, lakes, or muskeg swamps, and are without a permanent road. The often remote locations of bands contribute to a range of infrastructure deficits. For example, a 2006 Canadian Council on Learning study reported that only 13 percent of bands had broadband access, compared with 60 percent of urban communities and small towns with access to digital subscriber lines (DSL), cable, or wireless broadband services (Stewart 2008). Many Indigenous bands lack "connections to the basic infrastructure" such as telephone lines, underground cables, and cellphone towers (Stewart 2008). Improvements to land in the form of infrastructure is an important element in the entrepreneurship process.

Boettke and Coyne (2003) offer an economic perspective on the institutional and development discourse. In their discussion of the impacts of entrepreneurship on economic development, the authors suggest that consideration of economic progress and the institutions that facilitate entrepreneurship occurs at two levels. First, because competition and entrepreneurship are inseparable, institutional frameworks must be evaluated to gauge whether or not they provide support for entrepreneurship. Second, consideration must be given to the incentive structure of the institutional framework. Does the incentive structure allow the entrepreneur to exercise his subconscious alertness? Additionally, does it allow her to exploit economic opportunities? (72–73). The literature on the economic development of Canadian Indigenous communities consistently highlights the detrimental effects of federal legislation and policy and the departments responsible for their implementation (Helin 2006; Newhouse 2002; RCAP 1996). These communities have been adversely affected through the creation and maintenance of inefficient institutions such as the Indian Act and the imposed governance and institutional structures it authorizes, and the implementation of policy by the department responsible for bands.

Harper (2003) stresses the importance of institutions "that engender the processes of entrepreneurial discovery" (2). He elaborates on this by stating that research examining the conditions "conducive to entrepreneurship" must look at the changes to the institutional structures necessary to move to "more market oriented" economies (2). This is an important issue given the current situation, where many Indigenous communities have been shut out of market processes for legislative and social reasons. Harper's research diverged from other "economics contributions" by focusing on the antecedents of entrepreneurship rather than its consequences. This perspective is of particular interest because of its examination of the causal path from culture, institutions, and individual psychology to "entrepreneurial alertness" (3). This "path," Harper argues, exhibits a strong causal link between personal agency and the propensity of entrepreneurs first to recognize opportunities and then to exploit them (14). Personal agency relates to two cognitive issues: locus of control (contingency expectations) and self-efficacy (competence expectations). These are important factors when investigating Indigenous people. The passive welfare system has created a degree of dependence, both at the individual level and at the governmental level, that has effectively weakened both Indigenous governments and the people they serve (Trudgen 2000, 59; Helin 2006, 104). Is it possible for the Indigenous entrepreneur to both act as a catalyst for increased economic activity and, because of "his" behaviour, produce the conditions conducive to entrepreneurship? (Gartner 1985).

Stephen Cornell and colleagues have made extensive contributions to understanding economic development of American Indian tribes. Their research also supports the conclusion that the environmental context is important for business development. Cornell and Kalt (1992) offer three key ingredients of sustainable, self-determined development (6). The first factor the authors refer to as "external opportunity." It relates to the broader political, economic, and geographic "settings" that American Indian tribes exist in. The second consideration is that internal assets are a "critical factor." Internal assets are natural resources, human capital, institutions of governance, and culture (9). The third ingredient is the development strategy itself, which consists of the overall economic system and the choice of development activity (10). Cornell and Kalt argue that institutions are an important "piece of the development puzzle" (53). For these reasons, the quality of governance and institutions in Indigenous communities is also an important contextual/environmental factor.

Some Indigenous communities have successfully engaged in the entrepreneurial process and have made considerable efforts to create an entrepreneurial environment even within the confines of the legislation and processes outlined in previous pages.

Successful Indigenous Entrepreneurship

I visited the six communities between the fall of 2005 and the summer of 2006. I spent an average of six days in each community and interviewed an average of seven people in each band (a minimum of five and a maximum of ten). The distribution between male and female was fairly even, with 56 percent male (twenty-three men) and 54 percent female (eighteen women).

Three of the six Indigenous bands were each awarded the National Aboriginal Economic Developer Award from the Council for the Advancement of Native Development Officers. The awards go to "outstanding examples of Aboriginal economic development" (CANDO 2009). Each of these communities has exhibited a level of development of entrepreneurial ventures that places them in what I conjecture to be an "outlier" category simply because the success they have achieved is uncommon and exceptional in relation to the overall population of 615 Indigenous bands.

The three other cases were chosen for their theoretical replication possibilities (Yin 1994, 109). I conjectured that these communities would present contrasting results for anticipatable reasons as compared with the first three case studies, and that each would provide an opportunity to discover factors within Canadian Indigenous bands that act to constrain entrepreneurship. Each of these three commun-

ities is geographically close to one within the first set of communities. Therefore, each operates in a context featuring the same provincial, governmental, and non-governmental organizations and civil
sectors as the community that it is near. The criteria for choosing the
second set of communities was that each had to 1) be geographically
near one of the communities in the first set; 2) score lower on the
Human Development Index (HDI) as adapted by Beavan, Cooke, and
McHardy (2004) for the Aboriginal Affairs and Northern Development Research and Analysis Directorate. The modified HDI used
educational attainment, average annual income, and life expectancy
of Registered Indians to conceptualize on-reserve well-being in
relation to mainstream Canadians using 1981–2001 census data; and
3) agree to participate.

The new understanding developed from these case studies contributes to the discussion of the findings that concludes this paper.

Discussion

The multitude of factors involved in the creation of a new enterprise
within contemporary Canadian Indigenous communities point to an
environment that is much more convoluted and complex than that
experienced by entrepreneurs operating within the more structured,
well-defined markets that exist in Canada. For example, the imposed
legislative environment is characterized by many Indigenous leaders,
federal government officials, academics, and others as archaic and
a constraining factor within the communities under its authority.
However, some Indigenous communities have disregarded the challenges that exist, forging headlong into the formation of entrepreneurial environments that are conducive to new venture creation and
sustainability.

Three Indigenous bands that have gained considerable economic
success through the establishment of new entrepreneurial ventures
have done so with a sound understanding and acknowledgement of
the context in which they live. The Osoyoos Indian Band in south-
central British Columbia, Membertou First Nation on Cape Breton,
Nova Scotia, and the Lac La Ronge Indian Band in northern Saskatchewan have all developed successful entrepreneurial ventures

despite the environmental constraints that exist for Canadian Indigenous bands.[3]

Membertou First Nation, Lac La Ronge Indian Band, and the Osoyoos Indian Band have had very stable governments, in the sense of political leaders serving multiple terms. For example, Chief Clarence Louie of the Osoyoos band first took office in 1985 and has won re-election every two years since, except for one term from 1989 to 1991. Former chief Harry Cook was the political leader of the Lac La Ronge Indian Band for eighteen years—nine consecutive terms. His successor, Chief Tammy Cook-Searson, is now in her second three-year term. In Membertou, Terrance Paul became chief in 1984 and has been the political head of the community for thirty years.

In an attempt to improve their socio-economic circumstances through economic development, the Lac La Ronge Indian Band (LRIB) formed the Kitsaki Development Corporation (KDC) in 1981. For years the LRIB political leadership had recognized there was a lack of employment opportunities for band members. As well, leaders saw opportunities in the natural resource sector that, at that time, were being primarily exploited only by large non-Indigenous–owned corporations (Harry Cook, pers. comm.). Former chief Cook expressed his concerns by stating, "Why couldn't we, as Woodland Cree people, develop a strategy whereby over a period of time we could get involved in mainstream activities such as owning hotels, owning transportation systems, having contracts with major mining companies and being part of the forestry like Weyerhaeuser and other big companies that dominate the North?" (Harry Cook, pers. comm.). Therefore, with those views driving the political leadership, the LRIB initiated a long-term strategic planning process. The LRIB initially hired William Hatton as a consultant—then later appointed him general manager of the newly formed Kitsaki Development Corporation. Today, the Kitsaki Management Limited Partnership acts as the "economic development arm" of the Lac La Ronge Indian Band (Russell Roberts, pers. comm.). The KMLP group of holdings posted gross earnings of approximately $90 million in 2006 (Tammy Cook-Searson, pers. comm.).

Today, Chief Tammy Cook-Searson, the community's first female chief, holds the highest political office in the band and is also the president of all wholly owned companies. Chief Cook-Searson was previously a member of council for eight years, and for the past fifteen years she has been the owner of two businesses, Sundance Marina and Sundance Music. Political leadership is responsible for ensuring effective operation in a broad range of areas within the community, from education, health, social assistance, housing, preservation of heritage and culture, and forming new alliances to ensuring that the community's treaty and inherent rights are protected. The functions of government that the LRIB political body, with its administrative unit, has to perform are accomplished with much more specialization than in mainstream Canada. The functions that LRIB's government are responsible for have been delegated to a broad range of departments and agencies from the federal, provincial, and municipal governments, as well as non-governmental agencies. Moreover, LRIBs governance is all accomplished in an environment still under the legislative restraints of the Indian Act, amidst the vagaries of the mainstream market system, and within an Indigenous traditional and cultural system. This is a significant challenge that has not yet been effectively managed by many Indigenous communities in Canada. However, with a budget of over $50 million and more than a thousand people employed both in the administration of government and in the band's businesses, the community of Lac La Ronge has proven it can do it well (Tammy Cook-Searson, pers. comm.).

Bernd Christmas, former CEO of the Membertou Corporate Division, described the process his band used to facilitate the entrepreneurship that has occurred in his community as the "First Nations Progression Model" (McBride et al. 2002). The model consists of three stages—capacity building, preparation, and economic development—and it rests on four value pillars: conservation, sustainability, innovation, and success. The capacity-building aspect of the First Nations Progression Model involved inviting band members who had obtained higher education and now lived elsewhere to come back and help their community. Two people recruited early on played a significant role in Membertou's development. Sometime in 1994–95, Chief

Paul recruited Bernd Christmas as chief executive officer and general counsel and Dan Christmas as senior adviser to the chief and council (Membertou 2008).

Bernd Christmas earned his law degree at York University's Osgoode Hall Law School. At the time he was recruited, he was practising law with the Bay Street law firm Lang Michener (Thayer-Scott 2004, 5). Dan Christmas was working for the Union of Nova Scotia Indians, a provincial Aboriginal political organization, when he was invited back to Membertou (Dan Christmas, pers. comm.). Since then, there have been many more well-educated Membertou band members who have joined the team.

The creation of an accountable, transparent, and well-managed governance system that would attract investment and opportunity was the motivation for seeking ISO certification. Bernd Christmas, then CEO of Membertou Corporate Division, wondered why the private and public sector were not responding to the active marketing campaign the CEO was involved in—marketing the community as a debt-free First Nation offering opportunities. He was surprised by the lack of interest from the corporate and banking world (Dan Christmas, pers. comm.). Therefore, the possibility of ISO certification was investigated. ISO 9001: 2000 certification was achieved in January 2002. The achievement of ISO certification by Membertou, the first Aboriginal government in Canada—in fact, in the world— to do so, was the thing that was needed to "make the wave break" and "open the floodgates" for the business world to enter (McBride et al. 2002, 99).

In 1998, the Osoyoos Indian Band Development Corporation (OIBDC) was created, and "six or seven" already existing businesses were provincially incorporated and placed under the new organizational structure (Scott 2005). The creation of a separate arm's-length entity was the realization of Chris Scott, the newly hired economic development officer, who had come to the conclusion that "there was no such thing as a business decision, it was all politically motivated" (Chris Scott, pers. comm.). The new development corporation's governance structure included a group of five advisers on the board of directors, including "a mix of entrepreneurs, accountants, and bankers," people who Chris Scott and Chief Louie felt could "help guide this operation" (Chris Scott, pers. comm.).

Today, unemployment is almost non-existent in the Osoyoos Indian Band. In fact, Osoyoos now employs more people than its total membership! The employment stemmed from the community's entrepreneurial pursuits—pursuits that are still in operation today, along with several more new ventures (OIBDC 2009). Through the OIBDC (2009), the band owns and operates nine profitable enterprises. The motto of the development corporation is "working with business to preserve our past by strengthening our future." That sentiment can be found in the band's focus on what the chief refers to as "heritage and culture." Heritage and culture is exhibited through the branding of the OIBDC's enterprises, the design of a number of the businesses, for example the Nk'Mip Canyon Desert Golf Course, and through the manner in which human resources are managed. Most mainstream organizations define "immediate family" rather narrowly, with the nuclear family being the most-used definition (Beauregard, Bell, and Ozbilgin 2009, 48). This is a concern in First Nations communities, because it is contrary to the kinship systems many people of Indigenous cultures embrace. The Osoyoos Indian Band exhibits the collectivist value, where the community interests and extended family are "supposed to" take precedence over individual needs (Modesta Betterton, pers. comm.). This is why a policy regarding the employees' right to time off for family obligations extends further than the immediate family.

The Osoyoos people are still governed in many respects by the Indian Act. The band negotiates all lease agreements under the rules and regulations of this legislation. There are only two ways that a non-Indian can legally be in possession of reserve land. Section 58 (3) allows the minister to lease land in possession of any Indian for the benefit of the Indian (Imai 1998, 60). And Section 28 (2) provides the authority to the minister to issue a permit authorizing any person to occupy or use reserve land (Imai 1998, 35). In order for developers to gain access to reserve lands, a head lease must be negotiated between representatives of the band, the Department of Aboriginal and Northern Affairs, Lands and Trusts Services, and the developer. Payments on the lease will go to the Aboriginal Affairs department and then be transferred to the band. This process of leasing land is cumbersome and can take up to two years (Dave George, pers. comm.). However, the leasing of Osoyoos land has provided the opportunity for the band to release "dead capital" (Scott 2005). The band has realized significant profits from the leasing of their properties—revenues that have been used to get involved in other entrepreneurial ventures. This has all occurred within the restraints posed by the Indian Act.

The changes that the leadership has made within each of these communities have significantly transformed the business climates for these First Nations. Huge multinational corporations are seeking to partner with each of these communities on large, multi-million-dollar projects. These communities have created environments that are attractive to business, foster entrepreneurship and innovation, and facilitate rather than inhibit new enterprise creation.

Conclusion

There are many theories that suggest reform/development paths that could lead to enhanced quality of life amongst Indigenous peoples (see, for example, Alcantara 2007; Alfred 1999; Allard 2002; Cornell, Curtis, and Jorgensen 2004; Newhouse 2000; RCAP 1996). This article has described a range of challenges that Indigenous communities face when attempting to engage in economic activities that could lead to positive changes within their communities. For example, Indigenous bands struggle with the effects of the Indian Act in areas such as land and its usefulness as capital (Parkinson, n.d.) and governance (Abele 2007). The majority of on-reserve Indigenous people exist in very different financial, regulatory, and legal realities from most Canadians. The governments within these enclaves are largely responsible for working within the existing realities to form the social and economic environment that will facilitate entrepreneurship. Economic environmental factors include systems of land management that offer incentive for entrepreneurs, and institutions that "engender process-es of entrepreneurial discovery" (Harper 2003, 2). The Membertou First Nation, the Lac La Ronge Indian Band, and the Osoyoos Indian Band have each engaged in the development of institutions, policies, partnerships, capacity-building initiatives, infrastructure projects, and management practices that led to significant economic success from entrepreneurship.

Helin (2006) offered a solution in his book *Dances with Dependency*, which involved a return to the "simple tribal and human values that spawned the complex and beautiful Indigenous cultures in the first place." He didn't advocate a turning "back the clock." Rather, he suggested a renewal of the recognition of social interconnections and interdependence of families, "Tribes or Nations," and a return to the values of self-reliance, high moral conduct, loyalty, self-sacrifice, and leadership (2). Calliou (2005) argued a combined approach, with leaders of today revitalizing traditional principles and concepts of leadership while combining them with the modern competencies, knowledge, and skills required of mainstream managers. Doing this would allow Aboriginal leaders to direct their communities, organizations, and businesses "successfully in to the new economy" (48).

One of the key findings of the research discussed in this article relates to the notion of context and its importance to the entrepreneurial process. Understanding the context in which the entrepreneur operates is a fundamental concern of leaders responsible for policy and governance within their geographical realm. Helin's and Calliou's ideas are more than theoretical propositions positing future states; both arguments, which are generally quite similar, are in fact already being put into practice within the successful communities described above.

Calliou (2005) described three characteristics of great Indigenous leaders: 1) they had a strong sense of their identity, history, and culture; 2) they were visionaries who looked into the future and "had a vision or strategic direction of where they wanted their communities to go"; and 3) they were action-oriented, "They did not talk—they took action" (52). The evidence of a strategic focus and an action-oriented leadership within each of the three communities—Lac La Ronge, Osoyoos, and Membertou—is in plain sight. And, upon closer examination (such as I undertook), there is significant evidence of the recognition, honouring, and upholding of traditional value systems and histories, and a strong sense of pride in their respective cultural backgrounds. The people responsible for governance within each of the three researched communities strongly exhibit the characteristics of "great Indigenous leaders."

This is a key issue. People create the facilitative environments that attract investment and entrepreneurship. Leaders are responsible for initiating the evolution of their communities and addressing the challenges with innovation and action. Of course, these leaders need to know what actions to take, what strategies will lead to facilitative environments. However, without visionary, action-oriented people who have the legitimacy to act as leaders within their community, there would be no success. This last point concerning legitimacy is ultimately related to the manner in which the leaders of the three successful communities I visited engage and interact with their internal band membership. Culture, heritage, and language play a significant role in this regard.

The successful case studies described at the end of this book offer proof that it is possible to create an entrepreneurial environment within Canadian Indigenous communities, despite the many barriers and challenges that exist within those communities. They are practising successful self-government when they create sole productive communities. What is required is a development strategy that is led by the Indigenous people themselves—one that takes into account all of the various inhibiting and enabling factors within their own specific contextual circumstance, and is led by strong, visionary leadership who build the capacity and the environment necessary for entrepreneurial activity to flourish.

Notes

1   *Indigenous* is a generic term used to describe all the original (i.e. pre-colonial) inhabitants of Canada. The term is used throughout the chapter in reference to the one particular group that is talked about. First Nations belong to one of the three groups of Aboriginal people in Canada; the others are Metis and Inuit. In this paper the terms *Indigenous* and *Indigenous community* refer to the on-reserve population of First Nations.

2   *Entrepreneurial process* involves all the functions, activities, and actions associated with the perceiving of opportunities (Bygrave and Hofer 1991, 14) and the creation of value based on the perceived opportun-

ities, while acknowledging that the process is affected by relevant environmental contexts (Hindle 2010).

3   For more information, please read the case studies following this chapter.

References

AANDC (Aboriginal Affairs and Northern Development Canada). 2011. "A Taste of Success: Nk'Mip Cellars, Osoyoos, British Columbia." Accessed October 1, 2012. http://www.aadnc-aandc.gc.ca/eng/1311873422517/1311873529478.

Abele, Frances. 2007. *Like an Ill-Fitting Boot: Government, Governance and Management Systems in the Contemporary Indian Act.* Research paper, National Centre on the First Nations Governance.

Alcantara, Christopher. 2007. "Reduce transaction costs? Yes. Strengthen property rights? Maybe: The First Nations Land Management Act and economic development on Canadian Indian reserves." *Pubic Choice* 132 (3/4): 421–32.

Alfred, Taiaiake. 1999. *Peace, Power, Righteousness: An Indigenous Manifesto.* Toronto: Oxford University Press.

Allard, Jean. 2002. "Big Bear's Treaty: The road to freedom." *Inroads: The Canadian Journal of Opinion* 11: 109–69.

Anderson, Robert B. 1997. Corporate/indigenous partnerships in economic development: The first nations in Canada. *World Development* 25 (9): 1483–1503.

——. 1999. *Economic Development among the Aboriginal Peoples in Canada: The Hope for the Future.* North York: Captus Press.

——. 2005. "Aboriginal Economic Development in the New Economy." *The Saskatchewan Institute of Public Policy* 9: 1–8.

Anderson, Robert B., and Robert M. Bone. 1995. "First Nations Economic Development: A Contingency Perspective." *The Canadian Geographer.* 39 (2): 120–30.

Anderson, Robert B., and Stelios Loizides. 2006. "Growth of Enterprises in Aboriginal Communities." Ottawa: The Conference Board of Canada, publication 143–06: 1–20.

Anderson, Robert B., R. D. Camp II, Kevin Hindle, and Bob Kayseas. 2005. "Corporate Aboriginal alliances: A case study of the Osoyoos Indian Band." In *ASGE 2005: Regional frontiers of entrepreneurship research 2005:*

Compilation of papers of the second AGSE International Entrepreneurship Research Exchange, 225–42. Hawthorn, Victoria, Australia: Australian Graduate School of Entrepreneurship, Swinburne University of Technology.

Anderson, Robert B, Leo Paul Dana, Kevin Hindle, and Bob Kayseas. 2004. "Indigenous Land Claims and Economic Development: The Canadian Experience." *American Indian Quarterly* 28 (3&4): 634–48.

Armstrong, Robin. 2001. "The Geographical Patterns of Socio-economic Well-being of First Nations Communities in Canada." *Agricultural and Rural Working Paper Series* 46: 2–29.

Audretsch, David B., Max C. Keilbach, and Erik E. Lehmann. 2006. *Entrepreneurship and Economic Growth*. New York: Oxford University Press.

Beauregard, T. Alexandra, Myrtle P. Bell, and Mustafa Ozbilgin. 2009. "Revisiting the social construction of family in the context of work." *Journal of Managerial Psychology* 24 (1): 46–65.

Beavan, Daniel, Martin Cooke, and Mindy McHardy. 2004. "Measuring the Well-Being of Aboriginal People: An Application of the United Nations' Human Development Index to Registered Indians in Canada, 1981–2001." Strategic Research and Analysis Directorate, Indian Affairs and Northern Development Canada.

Bherer, Harold, Sylvie Gagnon, and Jacinte Roberge. 1990. *Wampum and Letters Patent: Exploratory Study of Native Entrepreneurship*. Halifax: Institute for Research on Public Policy.

Boettke, Peter J., and Christopher Coyne. 2003. "Entrepreneurship and Development: Cause or Consequence?" *Advances in Austrian Economics* 6: 67–88. http://ssrn.com/abstract=869770.

Boldt, Menno. 1993. *Surviving as Indians: The Challenge of Self-Government*. Toronto: University of Toronto Press.

Bratt, Rachel G. 2002 "Housing and Family Well-being." *Housing Studies.* 17 (1): 13–26.

Bygrave, William D., and Charles W. Hofer. 1991. "Theorizing about Entrepreneurship." *Entrepreneurship: Theory & Practice* 16 (2): 13–22.

Cachon, Jean-Charles. 2000. "Aboriginal entrepreneurship on reserves: some empirical data from Northern Ontario and considerations following the Supreme Court of Canada decision on the Delgamuukw v. British Columbia appeal." *Journal of Small Business and Entrepreneurship* 15 (3): 2–14.

Caldwell, David, and Pamela Hunt. 1998. "Aboriginal Businesses: Characteristics and Strategies for Growth." *Occasional Paper* 20: 1–96.

Calliou, Brian. 2005. "The Culture of Leadership: North American Indigenous Leadership in a Changing Economy." In *Indigenous People and the Modern State*, edited by Duane Champagne, Susan Steiner, and Karen Jo Torjesen. Vol. 10. Walnut Creek: AltaMira Press.

Calliou, Brian, and Cora Voyageur. 2007. "Aboriginal Economic Development and the Struggle for Self-Government." In *Power and Resistance: Critical Thinking about Canadian Social Issues*, edited by Wayne Antony and Les Samuelson, 115–34. 2nd ed. Halifax: Fernwood.

CANDO (Council for the Advancement of Native Development Officers). 2009. *Economic Developer of the Year Awards*. Accessed July 1, 2007. http://www.edo.ca/news-events/economic-developer-of-the-year-awards/past-winners.

Cardinal, Harold. 1969. *The Unjust Society: The Tragedy of Canada's Indians*. Edmonton: M. G. Hurtig Publishers.

Chataway, Cynthia. 2002. "Successful Development in Aboriginal Communities: Does It Depend upon a Particular Process?" *Journal of Aboriginal Economic Development* 3 (1): 76–88.

Chiste, Katherine Beaty. 1996. *Aboriginal Small Business and Entrepreneurship in Canada*. North York: Captus.

Clarkson, Linda, Vern Morrissette, and Gabriel Régallet. 1992. *Our Responsibility to the Seventh Generation: Indigenous Peoples and Sustainable Development*. Winnipeg: International Institute for Sustainable Development. http://www.ces.iisc.ernet.in/biodiversity/sdev/seventh_gen.pdf.

Coates, Ken. 2008. "The Indian Act and the Future of Aboriginal Governance in Canada." Research paper, National Centre for the First Nations Governance.

Corbin, Juliet M., and Anselm Strauss. 1998. *Basics of Qualitative Research: Techniques and Procedures for Developing Grounded Theory*. California: Sage Publications.

Cornell, Stephen. 2006a. "What Makes First Nations Enterprises Successful? Lesson Learned for the Harvard Project." *Joint Occasional Papers on Native Affairs* 2006 (1): 1–14. Tucson and Cambridge: Native Nations Institute for Leadership, Management, and Policy and Harvard Project on American Indian Economic Development.

——. 2006b. "Two Approaches to Economic Development on American Indian Reservations: One Works, the Other Doesn't." *Joint Occasional Papers on Native Affairs* 2006 (2): 1–25. Tucson and Cambridge: Native Nations Institute for Leadership, Management, and Policy and Harvard Project on American Indian Economic Development.

Cornell, Stephen and Joseph P. Kalt, eds. 1992. "What Can Tribes Do? Strategies and Institutions in American and Indian Economic Development." Los Angeles: American Indian Studies Center.

——. 2000. "Where's the glue? Institutional and cultural foundations of American Indian economic development." *The Journal of Socio-Economics* 29 (5): 443–70.

Cornell, Stephen, Catherine Curtis, and Miriam Jorgensen. 2004. "The Concept of Governance and its Implications for First Nations." *Joint Occasional Papers on Native Affairs* 2004 (2). Tucson and Cambridge: Native Nations Institute for Leadership, Management, and Policy and Harvard Project on American Indian Economic Development.

Dana, Leo Paul. 1995. "Self-employment in the Canadian Sub-Arctic: An Exploratory Study." *Canadian Journal of Administrative Sciences* 13 (1): 65–77.

Devaughn, Michael, Dale T. Eesley, Anne S. Miner, and Thekla Rura-Polley. 2001. "The Magic Beanstalk Vision: Commercializing University Inventions and Research." In *The Entrepreneurial Dynamic*, edited by Claudia Bird Schoonhoven and Elaine Romanelli, 109–46. Stanford: Stanford University Press.

Dorey, Dwight A., and Joseph Eliot Magnet. 2007. *Legal Aspects of Aboriginal Business Development*. Markham: LexisNexis Canada.

El-Namaki, M. S. S. 1988. "Encouraging Entrepreneurs in Developing Countries." *Long Range Planning* 21 (4): 98–106.

Frideres, James S. 1984. "Government Policy and Indian Natural Resource Development." *The Canadian Journal of Native Studies* 5 (1): 51–66.

Frideres, James S., and Rene R. Gadacz. 2001. *Aboriginal Peoples in Canada: Contemporary Conflicts*. Sixth ed. Toronto: Prentice Hall.

Gartner, William B. 1985. "A Conceptual Framework for Describing the Phenomenon of New Venture Creation." *Academy of Management Review* 10 (4): 696–706.

Harper, David A. 2003. *Foundations of Entrepreneurship and Economic Development: Foundations of the Market Economy*. New York: Routledge.

Harvard Project on American Indian Economic Development. 2008. *The State of Native Nations: Conditions under U.S. Policies of Self-Determination*. New York: Oxford University Press.

Helin, Calvin. 2006. *Dances with Dependency; Indigenous Success Through Self-Reliance*. Vancouver: Orca Publishing.

Hindle, Kevin. 2010. "How community context affects entrepreneurial process: a diagnostic framework." *Entrepreneurship & Regional Development* 22 (7): 599–647.

Hindle, Kevin, and Michele Lansdowne. 2005. "Brave Spirits on New Paths: Toward a Globally Relevant Paradigm of Indigenous Entrepreneurship Research." *Journal of Small Business and Entrepreneurship* 18 (2): 131–42.

Hindle, Kevin, and Peter Moroz. 2007. "Indigenous entrepreneurship as a research field: developing a definitional framework from the emerging canon." Babson College Entrepreneurship Research Conference, Frontiers of Entrepreneurship Research, Madrid.

Holcombe, Randall G. 2003. "The Origins of Entrepreneurial Opportunities." *Review of Austrian Economics* 16 (1): 25–43.

Hoy, Frank. 1995. "Researching the Entrepreneurial Venture." In *Advances in Entrepreneurship, Firm Emergence, and Growth*, edited by Jerome Katz and R.H. Brockhaus, 145–74. Greenwich, CT: JAI Press.

Imai, Shin. 1998. *The 1998 Consolidated Indian Act*. Scarborough: Carswell Thompson Professional Publishing.

Julien, Pierre-André. 2007. *A Theory of Local Entrepreneurship in the Knowledge Economy*. Cheltenham, UK: Edward Elgar Publishing,

Loizides, Stelios, and Wanda Wuttunee. 2005. "Creating Wealth and Employment in Aboriginal Communities." Ottawa: The Conference Board of Canada, publication 754–05: 1–14.

McBride, John, ed. 2001. *Our Own Vision, Our Own Plan: What six First Nations organizations have accomplished with their own economic development plans*. Burnaby, B.C.: Community Economic Development Centre at Simon Fraser University.

McBride, John, Graham McDonell, Colin Sanderson, and Charlene Smoke. 2002. *Rebuilding First Nations: Tools, Traditions, and Relationships*. Accountability and Governance Conference, June 10–11. Vancouver, B.C.: Aboriginal Financial Officers Association of B.C.

McHardy, Mindy, and O'Sullivan, Erin. 2004. "First Nations Community Well-Being in Canada: The Community Well-Being Index (CBW)." Research and Analysis Directorate, Indian and Northern Affairs Canada, Research and Analysis Directorate, Ottawa. Accessed July 15, 2009. http://www.ainc-inac.gc.ca/pr/ra/cwb/ index_e.html.

Membertou. 2004. "Membertou Community Plan." Membertou Geomatics Consultants. Halifax, Nova Scotia.

———. 2008. "Membertou Community Website." www.membertou.ca.

Newhouse, David. 2000. "Modern Aboriginal Economies: Capitalism with a Red Face." *The Journal of Aboriginal Economic Development* 1 (2): 55–61.

———. 2002. "Aboriginal Economic Development in the Shadow of the Borg." *The Journal of Aboriginal Economic Development* 3 (1): 107–13.

OIBDC (Osoyoos Indian Band Development Corporation website). 2009. Accessed January 15, 2009. www.oibdc.com.

Parkinson, John, M. n.d. *Sources of Capital for Native Businesses: Problems and Prospects.* Accessed July 15, 2010. http://www3.brandonu.ca/library/cjns/8.1/Parkinson.pdf.

Paul, Alexandra. 2008. "Government takes over Pine Creek management." *Winnipeg Free Press,* C10.

RCAP (Royal Commission on Aboriginal Peoples). 1996. *Report of the Royal Commission on Aboriginal Peoples.* Ottawa: Minister of Supply and Services Canada.

Romanelli, Elaine, and Claudia Bird Schoonhoven. 2004. "Introduction: premises of the entrepreneurship dynamic." In *The Entrepreneurial Dynamic,* edited by Claudia Bird Schoonhaven and Elaine Romanelli, 1–10. Stanford: Stanford University Press.

Scott, Chris. 2005. "Osoyoos Indian Band." Accessed October 15, 2008. http://www.sgog.bc.ca/uplo/OlChrisScott.pdf.

Shanks, Gordon. 2005. "Economic Development in First Nations: An Overview of Current Issues." Ottawa: Public Policy Forum..

Sibbeston, Nick, and Gerry St. Germain. 2007. "Sharing Canada's Prosperity—A Hand Up, Not a Handout." Final Report. Special Study on the involvement of Aboriginal communities and businesses in economic development activities in Canada.

Stam, Frederik Cornelis. 2003. "Why Butterflies Don't Leave: Lavational evolution of evolving enterprises." PhD diss. Universiteit Utrecht. http://igitur-archive.library.uu.nl/dissertations/2003-0922-092752/c1.pdf.

Statistics Canada. 2001. *Aboriginal Peoples of Canada: A Demographic Profile*, 2001 Census. Ottawa: Statistics Canada Census Operations Division, catalogue no. 96F0030XIE2001007, 1–26.

———. 2004. *Aboriginal Entrepreneurs in Canada: Progress and Prospects.* Ottawa: Industry Canada. Accessed November 4, 2008. http://strategis.ic.gc.ca/pics/ra/440_e.pdf.

———. 2008a. *The Canadian Labour Market at a Glance: Section O, Aboriginal people*, catalogue no. 71-222-X.

———. 2008b. *Aboriginal Peoples in Canada in 2006; Inuit, Métis and First Nations*, 2006 Census. Ottawa: Industry Canada, catalogue no. 97-558-XIE, 6–52.

Stewart, Monte. 2008. "First Nations lag behind in connectivity." *Business Edge* 8 (7).

Thayer-Scott, Jacquelyn. 2004. "Doing Business with the Devil: Land, Sovereignty, and Corporate Partnerships in Membertou Inc." Halifax: Atlantic Institute for Market Studies.

Trudgen, Richard. 2000. *Why warriors lie down and die: towards an understanding of why the Aboriginal people of Arnhem Land face the greatest crisis in health and education since European contact – Djambatj Mala.* Northern Territory, Australia: Why Warriors.

Ucbasaran, Deniz, Paul Westhead, and Mike Wright. 2001. "The Focus of Entrepreneurial Research: Contextual and Process Issues." *Entrepreneurship Theory and Practice* 25 (4): 57–80.

Van de Ven, A. H. 1993. "The development of an infrastructure for entrepreneurship." *Journal of Business Venturing* 8 (3): 211–30.

Wien, Fred. 2006. "Economic development: A Case Study of the Membertou First Nation." Published in part in *Growth of Enterprises in Aboriginal Communities*, Ottawa: Conference Board of Canada.

Whitecap Dakota First Nation. n.d. "Whitecap Dakota First Nation: Strengthening Community, Building Opportunity." Accessed October 1, 2012. http://www.afn.ca/uploads/files/policy_forum/whitecap_dakota_first_nation_governance_afn_presentation.pdf.

Yin, Robert K. 1994. *Case Study Research: Design and Methods,* 2nd ed. Thousand Oaks, California: Sage Publications.

Osoyoos Indian Band

The Osoyoos Indian Band (OIB) is one of the 198 bands in British Columbia. It is located in the southern tip of the Okanagan Valley, in the south-central area of the province. The southern extremity of the 13,062-hectare reserve is approximately six kilometres from the border between Canada and the United States. The OIB is located within Canada's only desert. The desert is the northern tip of the huge Sonoran Desert that ranges from Mexico up through the United States Midwestern Great Basin, reaching just over the border (Shangaan Webservices 2009). The OIB administration centre, the head office of the band government, is on the northwestern tip of the reserve land, adjacent to the community of Oliver. The town of Oliver has a population of 4,335, with an economy based on agriculture, fruit trees, and vineyards (Shangaan Webservices 2009). The Nk'Mip Project, the flagship economic development venture of the OIB, is situated on the southwest tip of the reserve, adjacent to the town of Osoyoos. Osoyoos is twenty-six kilometres south of Oliver and approximately six kilometres north of the United States border. It has a population of 4,599, with an economy based on tourism, fruit trees, and vineyards (Shangaan Webservices 2009).

The OIB was formed in 1877. There are a total of 435 registered members (AANDC 2009).

Creation and Development of an Entrepreneurial Environment

Chief Clarence Louie has been the leader of his community for almost three decades. During this time, he has been defeated by election only once. This is quite an accomplishment when you consider that elections occur every two years. In 1997, Chief Louie hired Chris Scott as an economic development officer. It was during those early years that Chief Louie formulated a plan for the OIB to develop a gaming establishment:

> The band made application for a casino. As you know the history of casinos on First Nations is one which there is a massive amount of wealth created. We prepared our RFPs [request for proposal] with a company from the United States and we made the application. It was a very good application but we got politically intercepted. We did not make the grade. The RFP was not accepted. We reached a crossroads then. (Chris Scott, pers. comm.)

It was after the defeat of the casino plan that Chief Louie proposed the creation of a "destination resort," suggesting that the "casino could come after" (Chris Scott, pers. comm.). Chris Scott advised the chief that a development on the scale envisioned by Chief Louie would be more efficiently managed under the auspices of a separate corporate entity. Chris Scott elaborates:

> In the year and a half that I had been in the community by then … the political interference was horrendous, horrendous! Every single problem, every employment issue, every request there was a lineup of people going in to see Clarence. There was no business decision being made … there was no such thing as a business decision, it was all politically driven. (Chris Scott, pers. comm.)

Therefore, in 1998, the Osoyoos Indian Band Development Corporation (OIBDC) was created and "six or seven" already existing businesses were provincially incorporated and placed under the new organizational structure (Chris Scott, pers. comm.). The new development corporation's structure included a group of five advisers that included "a mix of entrepreneurs, accountants, and bankers"— people who Chris Scott and Chief Louie felt could "help guide this operation" (Chris Scott, pers. comm.). Those advisers were non-voting members of the OIBDC, with all voting rights going to the chief and council in their capacity as directors.

Chris Scott's position has evolved during his tenure at the OIB. He is currently chief operating officer of the Osoyoos Indian Band Development Corporation.

Today, unemployment is almost non-existent in the OIB. In fact, as of November 2005, the last time the OIB reported these figures (Scott 2005), there were 153 Osoyoos band members employed in eight wholly owned businesses. There were also 57 other First Nations individuals from other communities working for the band, along with 291 people who were not First Nations, for a total of 501 positions. What is even more interesting is that of the 501 jobs in the OIB workforce, only 70 were government related (band administration, school, and daycare), with the remainder of the employment being in band-owned, for-profit businesses (Scott 2005). Moreover, this means that the Osoyoos Indian Band employs more people than they have total membership.

The above employment data is dated. However, the employment reported in 2005 by the OIB stemmed from the community's entrepreneurial pursuits—pursuits that are still in operation today, along with several more new ventures (Scott 2005). Through the OIBDC, the band owns and operates nine profitable enterprises—Nk'Mip Construction, Oliver Readi-Mix, Nk'Mip Canyon Desert Golf Course, Nk'Mip Vineyards, Nk'Mip Campground and RV Park, Nk'Mip Cellars (a winery), OIB Holdings (land leasing, commercial and residential), Nk'Mip Gas and Convenience, and Nk'Mip Desert Cultural Centre—and is a partner in the Mount Baldy Ski Corporation, Sonora Dunes Golf Course, and the Spirit Ridge Vineyard Resort and Spa.

The community has accomplished a great deal since the creation of the OIBDC. A measure of the strides the band has made, in economic terms, can be seen in the amount of self-generated income the OIB now earns through the OIBDC. In 1994, the OIB had revenues from commercial activities of $1.3 million; by 2002, that figure had increased to $14.3 million, a more than tenfold increase. In 1994, the value of payments received from the federal government exceeded these self-generated commercial revenues; by 2002, self-generated revenues were seven times the amount of federal government transfer payments (Anderson et al. 2005).

The motto of the development corporation is "working with business to preserve our past by strengthening our future" (Scott 2005). That sentiment is reflected in the band's focus on what the chief refers to as "heritage and culture."

A brief discussion of the underlying values that exist in the OIB and the OIBDC follows.

Entrepreneurship Philosophy

The band has done many things in the last twenty years that have positioned the community for growth and prosperity. The Osoyoos Indian Band provides an excellent example of an Indigenous community that has created a mode of development shaped by many external forces and yet still has a look and feel that is purely Indigenous. Evidence of this can be found in several areas, for example in management of human resources and in the design of the Nk'Mip Canyon Desert Golf Course.

Dave George is the manager of the golf course. It sits on the boundary line between the town of Oliver and the northeast portion of the OIB reserve. The company was started by two non-Indigenous entrepreneurs from the town of Oliver. The two developers leased enough property to construct a nine-hole golf course as well as a mobile home park. Dave George felt the OIB was not honestly dealt with in that arrangement. The terms of the agreement provided for the OIB to receive a portion of the annual profits from the golf course. George states, "[The developers'] main focus was the mobile home park.... [The golf course] was used as a tax writeoff.... They showed heavy losses each year" (Dave George, pers. comm.). The OIB purchased the property back in 1994 "lock, stock, and barrel" from the developers and proceeded to redesign the course. Several band members who were avid golfers, one of whom was also a member of the band council, designed another nine holes, and the OIB received bank financing to upgrade the course. In 2000, the OIB opened a championship eighteen-hole golf course that "is doing well" because it provides both an employment opportunity for band members and another source of revenue for the band administration (Dave George, pers. comm.).

The golf course is very different from most others. At the entrance is a large iron statue depicting an Indigenous man with a headdress on, pointing a bow and arrow at the sky. That artwork is found throughout the course. Dave George says, "[The artwork] is another way for us to

showcase our golf course and provide education to the public....
It's going to be an art gallery more than a golf course in the end"
(Dave George, pers. comm.). The artwork is not only a source of
cultural pride for band members, it is also a means for the community to market and brand itself through the use of images and the
name Nk'Mip. Brenda Baptiste elaborated on this, stating that "we
have created an OIB brand, we are stable, we are dependable, we are
successful, we are business people, that is our community" (Brenda
Baptiste, pers. comm.).

Chief Louie and members of his management team strongly
believe in the maintenance of heritage and culture. One of the main
themes that emerged from the interviews and the search of the
documentary evidence is the importance of heritage and tradition
to the people of Osoyoos (Brenda Baptiste, pers. comm.; Modesta
Betterton, pers. comm.; Dave George, pers. comm.; Clarence Louie,
pers. comm.; Chris Scott, pers. comm.). There *is* a real threat of a total
loss of the Okanagan language in the Osoyoos community. In fact,
"nobody under fifty-five speaks the language" within the OIB (Clarence Louie, pers. comm.). Moreover, as the band gets increasingly involved with the mainstream Canadian economy, there is an increased
threat to the Indigenous way of living. However, Chief Louie strongly
believes that heritage and culture can be maintained while engaging
in business ventures whose primary markets are non-Indigenous
consumers. These values extend further than the creation of language
programs for young students (there is such a program offered to
youth of the band and to non-Indigenous students who attend the
band schools). The importance of heritage and culture extends to the
operations of the band's businesses. For example, the following quote
provides an indication of Chief Louie's strong beliefs in this respect:

When people come here [Nk'Mip Canyon Desert Golf Course]
they are going to know that they are on a First Nations golf course.
And yeah, we may lose some customers over it, but I would rather
have a company that breaks even and showcases First Nation heritage ... [where] you know you are in a First Nations business, than
have a business that says you have a lot of money but you have sold

out and you have nothing there to identify that you are in a First Nations business. (Clarence Louie, pers comm.)

This statement provides a good example of what constitutes a successful venture to the chief of the Osoyoos Indian Band. It also provides evidence of how an Indigenous community is willing to maintain a "collectivist" orientation even while in competition with mainstream Canadian businesses. Another example of how Indigenous culture interacts with business operations is the way "family" is more broadly defined than in mainstream Canadian society.

The OIB has had to rely on the help of people from outside the community because of the lack of entrepreneurial experience within (Clarence Louie, pers. comm.). Regarding the OIB's entry into the business world at its current level, that help has come from people such as Chris Scott. Scott was awarded the British Columbia Exporter of the Year Award and the Entrepreneur of the Year Award before assuming his current position with the OIBDC. Scott was the founder and president of Okanagan Dried Fruits, a company with 120 employees that he eventually sold to a large multinational firm (OIBDC 2009). Chief Louie expressed his sentiments regarding the OIB's association with men like Chris Scott: "We are learning how to walk the walk and talk the talk with some of the most successful businessmen in Canada!" (Clarence Louie, pers comm.).

References

AANDC (Aboriginal Affairs and Northern Development Canada). 2009. *First Nations Profiles.* http://pse5-esd5.ainc-inac.gc.ca/fnp/Main/index. aspx?lang=eng.

Anderson, Robert B., R. D. Camp II, Kevin Hindle, and Bob Kayseas. 2005. "Corporate Aboriginal alliances: A case study of the Osoyoos Indian Band." In *ASGE 2005: Regional frontiers of entrepreneurship research 2005: Compilation of papers of the second AGSE International Entrepreneurship Research Exchange*, 225–42. Hawthorn, Victoria, Australia: Australian Graduate School of Entrepreneurship, Swinburne University of Technology.

OIBDC (Osoyoos Indian Band Development Corporation) website. 2009.

Accessed January 15, 2009. www.oibdc.com

Scott, Chris. 2005. "Osoyoos Indian Band." Accessed October 15, 2008. http://www.sgog.bc.ca/uplo/OlChrisScott.pdf.

Shangaan Webservices. 2009. "Osoyoos Indian Band." Accessed March 12, 2009. www.britishcolumbia.com.

Lac La Ronge Indian Band

The Lac La Ronge Indian Band (LRIB) is a Woodland Cree band located approximately 235 kilometres north of the city of Prince Albert, Saskatchewan. The LRIB is adjacent to the town of La Ronge, which has a population of 3,500. La Ronge is the service and transportation centre of northern Saskatchewan. The economy of the town of La Ronge is based on tourism, forestry, mining, commercial fishing, trapping, fur trading, dried meat products, wild mushroom and berry picking, and the wild rice industry. Northern Saskatchewan has a significant Indigenous population. In the late 1990s, of the forty thousand people who formed the overall northern Saskatchewan population, 87 percent were Indigenous, with almost 60 percent of those being Registered Indians.

The main administration offices of the LRIB are located on Lac La Ronge #156, which is one of the eighteen reserve land holdings of the LRIB. The other seventeen reserves that together form the total land base of 43,302 hectares (approximately 433 square kilometres) are located in six different communities spread out over a very large area in northern Saskatchewan, with Grandmother's Bay 100 kilometres to the northeast of La Ronge and Little Red River almost 200 kilometres to the south. The other three communities are Hall Lake, Nemeiben River (also known as Sucker River), and Stanley Mission.

Members of the Lac La Ronge band signed Treaty 6 on February 11, 1889, and the first reserve was surveyed in 1897 (Indian Claims Commission 1996, 5).

Creation and Development of an Entrepreneurial Environment

In an attempt to improve socio-economic circumstances through economic development, the LRIB formed the Kitsaki Development

Corporation (KDC) in 1981. For years, the LRIB political leadership had recognized there was a lack of employment opportunities for band members. As well, leaders saw opportunities in the natural resource sector that, at that time, were being primarily exploited by large non-Indigenous–owned corporations (Harry Cook, pers. comm.). Former chief Harry Cook expressed his concerns thus: "Why couldn't we, as Woodland Cree people, develop a strategy whereby over a period of time we could get involved in mainstream activities such as owning hotels, owning transportation systems, having contracts with major mining companies and being part of the forestry like Weyerhaeuser and other big companies that dominate the North?" (Harry Cook, pers. comm.).

With those views driving the political leadership, the LRIB initiated a long-term strategic planning process. The LRIB initially hired William Hatton as a consultant, then later appointed him general manager of the newly formed Kitsaki Development Corporation. Hatton, an American with extensive experience in community-based development projects, stated about his entry into the LRIB development process: "I went up to go moose hunting—I ended up writing business plans" (Dectar and Kowall 1993, 39). Hatton is credited with establishing "capacity building" as the foundation the KDC would build on.

> The objective of capacity building is akin to the oft-referred-to aim of human resource development. But, while human resource development programs tend to focus on improving employment and education levels, capacity building is aimed at developing a conducive business environment, controlled by knowledgeable individuals, with job creation as a secondary goal. (Dectar and Kowall 1993, 39)

The community was actively involved in those early years. Chief Cook and his council took questions to the members of the LRIB, such as: Who are we? Where do we want to go? How do we get there? Then, later: Would you agree with this direction? (Harry Cook, pers. comm.). With the chief and council as directors on the board of the Kitsaki Development Corporation, the Lac La Ronge Indian Band

then actively pursued opportunities. After several years, and after the
failure of three of four early business ventures for "various reasons,"
the development corporation's name was changed to the Kitsaki
Management Limited Partnership (KMLP) (Al Solheim, pers. comm.).
The political leadership and its economic development arm, the
KMLP, evolved. A learning process took place whereby political leaders
learned to "not physically interfere" in the KMLP business activities
(Harry Cook, pers. comm.). Qualified managers were appointed in all
businesses; managers were appointed based on expertise and knowledge and not affiliation. Al Solheim, the director of finance, articulated his views of politicians as board members by stating,

> I think where La Ronge has some advantages has been that we have
> always had chiefs who did a very good job of separating politics
> from business. That is what everybody says you have to do. That is
> true. But that takes special people. We have just been fortunate.
> (Al Solheim, pers. comm.)

Since the inception of the economic development arm of the
LRIB, there have been four different chiefs. However, Chief Harry
Cook was the political leader of the community throughout most of
the development of the corporation, occupying the office of chief for
eighteen years.

Today, the Kitsaki Management Limited Partnership acts as
the economic development arm of the Lac La Ronge Indian Band
(Russell Roberts, pers. comm.). The KMLP currently wholly owns or
has shares in the following companies: Athabasca Catering Limited
Partnership (food and janitorial services to mining operations),
Asiniy Gravel Crushing LP, Northern Lights Foods LP (exporter of
wild rice and wild organic mushrooms), Dakota Dunes Golf Links LP,
Canada North Environmental Services LP (environmental monitoring, impact assessments, baseline data acquisition, water quality, and
other biological services), First Nations Insurance, Keewatin/Procon
Joint Venture (underground and surface mining services), Kitsaki/
Procon Joint Venture (mining construction services), La Ronge Hotel
and Suites LP, La Ronge Wild Rice Corporation, Northern Resource

Trucking Limited Partnership, PANS Joint Venture, and Wapawekka Lumber. All of these businesses are under the management of the KMLP. There are several more businesses and/or revenue generators that are managed by the executive director of the LRIB Administration Centre. The Keethanow Group of Companies includes Keethanow Lumber and Furniture, Keethanow Bingo Hall, and the Keethanow Gas Bar and Grocery Store. The KMLP and Keethanow companies collectively employ 647 people (591 at KMLP), of whom 165 are LRIB members, 226 are "other" Indigenous, and 256 are non-Indigenous. The KMLP group of holdings posted gross earnings of approximately $90 million in 2006 (Tammy Cook-Searson, pers. comm.). There was no revenue data available concerning the Keethanow Group of Companies.

While the above are considerable assets on their own, the LRIB also owns shares in the Dakota Dunes Golf Course on the Whitecap Dakota First Nation near Saskatoon, and it owns a one-twelfth share of the assets that are managed by the Prince Albert Development Corporation (PADC). The LRIB is one of twelve bands belonging to the Prince Albert Grand Council, which is the political body that formed the PADC. The Prince Albert Grand Council owns a number of hotels in two cities, Prince Albert and Saskatoon, as well as a hotel in Meadow Lake and a share of West Wing Aviation, a northern air charter company.

The Council for the Advancement of Native Development Officers awarded the LRIB the distinction of Aboriginal Economic Developer of the Year in 1997 (Anderson et al. 2005). Then, in 2001, one of the LRIB companies, Kitsaki Meats, was the recipient of a Canada Export Award. The previous chief, Harry Cook, had the following to say about the export award:

> Because unemployment is so high in our community, it is a necessity that we continue to create jobs and training opportunities here at Kitsaki. One great way to do that is by selling our goods and services to people outside our community. (Anderson et al. 2005)

The LRIB has been a model of governance for more than thirty years. The community began to assume more and more control over delivery of programs and services after 1974, when it took over the Aboriginal Affairs and Northern Development's education program (Dectar and Kowall 1993, 31). The devolution of responsibility for delivery of programs and services continued throughout the 1970s and 1980s, and is still ongoing today. The band government is now responsible for a budget of over $50 million in transfers from various departments of the federal government (AANDC 2009).

Entrepreneurship Philosophy

The move to create the Kitsaki Management Limited Partnership development corporation was, as stated above, motivated by a desire to facilitate greater economic development in the community. There are four key principles that can be characterized as "business philosophy" that form the foundation of the operation of KMLP. Those key principles have been derived from the data obtained through interviews with LRIB community members as well as the documentary data obtained in the research process. The principles are: capacity building, employment creation through sound investments, creating an economic environment conducive to entrepreneurship, and doing all this within a framework of respect for the culture and traditions of the LRIB members, its resources, and the environment. Capacity building was briefly discussed above; it is briefly expanded on, along with each of the other three, in the following paragraphs.

Two of the four key commitments of the KMLP state:

1. We shall encourage and support education and training for people to prepare themselves for employment and economic opportunities.
2. We shall maximize Aboriginal employment in Kitsaki and Band enterprise through a "training oriented" work environment.

The principles of capacity building and employment through sound investments are found in the KMLP marketing information as well as in the manner whereby the company pursues investment opportunities. The above key principles indicate a focus on education and training and on the maximizing of employment through a "training-oriented" environment. The current CEO of KMLP pointed out several programs the company has initiated to create greater human capital within its workforce. For example, the KMLP has both entry-level and management training programs. The management training program is compulsory for the executive-level staff at the Lac La Ronge Hotel and Suites. There is education and training for chefs at Athabasca Catering that leads to "red seal" certification, and Northern Resource Trucking has a driving program that leads to Class 1A licences for new drivers (Russell Roberts, pers. comm.). The driving program has led to over a hundred LRIB members receiving the highest level of driving certification in Saskatchewan (Russell Roberts, pers. comm.). The former chief also expressed his views on this aspect of the LRIB development strategy. Former chief Cook stated, "We wish to better the standard of living of our members by creating opportunities...opportunity to have an education...so that people can have tremendous choices...young people can say, 'Yeah, someday I want to manage NRT or become an insurance agent'" (Harry Cook, pers. comm.).

In general, the business opportunities the LRIB has focused on have been "labour intensive" rather than "capital intensive" (Al Solheim, pers. comm.). That has allowed the LRIB, through its development corporation, to pursue opportunities—such as the catering company, wild rice and wild mushroom harvesting, hotels, and trucking—where band members, without the relevant prior education and experience, can be actively employed and are still investments that provide solid returns (Al Solheim, pers. comm.). Moreover, the LRIB is also facilitating greater capacity in its band members by exposing them to both the learning and the training required for the work they engage in, and by providing them with viable opportunities—exhibited through the portfolio of businesses owned by KMLP. The provision of employment opportunities is made possible through sound investments, and both are facilitating the creation of an environment conducive to entrepreneurship.

The comments by both former chief Cook and Al Solheim provide support for the assertion that the principles underpinning the creation of the KMLP were meant to serve a broader agenda than just revenue generation. In fact, the training, education, professional development, exploitation of entrepreneurial opportunities in key sectors—sectors that take advantage of the labour pool—creation of economic institutions, partnerships with large and small private and public corporations, and creation of the infrastructure required to support the businesses KMLP and the LRIB now own and manage are creating a facilitating environment for new entrepreneurial activity. In fact, former chief Cook spoke specifically about the creation of a nurturing environment in which individuals would be encouraged to engage in their new venture pursuits: "We encouraged individuals to go into small entrepreneur activity of their own. The economic activity that the band, through Kitsaki, would participate in would be in bigger things…something with assets over one million dollars" (Harry Cook, pers. comm.).

The fourth key principle noted above is related to ensuring that all development occurs within a framework of respect for the culture and traditions of the LRIB members, its resources, and the environment. Accordingly, the Development Philosophy of the Lac La Ronge Indian Band states:

> The Lac La Ronge Indian Band views its Traditional Lands as a heritage resource for future generations of its people. Our forest lands are for hunting, trapping, traveling, gathering of special forest products and medicinal plants, and for spiritual and cultural purposes. But we also view them as a renewable resource for sustainable long-term economic development and employment for our people. (LRIB 2005)

Former chief Harry Cook further illustrated the above sentiments noted in the LRIB (2005) *Traditional Land Use Policy* in a letter he wrote to the Canadian Environmental Agency in 2000: "You take care of the land, and the land will take care of you" (Canadian Environmental Assessment Agency 2000). The land and the Woodland Cree culture are important parts of the LRIB community. Many people in the community still live off the land, and that is one of the reasons why the KMLP chose to pursue opportunities in exporting both wild rice and wild mushrooms. The primary harvesters of both products are members of the LRIB (Russell Roberts, pers. comm.). The ties to the land extend to the current chief as well as the former leader. Former chief Cook lived on a trapline for most of his childhood—and he stated, "I still go out to the trapline" (Harry Cook, pers. comm.). The current political head, Chief Tammy Cook-Searson, was raised on the family trapline and continues to practise her skills as a competitor on the Northern Queen Trapper Circuit (Tammy Cook-Searson, pers. comm.). Language retention in the LRIB is an indication of the maintenance of the traditional lifestyle within the community: Statistics Canada reported that in 2001 more than 53 percent of the people in the LRIB spoke an Indigenous language at home (AANDC 2009).

References

AANDC (Aboriginal Affairs and Northern Development Canada). 2009. *First Nations Profiles.* http://pse5-esd5.ainc-inac.gc.ca/fnp/Main/index.aspx?lang=eng.

Anderson, Robert B., Robert J. Giberson, Kevin Hindle, and Bob Kayseas. 2005. "Relating Practice to Theory in Indigenous Entrepreneurship: A Pilot Investigation of the Kitsaki Partnership Portfolio." *American Indian Quarterly* 29 (1&2): 1–23.

Canadian Environmental Assessment Agency. 2000. Letter from Former Chief Harry Cook of the Lac La Ronge Indian Band. Accessed February 12, 2009. http://www.gc.ca/013/001/0002/0004/0004/laronge_e.html.

Dectar, Michael B., and Jeffery A. Kowall. 1993. "A Case Study of the Kitsaki Development Corporation." Accessed March 15, 2008. http://auspace.athabascau.ca8080/dspace/bitstream/2149/1002/1/P071_Kitsaki.pdf.

Indian Claims Commission. 1996. *Inquiry Into the Treaty Land Entitlement of the Lac La Ronge Indian Band.* Indian Claims Commission. Ottawa. Accessed March 15, 2009. http://publications.gc.ca/collections/collection_2009/indianclaims/RC31-66-1996E.pdf.

LRIB (Lac La Ronge Indian Band). 2005. *Lac La Ronge Indian Band Policy on Traditional and Contemporary Land Use.* Unpublished Band government policy.

Membertou First Nation

The Membertou First Nation is one of the thirteen First Nations in Nova Scotia. It is located on Cape Breton Island. The Indigenous population in the Maritimes only makes up approximately 6 percent of the national Registered Indian population (Statistics Canada 2008).

Membertou is one of the five Mi'kmaq communities on Cape Breton Island. It is an urban reserve located within the city limits of Sydney, Nova Scotia, a city with a population of approximately 105,000. Sydney's economy was largely based on the steel and coal industries. However, the decline of both industries and the closure of the Sydney Steel Corporation and the Cape Breton Development Corporation in 2000 and 2001 led to a diversification of the local economy. Today, the biggest economic engine in Sydney is tourism.

Membertou's main landholdings are 139.4 hectares situated close to downtown Sydney. Approximately 80 percent of its 1,067 band members reside in this area. The band has two other reserves: Caribou Marsh is a 219-hectare reserve and Lingan is a 5-hectare landholding (Membertou 2004).

Creation and Development of an Entrepreneurial Environment

Membertou is a community that has experienced many firsts in its history. For instance, the community was named after Grand Chief Membertou (1510–1611), the first Indigenous person to be baptized by the Catholic Church in Canada, on June 24, 1610 (Mi'kmaq Resource Centre 2005). It was also the first Indigenous government in Canada, and possibly the world, to achieve the ISO 9001:2000[1] rating for its management system.

Today, the community is well on its way to achieving another milestone: self-determination through active and meaningful participation in the economy. In the last fifteen years, the Membertou First Nation has moved from a massive operating debt and high welfare rolls to labour shortages, budget surpluses, capital reserves, and annual dividend payouts (Membertou 2008).

Until recently, Membertou was an average Canadian Indigenous community. It suffered from high unemployment, funding deficits, and social pathologies that offered little hope for a prosperous future for its residents. In 2005, Dan Christmas, senior adviser at Membertou, remembered the situation in his community during the early 1990s. He recalled:

> Well, ten, fifteen years ago, about 1990, Membertou was in a desperate situation. I was away at the time. But our band was in deficit and I think by 1994 our deficit hit rock bottom and it came to the point where it was a $4-million operation and we were running a million-dollar operational deficit. Today our budget is something like $65 million. But fifteen years ago we were $4 million and 99 percent of that was INAC or government dollars. HRDC, Health Canada, and INAC—those were the three main funding partners. Ninety-nine percent of our revenue was government, and when you are that far in deficit, there is very little room to move, you can't invest, you can't really train, your training dollars are limited, you have a limited amount of staff, there is only so much housing you can do. I think the biggest thing was the spirit of the people. People had their heads down. Today you see people walking on the road with their heads up, they're proud of their community, they are proud of who they are! But back then people looked for every two weeks for social to get their dollars; today it is payday, every two weeks everyone is buzzing because it is payday! But back then it was social. (Dan Christmas, pers. comm.)

Band operating deficits had been accumulating for a number of years prior to Terrance Paul being elected as chief. Chief Paul believed that erasing the deficit was a necessary step towards self-determination for the band: "If you are in debt, you have a noose around your neck, and the federal government controls all your decision-making power" (Membertou 2008).

The band's budget deficit situation worsened every year until the turning point in 1995. Chief Paul realized that something had to be done. He sought out band members who had moved away and asked them to return to the community. He gathered people together who he felt could form a new team and who would be willing to take an "unprecedented approach" in Membertou's development (Membertou 2008). When Membertou reached that critical point in the mid-1990s, the community received approximately $4 million in funding from the federal government to finance all of its programs and services.

In the beginning of that time period under review (1986–2002), Membertou was in debt and received almost all of its band funding from Indian Affairs (Dan Christmas, pers. comm.). However, by the end of the period under review, the band had increased its budget to $65 million (Membertou 2008), with most of that being self-generated. The band was able to turn its financial situation around in a relatively short period of time. In addition, the band now reports its workforce at 531—up from a mere 37 in the mid-1990s (Membertou 2008).

In fall 2000, the Membertou Corporate Division opened for business at Purdy's Wharf Tower on Halifax's waterfront, a four-hour drive from the Membertou First Nation. To pursue business opportunities with government and the private sector, it was believed the corporate division needed to be situated in Nova Scotia's business core (Membertou 2008). The Membertou Corporate Division developed four strategic objectives to guide its operations. They were:

1. Increase Membertou's business profile with other major companies by launching its first corporate office.
2. Establish new economic development while keeping in mind that Indigenous knowledge is based on the principles of conservation, sustainability of resources, and respect for the land, air, and water.
3. Create business partnerships.
4. Initiate proactive education and career-related training programs for Membertou's citizens in order to capitalize on employment opportunities resulting from newly established business partnerships and initiatives. (Membertou 2008)

Today, the Membertou Corporate Division manages a number of businesses that it developed across a diverse range of industries. Membertou's Corporate Division portfolio includes: the Membertou Trade and Convention Centre, Membertou Entertainment Centre, Membertou Market, Membertou Gaming Commission, Membertou Data Centre, Membertou Geomatics, Membertou Radio, Petroglyphs Gift Shop, Mescalero's Open Grill Steak House, and Membertou Radio Station, 99.9 FM (Membertou 2008).

The Membertou Trade and Convention Centre (MTCC) officially opened in October 2004. The MTCC is a 47,000-square-foot, $7.2-million meeting and convention facility equipped with state-of-the-art technology, video conferencing services, a sound and lighting system, and SMART Board technology (Membertou 2008). It provides conference and meeting services that range from a nine-hundred-seat concert hall in the 10,000-square-foot Great Hall to board meetings in the executive boardroom (Membertou 2008). Mescalero's Open Grill and Steak House is a 140-seat restaurant that offers traditional Mi'kmaq foods and Atlantic seafood. The restaurant opened in November 2004 and served over eighty thousand plates of food in its first six months of operation (Membertou 2008).

Membertou Market is best described as a hybrid: "It's bigger than a convenience store and smaller than a market" (Chris Cann, pers. comm.). The business has been steadily growing since it opened in December 2001, and today it serves about two thousand customers a day. It employs forty-three staff, with approximately half of them being band members (Chris Cann, pers. comm.).

The Membertou Gaming Commission operates five video lottery terminal (VLT) establishments. The nation has an agreement with the province that allows it to use the proceeds from 120 VLTs for community and economic development initiatives. The Province of Nova Scotia reported that between 1995 and 2006, approximately $250 million was generated for the Indigenous communities (Office of Aboriginal Affairs 2009).

The Membertou Gaming Commission establishments have taken a different approach to gaming from the other Nova Scotia bands. The province first offered bands the opportunity to run gaming operations in 1994. At that time, Membertou held a referendum to determine whether the venture would be supported by band members. The community chose not to be involved. Band members feared they would garner little benefit from gaming. They based their decision on what they had observed was happening to other Nova Scotia bands that had got involved with gaming. They saw that very few of the community members were benefiting. Membertou then held a second referendum on gaming after the Gaming Commission's proposal was rewritten to address their concerns. The new proposal saw the nation hold the gaming profits collectively for the band as a whole. The second referendum passed, with an 87 percent approval rating (Thayer-Scott 2004).

The Membertou Gaming Commission operates 24/7 and employs approximately fifty people. Membertou reported over $7.7 million in revenues from the Gaming Commission in its last publicly available audited financial report (Membertou 2008).[2]

Additionally, the band set up an Economic Development Fund to assist band members who are interested in establishing or expanding an individual business enterprise (Terrance Paul, pers. comm.). In October 2005, Membertou signed an agreement with the Sydney YMCA Entrepreneur Centre to allow Membertou's entrepreneurs to receive free training to help turn their ideas into viable businesses. Individually owned businesses include: Anthony's Convenience, Mi'kmaq Gas and Convenience, Herney's Convenience, H.K. Ranch, Satchel's Skate Sharpening, Kabaty 180/Hairstyling, Moore's Flooring, Sound Factory DJ Service, Edna's Antiques and Collectibles, Kukwes Consulting, Dozay's Art Gallery, Shaylene's, JR and Buck's Convenience, Jacob Marshall's Delivery, Kitpu Welding, Mi'kmaq Gifts and Collectibles, Simon's Autobody, and Marshall's Paintball (Membertou 2004).

Entrepreneurship Philosophy

Like the other nations featured in this paper, the community is always mindful of its commitment to recognize and respect its heritage and culture in its business practices. It has proven that it can thrive in the mainstream business world while staying true to its traditions of collective ownership and maintaining strong ties to culture and heritage.

Bernd Christmas, former CEO of the Membertou Corporate Division, commented:

> Conservation and sustainability, including stewardship of the land, are traditional native values that have been important to Mi'kmaq people over hundreds and thousands of years .... There is only one economy—the mainstream economy—but we have to bring our concepts into the monetary system built on innovation and success. There's no dishonour in measuring success through profit and return on investment. But it has to occur within a native cultural values framework. (Thayer-Scott 2004, 14)

The creation of an accountable, transparent, and well-managed governance system that would attract investment and opportunity was the motivation for seeking ISO certification. Bernd Christmas wondered why the private and public sector were not responding to their active marketing of the community as a debt-free First Nation with business opportunities. It was decided that pursuing an ISO certification would assure potential business partners of their trustworthiness and professional standards.

ISO 9001:2000 certification was obtained in January 2002. They were the first Aboriginal government in Canada (and the world) to reach this standard of business excellence. This accomplishment "made the wave break" and opened the "floodgates" for the business world to enter (McBride et al. 2002, 99).

The new organizational structure does not include a board of directors, as with most corporate bodies. The CEO reports to the chief and council, and each department has a director who reports to the CEO. The Membertou Corporate Division is also managed by the CEO, who has the final say in all "situations that impact the community, both resource-wise and financially" (Terrance Paul, pers. comm.).

The economic opportunities available to the band are now greatly improved. In fact, the opportunities and choices are not available in many other Indigenous communities. Moreover, the changes that the leadership has made within the community have transformed the business climate immensely. Multinational corporations are now seeking partnerships with the Membertou First Nation on multi-billion dollar projects. This is a result of Membertou creating an environment that is economically stable and reliable and that holds itself to a high professional standard. The community also has a governance system that fosters entrepreneurship and innovation among it members.

Notes

1. ISO 9001 certification is a set of quality management standards that are recognized in 159 countries (Membertou, 2008).
2. The Membertou First Nation makes its financial statements available on the community website.

References

McBride, John, Graham McDonell, Colin Sanderson, and Charlene Smoke. 2002. *Rebuilding First Nations: Tools, Traditions, and Relationships.* Accountability and Governance Conference, June 10–11. Vancouver, B.C.: Aboriginal Financial Officers Association of B.C.

Membertou. 2004. "Membertou Community Plan." Membertou Geomatics Consultants, Halifax, Nova Scotia.

———. 2008. Membertou Community Website. www.membertou.ca.

Mi'kmaq Resource Centre. 2005. "The Mi'kmaq." Halifax: University of Cape Breton. Accessed March, 12, 2006. http://mrc.uccb.ns.ca/mikmaq.html.

Office of Aboriginal Affairs. 2009. "First Nations Gaming." Accessed January 15, 2009,http://www.gov.ns.ca/abor/resources/first-nations-gaming/.

Statistics Canada. 2008. *Aboriginal Peoples in Canada in 2006; Inuit, Métis and First Nations,* 2006 Census. Ottawa: Industry Canada, catalogue no. 97-558-XIE, 6–52.

Thayer-Scott, Jacquelyn. 2004. "Doing Business with the Devil: Land, Sovereignty, and Corporate Partnerships in Membertou Inc." Halifax: Atlantic Institute for Market Studies.

Alberta Indian Investment Corporation[1]

Introduction

Founded in 1988, the Alberta Indian Investment Corporation (AIIC) is wholly owned by all the First Nations in the province of Alberta. AIIC is an Aboriginal capital corporation that provides loans to First Nations entrepreneurs as well as business support services. It is primarily a developmental lending institute, lending to First Nations start-up businesses and some business expansions. Thus, AIIC has been instrumental in business development for First Nations throughout Alberta. It is one of the largest of fifty-nine Aboriginal financial institutions in Canada and is a member of the National Aboriginal Capital Corporation Association. AIIC is one of four Aboriginal capital corporations in Alberta, the others being Apeetogosan (Metis) Development Inc., Settlements Investment Corporation, and the Indian Business Corporation.

Since it began lending in 1988, AIIC has loaned in excess of $50 million—over eight hundred loans. Its loan portfolio is currently about $3.5 million. But besides the financial services provided by AIIC, it has put as much effort into business support services, considering that much of its market comprises First Nations start-up businesses with relatively inexperienced business owners. AIIC proceeds on the assumption that First Nations people can govern and manage their own businesses successfully if they also receive the proper support. Such support includes business assistance in the form of counselling, mentoring, advising, and otherwise educating First Nations start-up entrepreneurs with the knowledge and skills to make their own business plan, manage their businesses, carry out financial controls, and understand business fundamentals.

The opportunity to diversify its operations to revenue sources beyond interest on loans led AIIC to develop two hospitality-based businesses whose interests are held through two wholly owned subsidiary companies: Wingate by Wyndham Hotel and the Homefire Grill restaurant and lounge, both located in west Edmonton. These investments are economically successful and provide new revenue that in turn can be utilized to support AIIC's mandate to serve the Alberta First Nations business community.

Context

Aboriginal capital corporations were developed to fill a gap in the lending market, because Aboriginal peoples in Canada were deemed to be a high-risk market and therefore had no access to regular bank loans. The purpose was to create a mechanism for providing commercial loans to Aboriginal entrepreneurs who could not get a loan from a regular commercial bank.

A primary obstacle to banks providing loans to First Nations entrepreneurs is Section 89 of the Indian Act, which does not allow any property of an "Indian" that is situated on a reserve to be seized in the event of default on repayment. Since banks could not secure their investment with collateral that could be seized, as they could with other clients, they refused or were and are very reluctant to provide loans to this risky market. There are now legal mechanisms in place to permit banks to collect on their loans, but unless an arrangement with the First Nation chief and council is made, such mechanisms cannot be enforced in reality. Thus, regular banks still see a risk of not being able to collect on a default on reserve.

Other factors that banks see as unfavourable to the development of successful businesses on reserves include: a lack of business and management skills; limited sector-specific knowledge and information; rural or remote location; and social or cultural limitations to business growth.

Institutional History

The parent company of AIIC, the Indian Equity Foundation, was established on November 1, 1976, as a result of the Syncrude Agreement signed by the Indian Association of Alberta, the Government of Canada, and Syncrude Canada Ltd. (Indian Equity Foundation 1986). This agreement arose out of a proposal to carry out open-pit mining of oil sands in northeastern Alberta. In order to obtain approval, Syncrude had to meet some of the interests of First Nations, such as employment, business, and other financial benefits related to the industrial development. The purpose of the Indian Equity Foundation was to provide no-cost start-up capital or equity to First Nations businesses through a $1-million fund established under the agreement. The initial intent was to have Indian Equity Foundation provide up to 20 percent of the capital cost for a First Nations business, thus enabling it to obtain a loan from the Department of Indian Affairs and Northern Development for the other 80 percent. Syncrude and the Government of Canada each invested $500,000 for the initial capital pool, with the Department of Indian Affairs and Northern Development providing some ongoing financial support for operating expenses. By 1986, the Indian Equity Foundation had current assets of $1.5 million in unallocated capital and $460,000 in current loans. It was a registered charity that did not have to pay income taxes and was registered under the Alberta Companies Act as a non-profit company, with no dividends to be paid to its shareholders, Alberta First Nations. The Indian Association of Alberta and Walter Twinn of the Sawridge First Nation each held one share in trust for Alberta First Nations.

The Indian Equity Foundation was governed by a board of directors who were appointed by the Indian Association of Alberta and chosen because of their business background and knowledge of First Nations communities, and who represented various geographical areas of the province and the three treaty areas. Fred Gladstone, a businessman from the Blood Reserve, was the original president of the foundation. The board's business involved setting policy, approving financing, and overseeing administration of the capital fund. The board would meet every two months to make decisions as a credit committee on individual loan applications over $10,000, whereas loans under this amount were approved by the executive. The foundation was administered by a general manager who worked closely with the board, making recommendations on policies and procedures, giving advice on investment of capital, managing all operations, supervising staff, analyzing loan applications, and monitoring loan performance based on repayment schedules. Other staff included an office manager, administrative clerks, and trainees. By 1986, the general manager was not authorized to recover bad loans and did not have the time or the resources to provide ongoing business management or mentoring services for borrowers.

The Indian Equity Foundation's initial socio-economic mandate saw its borrowers view the funds as a non-repayable contribution, like a grant. Obviously, such a model would see its capital continue to diminish, with applicants not repaying their "loans," and therefore would negatively impact the foundation's performance as a lending business. Thus, in 1979, the foundation changed its policy to clearly reflect that loans had to be repaid, even though these were no-interest start-up or operating loans. Although the financing by the foundation was a loan, conventional lenders treated it as equity because it was a subordinated, or second-place, loan with limited security taken against it. A promissory note and financing agreement were the only evidence of a debt against a new business; thus, the foundation was in the position of an unsecured creditor. Eventually, the foundation began to obtain personal guarantees as additional documentary evidence of a business debt. The foundation clarified its loan collection policy and began to collect on defaults on loan repayments by bringing borrowers who defaulted to court.

To be eligible for a loan, an applicant business had to be 51 percent owned by First Nations or controlled by a board of whom the majority were Alberta Treaty Indians, and the project had to be located in Alberta. Also, to qualify, projects had to be viable business proposals that would be capable of generating profits to be self-sustaining and not require further subsidy. The proposal had to illustrate management capability of the applicant, a business plan with a system to monitor performance, a market appraisal for the goods or services, a production system, and the capital requirements plus financial projections for five years.

At the same time, a sister corporation was established in 1976, the Indian Oil Sands Economic Development Corporation. This corporation was to work in tandem with the Indian Equity Foundation to provide business development and planning services to prospective First Nations businesses. Proposals were jointly prepared by the applicant and the Indian Oil Sands Economic Development Corporation staff, who would then present the business proposal to financial institutions. The name of this corporation was changed to Indian Business Development Services Ltd., which more accurately reflected its purpose and the nature of the services it provided. Indian Business Development Services, located in Edmonton, was also wholly owned by the Indian Association of Alberta and was governed by a five-person board, with seven staff in 1986. It relied on the Department of Indian Affairs and Northern Development for its operating budget.

Early on, there were some issues of Indian Business Development Services staff acting too much as advocates for the applicants and therefore not being objective enough on whether the business project was really viable. Some of the early track record actually bears out this view. As of 1986, over 50 percent of the Indian Business Development Services recommended loans turned out to be non-performing loans (meaning they were written off or were over three months behind in repayment and likely to be written off). One of the reasons for setting up these sister organizations was to address the need for separation of the development function from that of financing. However, it was noted that part of the problem rested with the lack of capacity of staff to adequately assess the financial viability of the business projects.

Another issue was that the board and staff of the Indian Equity Foundation saw the $50,000 lending limit as a restriction on the number of business projects they could lend to. They felt that the number and size of First Nations businesses would continue to grow. But they thought they could only feel secure in raising the lending limit if they had a larger pool of capital available for this growth, more reliable appraisal advice was developed, stronger security against a loan was provided, and more capacity was introduced to monitor the loans and provide follow-up management assistance and mentoring. Ultimately, the Indian Equity Foundation was able to grow its capital fund to $3 million.

This historical overview is important because the experience and issues faced by the Indian Equity Foundation carried over to the Alberta Indian Investment Corporation. The Indian Equity Foundation was tied to a contribution agreement until 1987, and became the parent company of a new entity that is currently known as the Alberta Indian Investment Corporation, which it founded in 1988.

Alberta Indian Investment Corporation

The initial capital pool of $8 million was provided by the Native Economic Development Program (NEDP), a program of Industry Canada, with the purpose of providing commercial loans to Alberta First Nations businesses. Despite research by Aboriginal capital corporations that documented the need for an investment of $11 million to $12 million for the organization to be self-sustaining, the NEDP decided to invest only $8 million. In the end, AIIC received the $8 million from the NEDP along with the $3-million capital pool built up by the Indian Equity Foundation, so it had $11 million available for lending. The Department of Indian Affairs and Northern Development also subsidized AIIC in the early years for strategic planning and other operational needs, but it discontinued this financial support in the early 1990s. With the ending of the contribution agreement with the federal government in 1997, AIIC board and staff took on a new frame of mind, with First Nations now wholly owning their own lending business and therefore enjoying a greater measure of self-government autonomy.

AIIC's strategic vision is to be "the lending institution which will ensure existing and potential First Nation entrepreneurs access to the capital they need." Its mission is to provide "a range of services to First Nation businesses, including business loans and business development assistance" (AIIC 2008). Thus, its purpose is to help Alberta's First Nations people achieve a level of economic self-determination by starting or acquiring businesses that will be commercially successful.

AIIC is a majority First Nations–run and –staffed entity. Since AIIC is owned and operated by First Nations, it has the ability to chart its own course to meet First Nations community needs with respect to business development. The board of AIIC is made up of First Nations leaders and business persons. It currently comprises an eight-member board of directors that represent seven Alberta First Nation tribal councils as well as one external business person with a finance background.

The eligibility criteria for a loan from AIIC require that the business be majority First Nations owned and derive the majority of its operational income within the province of Alberta. Assessment criteria includes: a viable business plan with financial projections; standard assessment of the applicant's credit, character, and available collateral; management capacity; and a minimum 10 percent owner's equity.

AIIC has the unique ability as a lending institute to place a greater emphasis on a community-based creditworthiness assessment. This willingness to accept a higher risk rate helps to make up for deficiencies in some clients' financial situation. In this way, AIIC is more willing than regular commercial banks to lend to start-up businesses and thus work towards the greater social goal of assisting more First Nations people to become business persons. It is playing a role in bringing investment onto First Nations reserves where little other means are available to do so. This in turn leads to the creation and ownership of capital on reserves. New wealth is created and then new investment decisions have to be made. Furthermore, money can circulate longer in the community before leakage occurs.

Much of the philosophy of AIIC staff and leaders is geared to making relationships a priority. AIIC staff feel a strong sense of community because they build connections to community, especially the personal business relationships they establish. They have worked on setting up offices close to First Nations communities and travel regularly out to the communities, which allows them to build relationships, educate communities on business loan opportunities, and market their services to potential entrepreneurs.

AIIC currently charges between 8.25 percent and 13 percent interest on its loans; the rate is determined via a borrow risk rating methodology. It has a loan portfolio of approximately $3.5 million. Its board and management have established strong lending policies and systems for their investments. They learned from the Indian Equity Foundation experience that in order to run a successful lending business, they had to have these mechanisms in place. AIIC diversified by investing in the hospitality industry, and now owns a hotel and a restaurant and lounge in Edmonton to bring in additional revenue.

AIIC has given out over eight hundred business loans since 1988, amounting to more than $50 million. It conducted an informal survey of 106 clients that revealed those 106 loans and associated support services had made a significant community impact, with the creation of approximately 375 full-time and 80 part-time jobs paying out an estimated $9 million in wages. Now AIIC has begun to see second-generation businesses obtain loans, following in their parents' footsteps as entrepreneurs. They also see that there are now new businesses subcontracting from the existing businesses that AIIC helped get started twenty-plus years ago.

There was always a concern among Aboriginal capital corporations about the high failure rate of Aboriginal start-up businesses, and especially the lack of business management support services, training, and mentoring to keep the start-ups sustainable. AIIC began offering business support services in 1995, but this was very limited due to lack of resources. In 2006–7, it was able to expand its business services with financial assistance from the Alberta government, with the Government of Canada coming on board the following year. This has allowed AIIC to assist approximately three hundred First Nations clients. It now provides business and accounting training, counselling, mentoring, and youth entrepreneurial initiatives. Federal funding has ended, and there is no longer any federal support for the business support services.

Challenges and the Future

AIIC is being governed and managed well, with strong policies and procedures. Its lending is very impactful in getting more First Nations businesses started or allowing existing businesses to expand. However, going forward, it still faces a shrinking capital fund for loans. In fact, many of the Aboriginal financial institutes across Canada that were created under the same program face a similar challenge. Thus, the financial model in its current state poses the challenge of a diminishing capital pool. The AIIC board has shown innovative leadership by diversifying into the hospitality sector to bring in more revenue.

As more Aboriginal people move to start up their own businesses, the demand for debt and equity financing also grows. The capital pool will have to grow to meet this demand. Furthermore, there is an increasing need for more varied types of financing as Aboriginal businesses get larger or expand into new markets. There is also more demand for seed capital and youth entrepreneur loans. AIIC leaders are working to meet these challenges and to continue to meet the lending needs of Alberta's First Nations entrepreneurs.

Notes

1. This case study is a summary of a longer case study written by Brian Calliou and Bob Hathaway in 2012 for The Banff Centre, titled "Alberta Indian Investment Corporation Case Study."

References

AIIC (Alberta Indian Investment Corporation). 2008. "Mission & Vision." Accessed June 6, 2014. http://www.aiicbusiness.org/Mission.htm.

Calliou, Brian, and Bob Hathaway. 2012. "Alberta Indian Investment Corporation Case Study." Banff: The Banff Centre.

Indian Equity Foundation. 1986. "Financing the Indian Private Sector." Report, property of the Alberta Indian Investment Corporation.

Blackfoot Crossing Historical Park[1]

Blackfoot Crossing Historical Park (BCHP) is a world-class cultural, educational, and entertainment centre built for the promotion and preservation of the language, culture, and traditions of the Siksika First Nation and its approximately six thousand members. It is located one hour east of the city of Calgary, just three kilometres south of the Trans-Canada Highway.

This $33-million world-class centre is entirely First Nations owned. It started as a vision by a number of Siksika First Nation elders but became a reality only after decades of planning, fundraising, and construction. The museum complex spans 62,000 square feet and houses a vast collection of Blackfoot artifacts and cultural materials. *Blackfoot* actually refers to four distinct tribes included in the Blackfoot Confederacy—the Blackfoot proper (Siksika), the Blood (Kainai), the Peigan (Pii'kani), and the Blackfeet nation—who share a common cultural background and history but who each have their own territory and leadership. The Blackfoot's history in the Treaty 7 area goes back more than seven thousand years.

The complex is built on a hill overlooking the site of a historical river crossing of the Bow called Soyopowahko by the Blackfoot. It represents a celebration of Blackfoot culture and was thirty years in the making. The story of Blackfoot Crossing Historical Park has two parts. The first part was bringing the dream to fruition—the building of the facility. The second part was sustaining the facility after the grand opening.

The Vision
The genesis of Blackfoot Crossing Historical Park was the very successful one-hundredth anniversary of the signing of Treaty 7[2]

that took place at Blackfoot Crossing in 1977. The festivities included a re-enactment of the signing by Queen Victoria's representatives. Visitors to the anniversary celebration included Charles, Prince of Wales, and his brother, Prince Andrew. The organizers were surprised by the turnout, estimated to be around thirty-five thousand people over the course of the weekend. They realized there was a need to educate others about Blackfoot history and its relation to Canadian society.

Blackfoot Crossing Historical Park was thirty years in the making. The project was moved forward under the leadership of the Siksika Nation elders, who had the initial vision, and of a number of chiefs and councils who provided community leadership during the planning and building phases.

The grand opening occurred on July 18, 2007, and drew many spectators, government officials, and dignitaries. Among those present were the then federal minister of Indian Affairs, Jim Prentice; the provincial lieutenant-governor, Norman Kwong; the National Chief of the Assembly of First Nations, Phil Fontaine; and the Province of Alberta's finance minister, Lyle Oberg. Chief Adrian Stimson presided over the grand opening as chief of the Siksika Nation.

Philosophy

The philosophy behind Blackfoot Crossing Historical Park comprises five pillars: culture, education, tourism, economic development, and social/political benefits. The culture component is featured in the preservation and display of cultural artifacts and iconography of the Blackfoot people. The education component is fulfilled by teaching Blackfoot members about their traditions and history. This aspect also provides a venue for non-Aboriginal people to learn about both the Blackfoot people and First Nations—in fact, about Canadian history in general. Tourism and economic development go hand in hand, exposing the culture to the outside world and thus bringing tourists and their capital to the area and generating employment in the community. The social/political component of the vision manifests itself in community and individual pride in the culture and traditions. It also provides a common bond between community members and fosters understanding between the informed non-Aboriginal people and the community members.

Part One: Bringing the Dream to Fruition

Realizing the dream of Blackfoot Crossing Historical Park took decades. Those responsible for bringing the dream to reality had an enormous job ahead of them, which included fundraising, designing the building, constructing it, and training staff.

Fundraising

Raising the funds required for this project was an enormous task. A major fundraising campaign in 2001, and a subsequent bid for grant money, produced $500,000. In 2002, Indian Affairs announced it would give a $2-million grant towards the project. With this money in hand, organizers applied for $4.5 million from the Alberta government. With the Province of Alberta's centennial in 2005, the Alberta government was prepared to award $200 million towards centennial projects. Those in charge were happy to hear, in 2002, that they had received the grant. Ultimately, Indian Affairs would come up with $6 million, while Siksika Nation provided the final $4 million.

The Building's Design

The 62,000 square feet span two levels. The main entrance, administrative offices, conference facilities, theatres, library/archives, gift shop, and cafeteria are on the upper level. The lower level houses the museum.

Ron Goodfellow of Goodfellow Architecture designed the structure. The architect felt it was of great importance to include the rich culture and traditions of the Blackfoot in the design of the building. He brought in numerous elders to help him gain this knowledge. These elders also provided suggestions on how to include the Blackfoot's history in the building's design. Design metaphors and concepts are seen throughout the building. For example, the main doors are situated so as to welcome the sun each morning. Other traditional touches include the yellow ochre teepees, meant to represent scraped buffalo hide; wall sconces that represent war or medicine shields and drums used by singers for powwows; and the eagle feather fan at the main entrance, which represents the sacredness of the eagle in the Blackfoot's ceremony and religion.

Construction

The economic boom in Alberta in the early 2000s put a strain on the construction industry. Due to high demand, skilled workers and tradesmen were both expensive and hard to obtain, which drove up construction costs. The cost jumped by $9.5 million, to $24 million. This put the entire project in jeopardy.

The community decided to hold a referendum on whether to attempt to get a loan or to scrap the project altogether. They voted to keep the project going. The management team was able to receive the $9.5-million loan, and the groundbreaking ceremony in 2002 would signal that the project—twenty-five years in the making—was finally becoming a reality.

There was plenty of support from the community for the building of the Blackfoot Crossing Historical Park, which was underscored by the referendum held in late 2002. At issue was whether or not to continue the project following the revelation that it was going to cost $15 million more than originally thought (not $9.5 million more, as first believed). The community supported the loan that would be required for the project to continue.

Training Staff

When the idea of a museum and cultural centre was conceived, there were no members in the Siksika community who were trained in museum studies. However, there was a wealth of individuals who could fulfill the cultural curatorial role.

The Siksika First Nation is fortunate to have Gerald McMaster, renowned artist, author, and curator, as one of its members. McMaster played a pivotal role in transferring curatorial skills and knowledge to those who would later work in those positions. Two individuals, Russell Wright and Irvin Scalplock, were trained to manage the museum's collection. The selection of community members meant that the employees had a vested interest in the success of the venture. This was more than just a job for these individuals; it was an opportunity to show their culture and heritage to the world and a means of transferring traditional knowledge to their own community members—especially the youth.

The project managers scanned the membership list to see who had the skills they needed to complete the task of training individuals for museum and curatorial work. As mentioned earlier, they were lucky to have a well-trained and well-respected professional within their ranks. He was able to transfer his knowledge and skills to the community members. However, the managers also looked to outside professionals to help train the needed workers. Blackfoot Crossing Historical Park worked closely with employees from the Royal Alberta Museum (located in Edmonton) and the Canadian Museum of Civilization (located in Gatineau, Quebec) to ensure that the needed skills were acquired by future employees.

Part Two: Sustaining the Dream

Blackfoot Crossing Historical Park has been in operation since July 2007. It has incorporated a number of income-generating departments that enable it to sustain itself financially. The departments include:

- **Museum:** The museum generates revenue by charging an admission fee. It houses a great number of artifacts and displays. The museum is also attempting to repatriate artifacts native to the area from Europe.

- **Library and Archives:** Library and Archives is dedicated to the history of the Blackfoot. The library also serves as an archival site containing newspaper articles, photos, and oral history. The library holds a number of books on Aboriginal history, culture, and contemporary issues. The librarian assists community members and others with document and information searches.

- **Conferences:** Conference rooms host numerous events. There is a main conference room with a capacity of three hundred people. There are also three smaller conference rooms that have a capacity of fifty people. Some of these rooms have hosted trade shows and women's shows.

- **Restaurant:** Restaurants generate revenue by offering a basic menu for breakfast, lunch, and dinner, as well as traditional Aboriginal foods. Some of these traditional foods include buffalo burgers, Indian tacos, and bannock. The restaurant also caters for meetings and trade shows held in the conference rooms.

- **Gift Shop:** This shop generates revenue by stocking souvenirs and mementoes of the Blackfoot Crossing Historical Park, as well as various books, DVDs, and music CDs. It also contains various arts and crafts made by people in the local communities. Also found in the gift shop is apparel such as moccasins, shirts, and blankets.

- **Vision Quest Theatre:** The theatre generates revenue by featuring short films about the Siksika, their history, and some of the features of Blackfoot Crossing Historical Park. The 100-seat theatre is also rented to organizations for events.

- **Events:** In order to draw more visitors to Blackfoot Crossing Historical Park, they decided to host a World Chicken Dance competition.

- **Teepee Village:** Teepee Village generates revenue by offering overnight accommodation to those who want to sleep in a teepee for a night and sample traditional Blackfoot cuisine. There is also an RV park with rental spots available.

- **Tours:** Tours provide a commentary to the park's visitors through a Siksika member's perspective. Tours begin with a short film in the theatre and continue with a commentary throughout the museum exhibits on the lower level. The knowledgeable guides inform visitors about the significance and meaning of the displayed items. An array of family teepee canvases are also featured on the lower level, and the iconography is clarified by the guide.

Conclusion

Blackfoot Crossing Historical Park is a success story. What began as a vision by a number of determined individuals has led to the establishment of a 62,000-square-foot facility that celebrates Blackfoot culture, bringing visitors from Calgary and around the world. It generates earned income, provides employment, and offers educational opportunities to Siksika Nation members and visitors from outside the community. It also brings pride to both young and old Siksika Nation members.

The facility is a testament to the persistence, ingenuity, and resourcefulness of those involved in the project. It was an exercise in long-term and short-term planning. A number of lessons were learned by the participants. During their difficulties they had to remember why they were doing it and what the vision was. Some of the obstacles they encountered were issues they could work at solving, such as the need for more funds to complete the project; the choice of the location, size, and scope of the building; and the selection of the architect and how the building would reflect Blackfoot culture.

The community planners remained true to their vision and to the five pillars (culture, education, tourism, economic development, and social/political benefits). They had the responsibility to ensure that these tenets remained first and foremost in their minds, and to not allow the prospect of short-term gain sway them from their long-term goal.

The planners were careful to enlist others to help them when they needed expertise that fell outside their areas of knowledge. By asking for help, they were more able to overcome some of the problems they encountered. They also had to be aware of the ever-changing political, economic, and social landscapes. Decisions had to be arrived at prudently, and adjustments had to be made when needed, while always keeping the focus on the museum.

Since money was an issue throughout the process, the project leaders had to remain vigilant in order to take advantage of funding opportunities when they arose. This meant that a lot of time and energy was spent writing grant proposals and making the case that this was a project worth investing in.

It was imperative that the planners keep the lines of communication open with the community members about the importance of the project for Siksika. They would need community support for some of their actions, such as borrowing money. If there had been dissension and suspicion among the community, then roadblocks would have been set up.

Since the location was off the beaten path, the planners had to get visitors to come to them, so had to ensure that the facility made the long drive worthwhile. Happy tourists would serve them well as word of mouth spread about Blackfoot Crossing Historical Park. The park was awarded a Travel Alberta ALTO award for sustainable tourism in October 2007.

Blackfoot Crossing Historical Park was thirty years in the making. It is a world-class facility that has fulfilled the wishes of its visionaries. As a tourist attraction, it tells the world about the history, tradition, and culture of the Blackfoot and the Siksika Nation. As a financial venture, it shows the world that First Nations people are capable managers who are able to sustain a world-class facility.

Notes

1. This case study is a summary of a longer case study written by Cora Voyageur in 2012 for The Banff Centre, titled "Blackfoot Crossing Historical Park Case Study."

2. A treaty is an agreement between two sovereign entities. Treaty 7 is one of the numbered, or post-Confederation, treaties between the Crown and the First Nations people of Canada. Treaty 7, as the name implies, was the seventh numbered treaty and was signed in 1877. It covers approximately 130,000 square kilometres in southern Alberta. The lieutenant-governor of the Northwest Territories and Special Treaty Commissioner, David Laird, negotiated Treaty 7 at Blackfoot Crossing with the nations of the Blackfoot Confederacy.

References

Voyageur, Cora. 2012. "Blackfoot Crossing Historical Park Case Study." Banff: The Banff Centre.

Metis Crossing[1]

Introduction

The story of Metis Crossing is more than just a story of economic success for the Metis Nation of Alberta; it is a story about the strength, resilience, and heart of the Metis people. Metis Crossing itself is a premier tourist attraction, possessing a vibrancy that draws visitors from across the country and around the world. It also serves as a Metis gathering place of such import that over three thousand people were present for its opening. All this was possible because Metis Crossing was conceived of and developed by Metis people in a manner that drew upon the lessons handed down by their elders and combined those lessons with a modern and strategic approach to business.

Historical Context

The Kisisskatchewan (North Saskatchewan River) has been important to Indigenous people for centuries. Indeed, this history is supported by archaeological digs undertaken in the area that date its use back six thousand years. Crossings over the river were highly valued as they connected the waterways with land routes. The river served as a highway: it supported the fur trade and provided access to fishing areas and grasslands for the annual buffalo hunts. This accessibility made the area now known as Metis Crossing a desirable place to settle.

The people who made the area home were Metis, proud members of a nation with its origins in the fur trade, who developed a distinct way of life and became instrumental in the development of Canada. Early on, the Metis primarily lived in the Red River Valley, in what is now Manitoba. As people of mixed heritage, the first generations of Metis were familiar with the customs and traditions of both the Europeans and Indigenous peoples.

While the Metis may have been vital to the fur trade, they became less valued by Canadian society as time passed, and they faced much discrimination. As the Hudson's Bay Company negotiated with Canada for the transfer of Rupert's Land, surveyors began to move onto Metis land in the Red River area with the intent of opening it up for European settlement. The Metis continually found themselves dispossessed; they were not given land for reserves, nor were they targeted for settlements like the Europeans. Instead, they could often be found along the roadside, which is how the phrase "roadside allowance" became part of their history.

The Metis Crossing site that drew the Metis to this spot had first seen newcomers arrive when a Methodist mission was started at Victoria Crossing in 1862, and the Hudson's Bay Company established a fort in 1864. Red River settlers began arriving in the area in 1865 along what became known as the Victoria Trail, which connected Fort Victoria to Fort Edmonton and was part of a larger trail system that led to Winnipeg.

Some Metis were farmers, and they introduced the traditional river lot system of land allocation into the area. The river lot system ensured that each family would have enough land to survive; bachelors would receive smaller parcels than those with families.

> Even today, the land tell[s] a story without actually saying anything because you could see the lines of trees and when they talked about river lots they talked about the old style where in the early history of the development of the province everybody needed access to the river because that was your transportation. Everybody needed a place to live, everybody needed a place to raise their livestock and everybody needed a wood lot where they could cut their wood.

These are the types of lessons to be learned by being on the actual sites.

Metis Crossing is located on what was formally six river lot titles given to the Erasmus, Norn, and Cromarty families in the late 1800s along the North Saskatchewan River. The Metis Crossing site is located within the Victoria District National Historic Site in Smoky Lake County, approximately one hundred kilometres northeast of Edmonton.

Demand for a Metis Cultural Site Grows

Metis people had expressed the need for a place of their own for many years. The Metis Association of Alberta, which would later become the Metis Nation of Alberta (MNA), began with organizational meetings in 1928 and was incorporated in 1932. In 1938 the provincial administration passed the Metis Betterment Act and created eight settlements that remain to this day the only constitutionally protected land base for the Metis in the country. While important, the establishment of these settlements was just one step forward in the fight of the Metis to have their rights recognized and their story told. Annual MNA assemblies began in 1961, and whenever there were gatherings of Metis, people would ask, "Why can't we have a place that's ours? Where we tell our story and everybody just knows we come back there every year?" In the larger context of Canada, the story of the Metis was primarily identified with areas such as the Red River Settlement in Manitoba and Batoche in Saskatchewan. However, there was no such historic Metis site in Alberta to facilitate the sharing of Metis culture and identity.

Decision on the Metis Crossing Site

It was not long after the constitutional recognition of Metis people in 1982 that the first opportunity to purchase the Metis Crossing land came about. In 1988, the owners of Riverview farm approached the MNA to sell the property. The owners, the Schaffers, knew that the land had played an important role in Metis history and they felt that the farm should be returned to them. In addition, they had a strong interest in conservation and were concerned about how their land might be developed if it was sold on the open market. Unfortunately, the MNA did not have the resources to acquire the land and asked the Schaffers if they could postpone selling the property until they were in a position to buy it. The Schaffers agreed to this, and the land was not put up for sale on the open market.

It is important to note that the initial discussions around the need to have a place to call their own did not specifically refer to tourism. The main goals in having a land base were to educate people about Metis history and culture and to be financially sustainable. Tourism was seen as a way to achieve both of these goals. Furthermore, the Metis people wanted a place where their own people could visit frequently.

While the Riverview farm was one area that the MNA was considering for development, it was not the only one. In 1999, a Metis Millennium Voyage Tourism Project was undertaken with the Alberta Metis Historical Society with the purpose of identifying three sites that were to be developed in 2000. The intent of the study was "to ensure that the chosen approach to development of a profit generating Métis tourism industry [was] workable" (Context Inc. and EXCELeration Corp. 2008, 8). A comprehensive review of sixty-three significant Metis areas was undertaken, and twelve locations were identified as being optimal. Of these twelve, the top three were: Buffalo Lake, Cyprus Hills, and St. Albert. While it did not make the top three, the Victoria Settlement site (Metis Crossing) was one of those identified. While these sites were considered to be of great importance and significance to the Metis people, the findings of the study included concerns regarding the "comparatively remote locations of the sites, the low volumes of local tourist traffic that exist now, and a distinct lack of impressive physical remains."

These problems were compounded by the lack of capital funds to invest in such a project. The feasibility study did provide strategies and recommendations to offset the limitations of a rural development. For example, the use of on-site accommodations, arts and craft sales, and incorporating educational components into any development could help ensure that profits were generated. In addition to the study being conducted, employees of the MNA were working hard to find possible funding sources for a potential development.

It was around this time that Lilli Schaffer approached the MNA for the second time about purchasing the Riverview farm. Circumstances were different this time: her husband had passed away and her need to sell the farm was pressing. Unlike the other sites, Riverview farm had buildings on the property, the six historic river lots were still visible, and it was close to the urban centre of Edmonton. The site appeared to address the issues identified in the study. However, if the MNA was to purchase the property, it would need to secure the funds quickly. There was no time to spare.

Realizing the Opportunity

Recognizing the constraints they were facing, the MNA decided to use the Riverview farm as its flagship tourism project. As stated in the Metis Crossing business plan:

> The location along the North Saskatchewan River was chosen because of its historic significance to Metis people, and proximity to a 1.2 million person local market. This region has a direct link to the success of the Hudson's Bay Company, the fur trade, and the opening of Western Canada. As such, it has received a National Historic site designation and will be marketed from this historical perspective to celebrate Métis people.

Now that the site was chosen, funding would need to be secured. The MNA needed capital funds in order to buy the land, as well as to develop the property. Also to be considered were the overarching goals of the Metis Crossing project: share the Metis story with all people, be a gathering place for Metis, achieve financial self-reliance, and build without amassing capital debt.

The last goal in particular would make finding financial resources difficult, as loan funding would not be sought. The MNA had worked hard to get out of debt and was committed to staying debt free; this was in keeping with the hard-working and entrepreneurial values shared by the Metis.

The first resources to be utilized were the human resources of the MNA. At the outset, Ron Harrison began writing proposals to various departments within the provincial and federal governments. Staff members were utilized, and not only those working in economic development: anyone with time to spare was asked to assist in the endeavour. Initially, only minor contributions were secured, such as $20,000 from Industry Canada, to assist in the development of

Phase I of the business plan. Overall, the development was to be a three-phase project with a total budget of $13.9 million. The projected activities and budget breakdown were summarized in the introduction of the Business Plan:

1. **Phase I ($3.6 million, 2005):** This phase of development focused on the restoration of the existing farmstead, the addition of a historical village, and the building of the basic infrastructure required by visitors (parking lot, washrooms). This phase could be completed in time for the site to be utilized in the Province of Alberta's Centennial celebrations.

2. **Phase II ($5.8 million, 2007):** Developments focused on market planning and building the main revenue-generating components, including the canopy walk, the training and retreat centre, and an events area. In addition to continued capital growth, seasonal operation would begin with the RV campground, educational programs, and interpretive programs in the historical village.

3. **Phase III ($4.5 million, 2008):** The development plan would again turn to cultural interpretation, with the completion of a year-round cultural interpretive building and exhibits. Overall completion of the project was planned for a 2009 opening.

The Metis have long struggled to build an effective relationship with the provincial government. This began to change when the MNA signed two agreements that enabled them to engage with government and work to realize their goals. First, an Alberta Framework Agreement was signed in 1988, which not only provided funding to the MNA but also established a working relationship with the provincial government. Second, a tripartite agreement was signed in 1992 between the Metis Nation of Alberta, the Alberta provincial government, and the federal government. This tripartite forum allowed the MNA to have direct access to government departments for their proposals.

In addition to working with government, the MNA began looking to individuals and businesses within the Metis community, as well as to the local non-Indigenous communities, for potential partners, sponsors, and contributors. In doing so, the MNA focused a lot of its attention and resources on building partnerships with the local communities. Corrine Card, executive director of Metis Crossing, described it as a cultural value because "that's kind of the Metis way...you work together, you find people to help you, but you have to be willing to do that work yourself! And you do that work, and you know what people have joined, and that's kind of the way the Metis people are and that's the way I was raised as Metis person." This partnership approach to doing business not only helped secure funding and resulted in valuable in-kind contributions, it also helped establish the legitimacy of Metis Crossing as an Albertan tourist destination.

Several key events occurred in 2000 that enabled the project to move forward. The Alberta government was planning centennial celebrations in 2005 and was funding cultural projects within the province. MNA president Audrey Poitras met with the premier and was encouraged to put in a proposal to access funding. In addition, the negotiations for the land were going ahead between the president of the MNA, the late Larry Desmeules, and Mrs. Schaffer. A price of $620,000 was agreed upon.

The MNA did not have the funding to purchase the property but wanted the bank to hold the mortgage until the funds could be found. President Poitras recalls expressing to their bank manager:

> We would like to be able to buy this land and at least have a bit more time to try to meet our dream. We are asking you to purchase this land for us, with the intent that we will find money to pay for it. Because we know that we can't pay a mortgage on the land and we can't develop and do everything and still exist. We know that we have to find someone. We know we have to find people who believe in us. We know we have to find grants that will pay for our land. That's one of the things we've committed to. We will find somebody. And then we will access grants or capital and we will develop our plans so each of the phases of our development will be self-sustaining.

Accompanying the request was the good credit of the MNA and letters of support for the project from individuals and businesses. In the end, the bank agreed to hold the mortgage in three-month intervals, with MNA paying the interest—a testament to the business sense of the Metis people and the importance of this project.

There was one issue that would remain even if the MNA was successful in securing centennial grant funding: the funding could not be used for capital purchases, so another source would be needed to purchase the farm. The president of the MNA approached Dr. Herb Belcourt, OC, who, along with several partners, was in the process of setting up the Belcourt Brosseau foundation. Dr. Belcourt has been described in the media as a "Metis entrepreneur, philanthropist, and activist" (Buehler 2010) and he was interested in the Metis Crossing project because of the Metis educational component. Dr. Belcourt told the MNA that he and his partners would be willing to provide the capital if they were able to secure the centennial grant for the development of the property.

An extensive lobbying effort was undertaken with respect to the provincial centennial grant. In the end, the MNA was successful in securing a Centennial Legacies grant of $1 million to be put towards development of the site. The Riverview farm was purchased in 2001. On June 17, 2003, a donation agreement was signed between Belcourt's company, Canative Housing Corporation, the Metis Nation of Alberta, and the Metis Nation Holdings Ltd. A donation of $620,000 was made to the Metis Nation for the purpose of purchasing the property and enabling the construction and establishment of an interpretive centre. The Victoria Landing Developments Ltd. was incorporated and the property was transferred from the holding company. The donation allowed the mortgage to be cleared and Metis Crossing to remain debt free.

Organizations were continually approached to support the project. Metis Crossing project manager Juanita Marois stated that "organizations agree to support projects with teams of people that they trust to achieve the goals outlined," and it speaks to the respect and recognition Metis Crossing was garnering from the local community that they received so many offers of help. Thus, external partners were approached to support or invest in the project, from local businesses to government and private industry.

Organizational Structure and Governance

The Metis Nation of Alberta is the owner and sole shareholder of Metis Crossing Ltd., a registered company. It is one of seven organizations owned by the MNA. The initial corporation that was set up to steward the project was called the Victoria Landing Developments Ltd., with a board of directors appointed in 2003. The name of the corporation was later changed to Metis Crossing Ltd. The structure and systems that were developed ensure that ultimate responsibility rests with the elected leadership of the MNA, so Metis Crossing board members and their general manager report regularly to the MNA leadership. Metis Crossing is governed by a volunteer board of directors made up of four Metis persons, two men and two women. They were chosen for their skills and expertise as well as to represent regions of the province. Metis Crossing is run as a separate for-profit entity. The setting up of a separate legal entity ensures that any legal liabilities are limited to the corporation, thereby protecting the MNA. There is a small staff of full- and part-time workers, with a general manager who runs the operations and business. The board has developed a thirty-year work plan to see the site grow and continue to develop.

Metis Crossing Business

Metis Crossing is a destination for both Metis and tourists interested in exploring and learning more about Alberta's Metis culture and history. The historical site includes many old buildings that give a sense of a traditional Metis village, along with a farmstead. There is a museum-like Metis Cultural Exhibit, which has a collection of artifacts, books, and crafts. There is also an area where genealogical research and documentation is displayed and where people interested in learning family histories can explore their roots. There are interpretive programs and tours of the site and its historical buildings, York boats, and Red River carts. There are also education programs for local and regional schools. The infrastructure includes a parking lot, RV camping area, playground, washrooms, zip line, and a permanent stage for music, dance, and other events. Thus, Metis Crossing is a draw for tourists interested in learning about Metis history and culture, but more importantly, it is a historical Metis site used for contemporary Metis gatherings and celebrations.

Conclusion

Metis Crossing is a successful cultural tourism enterprise that is able to generate revenue that allows it to operate. However, another important objective of Metis Crossing is to serve Alberta's Metis as a cultural gathering site, where they can come together to celebrate their culture and history. The Metis of Alberta had a vision for such a site, and through the leadership of the Metis Nation of Alberta they were able to turn that dream into a reality. It took a lot of planning and work to make it happen, but in August 2005 over three thousand Metis and friends showed up at the new historical site to celebrate the Metis Crossing Centennial Voyage. Thus, we see here an example of a social enterprise where social and cultural goals are met while generating revenue.

Notes

1. This case study is a summary of a longer case study written by Sarah Morales and Cheryl Simon in 2012 for The Banff Centre, titled "The Forgotten People No Longer: The Metis Crossing Case Study."

References

Buehler, Clint. 2010. "Herb Belcourt Chosen for Order of Canada." *First Nation Drum*. Accessed June 11, 2014. http://www.firstnationsdrum.com/2010/07/herb-belcourt-chosen-for-order-of-canada/.

Context Inc. and EXCELeration Corp. 2000. "The Voyage Has Begun: The Métis Millennium Voyage Tourism Feasibility Study." Calgary.

Morales, Sarah, and Cheryl Simon. 2012. "The Forgotten People No Longer: The Métis Crossing Case Study." Banff: The Banff Centre.

Mikisew Group of Companies[1]

The Mikisew Cree First Nation (MCFN) is located in Fort Chipewyan, in the northeast corner of Alberta, along the western shore
of Lake Athabasca. The MCFN established the Mikisew Group of
Companies in 1991 in order to invest monies from a $26.6-million
land claim settlement with the governments of Alberta and Canada.
The Mikisew Group of Companies has achieved remarkable success,
evident in the business awards its companies have received. Although
the Mikisew Group is a business, it is also part of the MCFN's overall
self-determination strategy of practising self-governance through
increasing economic self-sufficiency. Success in these terms is evident
in the substantial revenues it generates, the employment, training,
and career opportunities it provides for the nation members, and the
political and economic clout it exercises in promoting the MCFN's interests in the industrial development decisions that affect the nation's
traditional territory.

Background

The Mikisew Cree have been in what is now known as northern
Alberta for centuries, hunting, trapping, fishing, and gathering. They
became very involved in the fur trade after a fur trading post was
set up in 1788. Once the Dominion of Canada was established in
1867, it was determined that in the division of powers between the
provinces and the federal government, it would be the latter who had
the jurisdiction and responsibility over Indians and lands reserved
for Indians. The federal government established an Indian Act and
various policies to control First Nations, thus formalizing the colonial
relationship. Soon after, the Dominion government began entering

into treaties in order to open up the land to European settlers. What is now known as northern Alberta became Treaty 8 in 1899, with the Mikisew Cree joining other First Nations at the negotiations and signing. The Mikisew leaders, as well as other First Nations leaders during the Treaty 8 negotiations, took very strong stands to protect their interests in the land and resources, especially their traditional livelihood. The majority of community members of the MCFN were able to maintain their traditional livelihood well into the 1960s, and some still practise traditional hunting, trapping, and fishing today along with their wage labour.

There were external forces beginning to make themselves felt that impacted the Mikisew Cree's (and the Dene's and Metis's) ability to practise their traditional livelihood. Firstly, the federal government established the Wood Buffalo National Park right near Fort Chipewyan and imposed no-hunting regulations. Secondly, the British Columbia government approved the construction of the Bennett Dam upstream on the Peace River, which affected water levels, disrupting the fish and animal populations along the river. Thirdly, the Alberta government approved and promoted the exploitation of the oil sands upstream on the Athabasca River, which led to huge strip mining and a rapid influx of outside workers into the region. In response, the MCFN leaders pursued a land claim for reserve lands based on the terms of Treaty 8. A land claims agreement was ultimately reached with the MCFN for nine small reserves, giving the nation control over 4,973 hectares. It reaffirmed for MCFN members their hunting, fishing, and trapping rights in Wood Buffalo National Park, and accorded a financial settlement of $26.6 million.

Vision and Strategy Leading to the Mikisew Group of Companies

The MCFN political leaders were faced with the question of what to do with the land claim monies. They saw this as possibly a one-time opportunity to do something important that would help the Mikisew Nation. Chief and council at the time consulted with the MCFN members to gain input towards a strategic plan and strategic investment. From this community dialogue, they formulated a strategic vision that included developing the following:

- Skilled MCFN members who could run and operate any MCFN businesses
- MCFN professionals
- MCFN lands in ways that protect treaty rights and the environment
- An economically self-sufficient First Nation
- Excellence in cultural, educational, and business planning

With this vision in place, the MCFN leaders decided to pursue their community development plan with a strong business-based strategy. In order to practise financial stewardship, the MCFN leaders began by setting up the Mikisew Commercial Trust, with stringent rules on how the settlement monies could be used. The MCFN leaders also decided to transfer ownership of the Mikisew Group of Companies to the separately chartered Mikisew Commercial Trust, which limited liability of the MCFN to the Trust and its companies. Investment decisions were thus concentrated in one place. The Mikisew Commercial Trust operates as a holding company to manage the land claim monies and business revenues. It has a board of directors who govern the organization, determine its strategic direction, and hire a general manager to control the operations.

MCFN is an isolated, fly-in community for most of the year, so economic opportunities in Fort Chipewyan were limited. However, just upstream on the Athabasca River to the south was a growing oil sands industry, so the MCFN leaders decided to concentrate initial business efforts in Fort McMurray.

Establishing Mikisew Group of Companies

These efforts bore fruit when Syncrude Canada offered to hire MCFN members to work at their huge industrial plant site, which prompted MCFN to establish a new band-owned company, 2000 Plus Limited Partnership, in 1991. A contract was secured for 2000 Plus to provide labour services to Syncrude in areas of general labour, janitorial, safety, plant and fleet maintenance, heavy machinery operations, and construction. From this first successful business venture, MCFN established over time a number of businesses that became known as the Mikisew Group of Companies. They hired experienced managers to run their businesses at the start to ensure they operated successfully, but they also put great effort into training, offering opportunities to gain experience, and mentoring for their own members so they could eventually move into management positions.

By 2012, the Mikisew Group of Companies had become a multi-million dollar conglomerate that included nine businesses:

1. **Mikisew Energy Services Group (MESG)**: The flagship within the Mikisew Group of Companies, MESG is an International Organization for Standardization (ISO)–certified union company located in Fort McMurray. It is a group of industrial labour and maintenance companies that serve the oil and gas, forestry, and mining industries. In 2008, MCFN's first company, 2000 Plus Limited, was folded into MESG.

2. **Mikisew Industrial Supply, Ltd.**: This ISO-registered company manufactures load tie-downs, round slings, and web slings (products for securing loads to trucks, cranes, and other transport mechanisms), as well as specialized products for clients. It is located in Edmonton.

3. **Mikisew Sport Fishing**: Advertised as the premier sports fishing operator in northern Alberta, Mikisew Sport Fishing is a seasonal business based in Fort McMurray. It provides guides, accommodation, and boats at rustic fishing camps on Mikisew Cree land north of Lake Athabasca.

4. **Super 8 Fort McMurray**: This hotel with one hundred guest rooms, in which the Mikisew Group owns a 75 percent share, is located in Fort McMurray on land controlled by another Mikisew Group company, Mikisew Property Development. It caters primarily to long-term guests and oil and gas industry employees.

5. **Fort Petroleum**: The main supplier of gasoline and diesel fuel in Fort Chipewyan, Fort Petroleum is also headquartered in Fort Chipewyan. It supplies bulk fuels, retails a wide assort-

ment of oil and lubricant products, and offers heavy equipment rental services to residential, commercial, and government-sector customers. A key company goal is to be a consistent, affordable fuel supplier for MCFN citizens living in Fort Chipewyan.

6. **Mikisew Fleet Maintenance:** This Canadian Welding Bureau and Alberta Boilers Safety Association–certified company is located in Fort McMurray and performs light- and heavy-duty service for large vehicle fleets. The company aims to be the area's premier heavy-duty and automotive vehicle inspection and fleet maintenance facility. Expansion plans feature a larger shop and enhanced field services.

7. **Mikisew Property Development:** Formed to pursue appropriate revenue-generating commercial development activities on strategically located properties owned by MCFN and the Mikisew Group, Mikisew Property Development currently operates only in Fort McMurray. It holds the land on which the Super 8 is located, leases nearby parcels to a Burger King and to a Shell station, and has plans to develop more land in this focus area. Over time, the company aims to operate throughout the Regional Municipality of Wood Buffalo.

8. **M2, Ltd.:** A joint venture with Mammoet Canada Western, Ltd.—a specialized heavy load transportation and lifting company for the petrochemical, civil, power, and construction industries—Edmonton-based M2, Ltd. provides pilot car services for Mammoet's wide-load vehicles. With a particular focus on skill and career development, M2 business plans include growing services to complement more of Mammoet Canada's current lines of business.

9. **Mikisew/AMECO Group:** This Mikisew Energy Services Group and AMECO team was formed to service 215 of AMECO's light-duty vehicles. The joint venture provides employment and career development opportunities in skilled trades. It is based in Fort McMurray.

The MCFN leaders made a decision to avoid being passive investors and instead to become investors who would actively oversee their investments, manage for a triple bottom line, and develop MCFN members' capacity to manage the companies. Thus, they invested in human capital development for their people. Aaron Kaskamin, regional manager of MESG, stated that his company does an average of $2 million per year in skills and career development for its First Nations employees (Aaron Kaskamin, pers. comm.). To ensure that employment opportunities for Mikisew members is respected as a strategic objective, the Mikisew Group of Companies developed a policy of Mikisew-focused hiring. As part of this strategy, Mikisew companies will work to make special arrangements for MCFN members, such as a single mother who might need a flexible schedule. The MCFN set up companies in Fort McMurray because that is where many of its members live and because of the business opportunities offered by oil sands development. However, with many of its members also living in Edmonton, it established one of its businesses, the Mikisew Industrial Supply Ltd., there. Mikisew Group of Companies, through its partnerships and joint ventures, along with its subcontractors, presses for further opportunities for its members to receive training and employment. Mikisew Group of Companies also makes great efforts to promote and advance the careers of its First Nation members, with several now in senior management roles.

The Mikisew Commercial Trust made a significant effort to communicate the objectives of the Trust, its investment in the MCFN's future, and the use of dividends for social purposes so that it had strong community support for how the settlement monies and the revenues generated were being used. The Mikisew Group of Companies has been financially successful enough to provide some dividend payments to the general membership. The continued growth of the Mikisew Group, and its ability to produce revenues for reinvestment, transfers to the MCFN government, and dividends to members, illustrates that the MCFN has set up the structures and processes to separate politics from business decision making. Leaders and managers also understand these community objectives, so we see the chief and council, board directors, and managers all operate with the understanding that their work and the revenues they create are for the bene-fit of the MCFN as a whole. These leaders and managers understand that their true bosses are the MCFN members. The Mikisew Group of Companies reports regularly to the community via general meetings, shareholder meetings, annual reports, newsletters, and its website.

Although the MCFN people are proud of their band-owned busi-ness success and are appreciative of the revenues generated for social purposes, they are nevertheless very concerned about the pace of oil sands development and its environmental impact. The MCFN leaders wanted to play an active role in the industrial development decisions that impact their traditional territories. One of the first steps in this strategy was to become a corporate colleague with industrial de-velopers. This corporate connection can often provide more practical impact than trying to create dialogue with provincial government officials. In this corporate space, the MCFN is able to voice its interests and concerns about environmental impacts and push for such issues to be addressed in the day-to-day business of the multinational cor-porations involved in oil sands development. Through the Mikisew Group of Companies' business relationships, MCFN is able to have a presence and a voice where its ideas have relevance because it is a player. Its message about balanced development is couched in the MCFN's long-term systems thinking, because the Mikisew Cree know that once the natural resources are depleted, the multinational com-panies will move on, but they will remain there in their homelands.

The MCFN also uses other political and legal strategies to protect its nation interests. The duty to consult forces the provincial government to consult with the First Nation on regulatory or governmental action that could impact its treaty and on Aboriginal rights, and accom-modate any concerns. Government regulations and approvals also require the multinational companies to consult with and accommo-date First Nations. And MCFN developed its own consultation policy that industry players follow. Thus, besides the economic benefits MCFN can negotiate, it also has a powerful mechanism through which to bring its environmental and social impact interests to the table to be considered and accommodated.

MCFN also has a Government Industry Relations Office, where

some Nation members work closely with the oil industry to voice their interests on business as well as environmental, social, and cultural impacts. MCFN plays an active role in environmental and social impact studies along with traditional land use studies to map out its sacred sites and sensitive areas, such as traditional-livelihood areas. One cause of concern is the cumulative impact of the new oil sands projects in the region. MCFN is represented on the new Cumulative Environmental Management Association, a watchdog group monitoring such impacts. One Mikisew member, Melody Lepine, who is also the government industry relations director for MCFN, illustrated the tension that MCFN leaders live with when she stated, "We kind of play two roles in that sense, in trying to work with companies in seeking benefits and at the same time ... trying to minimize the impacts on the environment, which is very important to Mikisew" (Melody Lepine, pers. comm.). These multiple strategies give the MCFN a strong political and economic influence in the oil sands development in its region.

Conclusion

The Mikisew Group of Companies is a successful enterprise, not only in financial terms but in the ways it promotes self-sufficiency and self-determination for the MCFN. The following is a brief summary of the decisions and practices, described in this case study, that underwrite the Mikisew Group of Companies' effectiveness:

- Community involvement in strategic discussions, which leaders framed as discussions about self-reliance, good stewardship, and the community's desired future.

- Strong linkages between the Mikisew Nation's identified strategy and its business investment and management practices, including management towards multiple bottom lines (revenue generation and job and skill development).

- An emphasis on maintaining and growing the value of the land claim settlement monies, especially the decisions to pay per capita distributions only from corporate profits and to limit the proportion paid.

- Creation of a separate organizational entity as a forum for business decision making and a helpful mechanism in managing the boundary between business and politics.

- Willingness to engage productively with resource extractors as a strategy for gaining respect and attention for their interests.

- Development of a full-bodied consultation policy and a First Nation government office through which to implement the policy.

In sum, the Mikisew Cree First Nation and Mikisew Group of Companies have a powerful record of success. Their current challenge is to continue to move from strength to strength. Other First Nations seeking to protect and leverage community financial resources, manage businesses for financial and human capital growth, and gain a voice in regional development can learn from this success story.

Notes

1. This case study is a summary of a longer case study written by Miriam Jorgensen and Rachel Starks in 2012 for The Banff Centre, titled "Forwarding First Nation Goals through Enterprise Ownership: The Mikisew Group of Companies Case Study."

References

Jorgensen, Miriam, and Rachel Starks. 2012. "Forwarding First Nation Goals through Enterprise Ownership: The Mikisew Group of Companies Case Study." Banff: The Banff Centre.

Conclusion

Restorying Indigenous Leadership

Cora Voyageur, Laura Brearley, and Brian Calliou

The interplay between stories, sustainability, and community in Indigenous leadership and community development is a key feature of the research described in *Restorying Indigenous Leadership*. The stories reflect the collectivist nature of effective leadership and community development practices. In their complexity, the stories reveal the interconnections between revitalization, relationships, and research itself. In order to develop sustainable communities and enterprises, the research in this book highlights the importance of collaborative approaches to leadership and a willingness to invest in relationship building within and beyond communities.

What the stories share is an understanding of how to work with the interrelationships between context, culture, and knowledge. This focus on interconnectedness and relationality places this work at the leading edge of research on leadership.

The contributors to *Restorying Indigenous Leadership*, as strength-based storytellers, acknowledge the complexities inherent in our relationships with culture, with each other, and with the mainstream economy. Their stories reveal the dynamic tensions inherent in fostering Indigenous leadership and community development in competitive contexts shaped by economic imperatives. The stories contain examples of Indigenous leaders who understand that relationships and partnerships are key to building vibrant enterprises and communities, as well as creating economies of scale. The research calls for

capable leaders of self-determined communities with legitimate and accountable governance structures, yet grounded in their culture and local knowledge and experience.

The Practice of Restorying

Restorying is a strength-based approach to narrative research. Many scholars writing on Indigenous leadership argue that the effects of colonization and oppression suffered by Indigenous peoples must be overcome by returning to the strength of traditional values and principles (Begay 1997; Ottmann 2005; Calliou 2005; Simpson and Turner 2008; Metoyer 2010; Fraser and Kenny 2012). The research and stories told in this book, while presenting a strength-based approach, also acknowledge the problems Indigenous communities face. In that regard, *Restorying* brings together stories of knowledge and healing within the cultural context of their Indigenous communities—with pain and despair intertwined with creativity and possibility. There are discussions of successful Indigenous communities and leaders told against the backdrop of the statistics of unemployment and disadvantage that resemble the conditions of developing countries. This approach to research into Indigenous leadership and community development is holistic, and the stories within *Restorying* compellingly reveal the full legacy of colonization and dispossession and the associated intergenerational trauma. As well, the research within this anthology is sufficiently textured so that the stories of success are told in a way that recognizes the difficulties faced while still fostering a sense of agency.

It is important that all aspects of stories are acknowledged and represented. It is not about an either/or approach, which implies a duality: interconnectedness is about coexistence. Melanie Yazzie, a Navajo artist and educator, says:

> In our Navajo belief, the good and the bad coexist. Nothing is entirely good and nothing is entirely bad. It all exists together to make something whole. This is what leads to healing. When we are getting well, we have to strip everything back to the basics and then we can re-create ourselves into being whole again. (Melanie Yazzie, pers. comm.)

The stories of wise practice in this book are told against the backdrops of dispossession and despair, but also that of possibility; they recognize the strength of Indigenous wise practices. Nature writer and philosopher Barry Lopez (2010) contends that everything is held together with stories and we need to share them, as much as we need to share food. We need to be reminded of who we are, what we intend to do, and how we want to conduct ourselves in the world. Storytelling, he claims, is the best and only protection against forgetting. Restorying is a restorative process in which we remember who we are. It has the potential to generate healing at both the individual and community level.

Culture, Context, and Knowledge Matter

A central theme running through this book is that in a restorative approach to Indigenous leadership development, culture matters, context matters, and knowledge matters. The stories reveal the importance of documenting experience as well as the significance of asking the right questions: What matters? and What matters most?

A wise practices approach to leadership involves listening deeply to the voices of our elders, our artists, and our philosophers. To illustrate the wisdom that leaders need to exhibit in the action they take to lead us into the emerging future, here are some thoughts from Tom Crane Bear, a Blackfoot elder, pipe carrier, and cultural adviser for The Banff Centre's Indigenous programming. His words of wisdom reveal the significance of culture, context, and knowledge and why they are important in building community and restorying Indigenous leadership.

On Why Culture Matters
Culture is the backbone of existence of the people. Culture is very important to us. Culture is a way of life. We have to keep at it. It teaches us how to be respectful to each other and to the Creator. Spirituality is our culture. It underpins how we look at life and what we do. Spirituality is a strong principle for the people. A lot of people have forgotten culture, language, spirituality, and beliefs. They have forgotten how to be themselves. It's important to have a daily awareness of who you are in relationship to the Creator. We are meant to love each other, care for each other, and look after each other.

We have stories right from time beginning. Storytelling is our culture. Without stories, we wouldn't know where we came from. When I was young, my grandmother told me stories about Creation and how the world began. She remembered the stories of the old times. We come from Napi, who created the trees, the mountains, the rivers, all the animals that you see running around. He created man and woman, and from there we branched out into different branches of a tree. All the nations in Canada, in America, in Australia, all over the world, they all have stories. Without stories you won't know who you are or where you came from. We become the stories that we are told.

On Why Context Matters
We have come to learn the ways of other people. It's important that they understand our way of believing, too. We are willing to share in this way. Today, education is a must. Education is an avenue out

of dependency on the monthly welfare cheque. If people don't get an education and sit around doing nothing, the Indian Act is still controlling us and containing us.

When I was young, Indian policy on the reserve meant I could not go beyond grade eight. I had my education in the school of life and upgraded my formal qualifications later in life. It's come a long way since I was a child. People who continue their education can go off-reserve and have the opportunity to mix with other races and broaden their perspective. Once they graduate, they can come back to the reserve. They return to the community with master's degrees and PhDs. They know the law and they know how to negotiate. They can be on council, a chief, or a consultant. Education is about broadening the frame and getting a wider picture.

On Why Knowledge Matters

You come into the world as a baby and you begin learning. You grow and become a young person and begin to work. As you grow older, you take on more and more responsibilities in the family. You learn to take care of others and to be kind to your elders and your family members. As you continue on in life, you learn about the four key dimensions of life: kindness, honesty, trust, and love.

You will walk into wisdom as you live, and wisdom grows with life. Kindness and how to accept people, that's part of our training. With an elder, there is both kindness and firmness. You can say your piece in an honest way, without hurting anybody or denying anybody. Eventually, if you practise to be kind, to be honest, to be trustworthy, and to love, these things can push you right through to wisdom. You can't talk about wisdom without these four principles. You can become a pipe carrier, you help anyone out, you pray for people, and you know a lot of old songs. If you know the four principles, you know who you are and you can be a leader. To obtain wisdom, you have to earn it. You have to go through life with openness and honesty and come to know who you are. When you are on the path of wisdom, learning how to behave, smudging and practising culture, talking about culture, nothing can hold you back. It works. (Elder Tom Crane Bear, pers. comm.)

Such wisdom and teachings are what a new wave of Indigenous scholars argue are essential for developing and training Indigenous leaders (Nicholas-MacKenzie 1999; Washington 2004; Ottmann 2005; Calliou 2005; Simpson and Turner 2008; Metoyer 2010; Fraser and Kenny 2012).

Stories of Wise Practice and Community Strengthening

The research and stories presented in this book also represent this current wave of scholars calling for the development of Indigenous leaders who need to learn the knowledge and skills required to lead their communities and organizations through the complexity of this modern, globally connected world while also returning to the teachings of our elders to ground them in their local community and identity.

Identifying Success Factors

In her contribution to *Restorying Indigenous Leadership*, Miriam Jorgensen draws on decades of research with her colleagues from the Harvard Project on American Indian Economic Development and its sister organization, the Native Nations Institute for Leadership, Management, and Policy at the University of Arizona. She identifies five key areas that have emerged from the Harvard Project as central to Indigenous economic and community development: Sovereignty Matters; Institutions Matter; Culture Matters; Strategic Thinking Matters; and Leadership Matters. Jorgensen frames Indigenous leaders, whether elected, community, or spiritual, as people who introduce new knowledge, challenge assumptions, convince people that things can be different, propose change, and mobilize the community to take action. She articulates the need for stability and accountability in governing institutions and responsibility in leaders within a context of respect for culture and the environment. In her advocacy of seventh-generation thinking, Jorgensen compellingly articulates the need to move from an individual/present focus to a collective/future focus. In this approach, sustainability is a central concern and decisions need to factor in the impact of today's decisions on the future survival of a collective body.

There are significant overlaps between the key priorities identified by the Harvard Project and The Banff Centre's wise practices
approach. This research identifies what's integral to community
development through a model featuring seven elements that contribute to success: identity and culture; leadership; strategic vision
and planning; good governance and management; accountability
and stewardship; performance evaluation; and collaborations,
partnerships, and external relationships. In their chapter sharing this
research, Brian Calliou and Cynthia Wesley-Esquimaux recognize
the need for making space for the Indigenous knowledge, experiences, and stories learned on the front lines. A wise practices approach
acknowledges the complexity and uncertainty of the times we live
in and the need to make decisions that encompass the welfare of
others and also the planet. The researchers affirm the importance
of culture and advocate that Indigenous knowledge and wisdom
be complemented by proven knowledge and skills of the modern
business and organizational development world. The incorporation
of Indigenous traditional knowledge into practice means that people
live as good human beings, respectful to each other and to the environment. This approach strongly resonates with Elder Tom Crane
Bear's teachings.

Constraints and Possibilities
In his chapter on three economically successful Indigenous case
studies, Bob Kayseas describes the challenges of dealing with market
constraints and the legacy of the Indian Act. He identifies the oppor-
tunities and enabling factors for Indigenous entrepreneurship and
community development. His case studies of Indigenous on-reserve
Canadian enterprises from British Columbia, Saskatchewan, and
Nova Scotia invite us to learn from stories through a process of critical
reflection and questioning. The stories of entrepreneurship in Dennis
Foley's chapter reveal similar constraints and possibilities within the
Australian context. He argues convincingly for the incorporation of
Indigenous ways of knowing into business practices, business educa-
tion, and research.

Collaboration and Community

The importance of strengthening communities and enterprises through collaborative approaches is a key theme explored in *Restorying Indigenous Leadership*. Cora Voyageur's chapter demonstrates the range of strengths that Indigenous women leaders bring to politics and businesses in communities through their collectivist approach and their strengths in community building. She describes how Indigenous women are entering positions of power and authority in increasing numbers, with the number of women chiefs more than doubling in the last twenty years. The growing influence of women in education, politics, and entrepreneurship is being felt both in Indigenous communities and in mainstream society. This trend is likely to continue in the future, with Indigenous women playing an increasing role in community leadership.

A diverse range of collaborative Indigenous leadership training models is examined in Christopher Wetzel's chapter. He explores private and public models of training Indigenous leaders in the United States, as well as specialist and general approaches. Wetzel recognizes the widespread influence in training organizations of the Harvard Project's holistic model of sustainable economic development predicated on an interwoven model of institutions, sovereignty, and culture.

Relationality and Reciprocity

Michelle Evans's chapter based on her doctoral research with Indigenous arts leaders recognizes the co-constructed nature of leadership. This approach transcends a charismatic, attribute-based model of leadership and reframes it as a relational process co-created within emotional, historical, socio-economic, and cultural contexts. Relationality and reciprocity are also key themes in Laura Brearley's chapter about community leadership. In a Deep Listening and Leadership model, leaders can broaden the range of their practice in different contexts as collaborators, learners, facilitators, artists, storytellers, custodians, and messengers. An increased awareness of the interplay between culture, context, and knowledge is central to the Deep Listening and Leadership model.

Indigenous Leadership Research into the Future

Indigenous researcher Russell Bishop (1996) strongly advocates that researchers take ownership of the sociological, cultural, psychological, and educative roots of traditional Indigenous ontology and epistemology. He claims that indigenizing the narrative "corrects the stereotyping and mythologizing of the native" (528). Linked to this is his promotion of the use of "alternative research designs and creative presentation formats" (528). Making room for voices that are "silenced, othered and marginalized by the dominant social order" requires "flexible and fluid qualitative research methodologies" (Liamputtong 2007, 7) and an approach that is open to working with complexity and multiple forms of representation.

Leadership literature encompasses a range of perspectives that span the simplistic to the complex. Some literature focuses on individuals as having the locus of control, for example vision-led change (Belasco 1990) and charismatic leadership (Peters and Waterman 1982). The literature of leadership over recent decades tracks a move away from top-down coercive approaches dependent on the charisma of individual leaders. In such models of leadership, a leader creates and communicates a vision and then organizes and aligns people to that vision (Belasco 1990). Dexter Dunphy and Doug Stace (1996) argue that such models of alignment perpetuate cultures of dependence, conformity, and ultimately alienation. Such individually focused models of leadership frame leaders as heroic manipulators of culture who use stories, symbols, and metaphors to align and control (Peters and Waterman 1982; Kanter 1985; Deal and Kennedy 1982). These approaches do not generally attend to issues of cultural diversity, relationality, or context.

Contingency theory resulted in the development of models of leadership that challenged prescriptions of universal solutions to complex organizational and community issues (Fineman, Gabriel, and Sims 1993). This literature focused on issues of relationship between structure and leadership (Burns and Stalker 1961; Woodward 1965; Fiedler 1967) and argued against ideal or replicable forms or styles, acknowledging the influence of multiple factors such as cultural, environmental, and organizational contexts. The emergence of meaning-making in leadership literature was also a move away from singular interpretations to the recognition that there were variable ways in which people could interpret events (Morgan and Smirch 1982; Daft and Weick 1984; Isabella 1990).

According to Bishop (1996, 519), the acknowledgement of the value of multiple realities "creates space for multiple audiences, convenes conversations that critique the approach within local and global contexts, and directs learning and inquiry toward community empowerment." This approach makes room for the space "in be-tween" described by Indigenous researcher Leilani Holmes (2000, 50) as the place "where both the knowledge of our elders and the knowledge of our colleagues or professors may enter, live, and be voiced." The research and stories in this book reflect and argue for this same approach to the study of leadership. Indeed, the stories of the future will emerge from what bell hooks (2003, 23) has referred to as the "in-between" space and, like the stories of the past, will bring with them "transformative potential."

Expanding the Frame

In the development of Indigenous leaders, there needs to be an emphasis on learning the knowledge and skills of modern leadership, management, and business. However, as is argued throughout this book, traditional teachings must be reintegrated into the development of emerging leaders. In other words, as Franceen Reihana and Martin Perkison (n.d., 1) put it, leadership today requires "new expertise and old wisdom." Indigenous leaders need to be competent as orators and storytellers. They need to tell a new story—a story of what is possible, of what is important, of what is necessary to build successful, healthy, and balanced communities.

Underpinning the contributions in this book is the recognition that a restorying process involves looking at the big picture, working with both the pain and the potential in Indigenous communities. This understanding is strongly evoked in the work of Australian Aboriginal storyteller and artist Lisa Kennedy, a descendant of Woretemoetey-enner, a Trawlwoolway woman from northeast Tasmania, Australia, who was one of the women taken by the sealers in the early years of colonization. By first acknowledging and understanding this history of dispossession and tragedy, Lisa's storytelling, artwork, and leadership are motivated by a deep sense of responsibility to the whole. Her words below illuminate this understanding, which also illustrates a wise practices approach to becoming a great leader.

Creative Cultural Connections

The spirits of the land have compelled me to speak
    with what I know
I have looked for creative ways to bring out what I feel inside
I have always felt a responsibility
And a need to share

Over time I have become more open
And learned to trust more deeply
These days I feel connected and part of a continuity
Of playful, imaginative, creative ways of knowing

I have learned to hold back and not push so much
Working in more collaborative ways
Bringing knowledge and the environment together
Providing opportunities for others to create something together

I know I'm working at the edge and I know I'm lucky
I'm grateful to the Old People for what I've been given
I feel a responsibility to do things the right way
It takes time and the process needs to be respected

I feel I am in service to the larger community
It is exciting to see the potential in others
Knowing that if we work together
Something great could happen

It's important to know where we have come from
Recognizing where we are now
Drawing from the best of it all
And then communicating it creatively
Culture lives in us all
It is what we share

It's a portal to the Old People
A place of direct connection to spirituality

Sitting with the Ancestors is a path to healing
Enriching us with insights
I feel the Old People here
I can feel the release and the responsibility that comes with that

We help people connect with their own imaginative source
Providing the creative tools of art, earth, land and food
Individual and universal
Recognizing that we all drink from the same well.

(Lisa Kennedy, pers. comm.)

The research and stories told in this book reveal that culture lived as a dynamic and evolving process will ensure that its practice is restoried, restored, and revitalized. Many of the Indigenous traditional teachings remind us that as human beings from diverse cultures, we drink from the same well, while at the same time we work within and between diverse economic, political, and socio-cultural contexts. Developing leaders who are well educated but also grounded in their local and cultural knowledge and wisdom will result in more healthy, prosperous, and balanced communities. The development of such leadership is predicated on a sensitivity to these contexts in combination with a blend of cultural wisdom, sustainable business practices, and environmental responsibility.

References

Begay, Manley, Jr. 1997. "Leading by Choice, Not Chance: Leadership Education for Native Executives of American Indian Nations." Unpublished PhD diss., Graduate School of Education, Harvard University.

Belasco, James A. 1990. *Teaching the Elephant to Dance: Empowering Change in Your Organisation*. New York: Crown.

Bishop, Russell. 1996. *Collaborative Research Stories: Whakawhanaungatanga*. Palmerston North, New Zealand: Dunmore Press.

Burns, Tom, and G. M. Stalker. 1961. *The Management of Innovation*. London: Tavistock.

Calliou, Brian. 2005. "The Culture of Leadership: North American Indigenous Leadership in a Changing Economy." In *Indigenous Peoples and the Modern State*, edited by Duane Champagne, Karen Jo Torjesen, and Susan Steiner, 47–68. Walnut Creek: AltaMira Press.

Daft, Richard L., and Karl E. Weick. 1984. "Toward a Model of Organizations as Interpretation Systems." *Academy of Management Review* 9 (2): 284–95.

Deal, Terrence E., and Allan A. Kennedy. 1982. *Corporate Cultures: The Rites and Rituals of Corporate Life*. Workingham, UK: Addison-Wesley.

Dunphy, Dexter, and Doug Stace. 1996. *Beyond the Boundaries: Leading and Re-creating the Successful Enterprise*. Australia: McGraw-Hill.

Fiedler, Fred Edward. 1967. *A Theory of Leadership Effectiveness*. New York: McGraw-Hill.

Fineman, Stephen, Yiannis Gabriel, and David Sims. 1993. *Organizing & Organizations: An Introduction*. London: Sage Publications.

Fraser, Tina Ngaroimata, and Carolyn Kenny, eds. 2012. *Living Indigenous Leadership: Native Narratives on Building Strong Communities*. Vancouver: University of British Columbia Press.

Holmes, Leilani. 2000. "Heart Knowledge, Blood Memory, and the Voice of the Land: Implications of Research among Hawaiian Elders." In *Indigenous Knowledges in Global Contexts: Multiple Readings of Our World*, edited by George J. Sefa Dei, Budd L. Hall, and Dorothy Goldin Rosenberg, 37–53. Toronto: University of Toronto Press.

hooks, bell. 2003. *Teaching Community: A Pedagogy of Hope*. New York: Routledge.

Isabella, Lynn A. 1990. "Evolving Interpretations as a Change Unfolds: How Managers Construe Key Organizational Events." *Academy of Management Journal* 33 (1): 7–41.

Kanter, Rosabeth Moss. 1985. *The Change Masters: Innovation & Entrepreneurship in American Corporation*. New York: Counterpoint.

Liamputtong, Pranee. 2007. *Researching the Vulnerable: A Guide to Sensitive Research Methods*. Thousand Oaks: Sage Publications.

Lopez, Barry. April 30, 2010. In conversation with Bill Moyers. *Bill Moyers Journal*. PBS. Accessed December 31, 2013. http://www.pbs.org/moyers/journal/04302010/watch3.html.

Metoyer, Cheryl A. 2010. "Leadership in American Indian Communities:

Winter Lessons." *American Indian Culture and Research Journal* 34 (4): 1–12.

Morgan, Gareth, and Linda Smircich. 1982. "Leadership: The Management of Meaning." *The Journal of Applied Behavioral Science* 18 (3): 257–73.

Nicholas-MacKenzie, L. 1999. "Lessons From Our Ancestors: A Legacy of Leadership." Unpublished PhD diss., Royal Rhodes University, British Columbia.

Ottmann, Jacqueline. 2005. "First Nations Leadership Development." Report for the Banff Centre, Indigenous Leadership and Management. Accessed January 1, 2014. www.banffcentre.ca/departments/leadership/aboriginal/library/pdf.

Perkinson, Martin, and Franceen Reihana. n.d. "Tikanga Māori Leadership: Understanding the Dynamics of Maori Leadership in a Changing World." Research project abstract, http://www.firstfound.org/reihana.htm.

Peters, Thomas, and Robert H. Waterman, Jr. 1982. *In Search of Excellence: Lessons from America's Best-Run Companies*. New York: Harper and Row.

Simpson, Audra, and Dale Turner. 2008. "Indigenous Leadership in a Flat World." Research paper for the National Centre for First Nations Governance, Vancouver, British Columbia. http://fngovernance.org/ncfng_research/turner_and_simpson.pdf.

Washington, Siemthlut Michelle. 2004. "Bringing Traditional Teachings to Leadership." *American Indian Quarterly* 28 (2): 583–603.

Woodward, Joan. 1965. *Industrial Organization: Theory and Practice*. Oxford: Oxford University Press.

Contributors

Editor Bios

DR. CORA VOYAGEUR is a sociologist at the University of Calgary. Her research explores the Indigenous experience in Canada. Her books include *Firekeepers of the Twenty-First Century: Women Chiefs in Canada* and *My Heroes Have Always Been Indians*. She co-edited *Hidden in Plain Sight: Contributions of Aboriginal Peoples to Canadian Identity and Culture*, Volumes I and II. She is a member of the Athabasca Chipewyan First Nation.

DR. LAURA BREARLEY is a creative research specialist and coordinates the Deep Listening Project, an international creative exchange and research project involving Indigenous and non-Indigenous artists, musicians, and researchers. The project grew out of the Koori Cohort of Researchers that Laura established at RMIT University and Monash University. Laura is an adjunct professor at Swinburne University, where she works with masters students in the Faculty of Design.

BRIAN CALLIOU has been the program director of The Banff Centre's Indigenous Leadership and Management program since August 2003. His work has appeared in various academic journals and books including *Indigenous Peoples and the Modern State* and *Power & Resistance: Critical Thinking about Canadian Issues*. His research interests include Aboriginal leadership, self-government, economic development, and treaty rights.

Contributor Bios

DR. MICHELLE EVANS, originally from the Hunter Valley, NSW Australia, is a Bathurst-based academic, writer, facilitator, and cultural producer. Michelle holds a senior lectureship in leadership at Charles Sturt University and is a research fellow at Melbourne Business

School and fellow of the Research Centre for Leadership in Action at NYU. Michelle leads Australia's first Indigenous Business Master Class series, MURRA, established to skill up Indigenous entrepreneurs. Michelle is a Fulbright Scholar (2013), a visiting fellow of the Centre for Co-operative and Community Based Economy at the University of Victoria, Canada (2012), and is trustee of the Yvonne Cohen Award for Indigenous Creative Young People.

DR. DENNIS FOLEY is Aboriginal, researching in the fields of management/entrepreneurship, history, and education. A Fulbright Scholar, double Endeavour Fellow, and recipient of other prestigious research grants and awards, he has lived and worked with Indigenous colleagues in the United States, Aotearoa, Canada, Hawaii, Ireland, and Taiwan, as well as urban and remote Australia.

DR. MIRIAM JORGENSEN, MA, University of Oxford, and MPP and PhD, Harvard University, is the research director for the University of Arizona's Native Nations Institute and the Harvard Project on American Indian Economic Development. Her books, *Rebuilding Native Nations*, *The State of the Native Nations*, and *Structuring Sovereignty*, are leading texts in Indigenous affairs.

DR. BOB KAYSEAS, a Saskatchewan-born First Nations scholar, is an associate professor at First Nations University of Canada, located in Regina, Saskatchewan. Bob is a member of the Fishing Lake First Nation, a Saulteaux community in east-central Saskatchewan. Bob obtained a degree in business administration and a master of business administration from the University of Regina and a PhD (Enterprise and Innovation) from the Australian Graduate School of Entrepreneurship, Swinburne University of Technology in Melbourne, Australia. Bob has established a recognized scholarly program of research centred on Aboriginal entrepreneurship and economic development, and he is actively engaged in the research and practice of both, as is evidenced in the number of publications he has on Indigenous entrepreneurship and the economic development of Canadian Indigenous bands, and in the number of consultancy projects he has successfully completed.

DR. CYNTHIA WESLEY-ESQUIMAUX is the vice-provost, Aboriginal Initiatives, at Lakehead University. She serves as a status-only assistant professor at the Factor-Inwentash Faculty of Social Work at the University of Toronto, an adjunct assistant professor at Carleton University, a board member at Healthy Minds Canada, and is an active and engaging media representative.

CHRISTOPHER WETZEL is an associate professor and chair of the Department of Sociology and Criminology at Stonehill College. His book *Potawatomis: One Spirit, One Nation,* which analyzes the national revitalization movement among Potawatomi Indians in the United States and Canada, will be published by the University of Oklahoma Press in 2015.